W9-CUO-168

Web Content Management
Systems, Features, and Best Practices

Deane Barker

Beijing · Boston · Farnham · Sebastopol · Tokyo

Web Content Management

by Deane Barker

Printed in the United States of America.

Published by O'Reilly Media, Inc., 1005 Gravenstein Highway North, Sebastopol, CA 95472.

O'Reilly books may be purchased for educational, business, or sales promotional use. Online editions are also available for most titles (*http://safaribooksonline.com*). For more information, contact our corporate/institutional sales department: 800-998-9938 or *corporate@oreilly.com*.

Editor: Allyson MacDonald	**Indexer:** WordCo Indexing Services
Production Editor: Colleen Cole	**Interior Designer:** David Futato
Copyeditor: Rachel Head	**Cover Designer:** Randy Comer
Proofreader: Susan Moritz	**Illustrator:** Rebecca Demarest

March 2016:   First Edition

Revision History for the First Edition

2016-03-09:   First Release

See *http://oreilly.com/catalog/errata.csp?isbn=9781491908129* for release details.

978-1-491-90812-9

[LSI]

For Mom.

I finally figured out what I want to be when I grow up.

Table of Contents

Part I.   The Basics

Foreword

The web content management industry has evolved substantially over the past two decades. Today, CMS vendors and industry pundits put overarching emphasis on "customer experience management," the idea that successful customer interactions should drive all your digital investments. This is a useful prioritization, inasmuch as we should all be thinking "screen first" (i.e., how do customers experience our digital incarnations?) After all, why produce digital content unless people actually want to consume it?

But this emphasis on experience management sometimes relegates the process of producing and publishing high-quality information to the backseat. We can all understand why marketers pay more attention to frontend design, mobile strategies, and social micromessaging, but in doing so they risk losing focus on deeper forms of information-based engagement.

Consider the nearly ubiquitous desire to create more personalized digital interactions. Many personalization strategies start with the premise, "assume suitable content for each interaction." This begs many questions. Suitable content from where? How will it be managed? How will it get chunked? How will we vary it for each and every audience? How will it get assembled? How will we simulate all the permutations? Behind those questions lie some thorny content management challenges.

On the brighter side, the last few years have seen the rise of "content strategy" as an important digital discipline. What exactly people mean by content strategy will vary, but the general idea is that you need to have your content house in order before you start executing business strategies across various digital channels.

The emergence of a new generation of digital content strategists is a welcome development, though I sometimes wish they would better understand the organizational environments where their strategies need to live. Content strategies that look great on day 1 can get messy by day 365, let alone day 730. You need to sort out simple authoring and approval regimes; you need to find and modify previous versions of campaigns; you need to integrate analytics into subsequent iterations; you need to archive older information so it doesn't clog up your search engine results. And so on.

So, the WCM industry is experiencing some key gaps today, and we need people who can effectively bridge those gaps. Like the gap between content creation and content consumption. The gap between content strategies and CMS implementations. Between business needs and architectural patterns. Between authors and marketers. Between developers and campaign managers. Between strategists and implementers. Deane Barker is the rare individual who can speak to all those concerns.

As a New Zealander happily transplanted to North America, Deane has the ability to get passionately engaged yet also take the outsider's critical perspective. At first blush this book is a primer on essential CMS topics, but when you read more deeply you'll find it's really an argument—a passionate call to treat web content and processes around it as seriously as you treat any other business or marketing asset.

So, you should read the book cover to cover, but I particularly recommend you book-mark the chapters on the CMS team, content modeling and aggregation, migration, and implementation. These are the tough topics that consultants and vendors often don't like to discuss, but that could make or break your CMS program. Deane covers them with the right mix of breadth and efficiency that can only come from someone who's gone through them many, many times.

Although this book is written for the business generalist, if you are a developer or architect it's a very worthwhile read, and would have been even if Deane hadn't included all the useful code snippets (though he did include them, to my delight and hopefully yours). Check out the early chapter on "points of comparison" for some key logical distinctions you'll want your team to follow.

If there was a magical machine that could make the perfect CMS, I would put Deane at the controls. In the absence of such a machine, the rest of us need to figure out best practices the old-fashioned way: by testing and experience. I hope you get the chance to test many CMS tools, just to get a firsthand feel for the surprising variations in approach among them. But if you are looking for a single source of received wisdom and experience on CMS best practices, then drop what you're doing and read this book.

— Tony Byrne
Founder, Real Story Group
www.realstorygroup.com
December 2015

Preface

Back in 1995 or so, I wrote my first HTML document.

I wrote it in Notepad on my 90 MHz Pentium tower from Gateway 2000. I still remember adding a TITLE tag, refreshing the page in Internet Explorer, and watching with awe as my document title filled the title bar of the browser window (the idea of tabbed browsers was still years in the future, so the document's TITLE tag became the title of the entire window).

That first web page quickly grew into an entire website (the subject and point of which I honestly can't remember—I suspect it was just a list of links to other sites). Mainstream adoption of CSS and JavaScript was still a few years off, so I didn't have scripts or stylesheets, but I had a handful of HTML files and a bunch of images (you were nobody if you didn't have a tiled, textured background on your page of links).

Quickly, I ran smack into the first problem of webmasters everywhere: *how do I keep track of all this stuff?* I don't even think the word "content" had been popularly applied yet—it was all just "stuff."

As websites inevitably grew, so did all the stuff. Since we were largely bound to the filesystem, we had copies of everything on our local computers that we would FTP to our servers. Huge problems resulted if you had more than one editor. With two people trying to manage files, they would inevitably get out of sync and changes would be unintentionally overwritten. Occasionally, you had to sync against the server by downloading everything and overwriting your local copy, just to make sure you had the latest version of the entire site.

The process of managing a website was enormously tedious. Linking from one page to another assumed the two pages would always exist. Broken links were common, and if you decided to reorganize the structure of your site or rename pages, you had to hunt through all your files to find where the previous name might have been used.

The most valuable thing in my toolkit might have been the global search and replace utility that let me look for—and correct—links in hundreds of files at once.[1]

This was the story of being a webmaster in the mid-'90s, before content management arrived. It was a tedious experience of manually managing hundreds of files, making sure you had multiple backups of everything, and trying to cobble together a toolset that gave you some modicum of control.

Fast-forward almost 20 years, and web technologies have evolved to remove most of the tedium. Today's web manager largely works with abstract notions of content rather than actual files, without needing to understand the underlying technology, file-system, or programming languages.

But even abstracting content from technology has still left us with eternal problems to solve: How do we structure or "model" our content? How do we allow for its organization? How do we search it? How do we work together on content without causing conflicts?

In short, how do we *manage* content?

Who Is This Book For?

This book is an attempt to approach web content management from the outside, without pushing any particular technology or methodology. It is designed for readers who want to understand the larger context in which a specific content management system (CMS) might work, or understand the underlying content management problems that any particular system will need to solve.

These readers might be:

- Project managers tasked with managing the implementation of a new CMS
- Experienced developers who might be new to content management in particular
- Web managers embarking on an evaluation project to acquire a new CMS
- Content producers transitioning from offline content to web content management
- Existing CMS developers wanting to step outside their chosen platform and look at their discipline from a new perspective

---

1 It was called—appropriately—"Search and Replace" from Funduc Software, and actually still exists as shareware (*http://www.funduc.com/search_replace.htm*). Sadly, it had no backup or undo features at the time. Remind me sometime to tell you the story of how I accidentally did an irreversible find and replace on the letter "e."

- Designers or content strategists wanting to understand more about the technological context of their work
- Anyone trying to understand and justify a new CMS-related project

What Is Not in This Book?

This book is *not* a technical programming manual. There are some code samples scattered throughout, but many are in a fictitious templating language, and all are meant to be purely illustrative, not practical.

Additionally, this book is intended to be language- and platform-agnostic. I will discuss many different systems, technologies, and platforms. I neither explicitly endorse nor condemn any of them. I have made an attempt to draw examples and screen captures from a wide variety of systems.

How Is This Book Organized?

The book's chapters are grouped into three parts:

Part I, "The Basics"
> This part will lay the groundwork for the larger discussion of content management. We'll talk about what content is, paradigms with which to compare different systems, the roles that make up a CMS team, and how your organization might acquire a CMS.

Part II, "The Components of Content Management Systems"
> This part will analyze the major functional areas of modern CMSs—how they model content, aggregate content, coordinate workflow, manage assets, etc.

Part III, "Implementations"
> This final part will discuss the scope and structure of a CMS implementation project, and the best practices and process of running one successfully (or even just surviving one). Additionally, we'll talk about the oft-overlooked practice of migrating web content, and how you might work with an external CMS integrator, if you need one.

A Note on Generalities

A large portion of this book is about content management systems, but not any *particular* system. This means I'll be trying to discuss every variety of content management system at the same time, which is a semantically challenging task.

One of the challenges of writing this book has been coming up with different phrasing to subdivide the entire domain of CMSs into groups. In the following pages, you'll see countless phrases such as "most systems," "some systems," and "almost all systems," as well as a lot of qualifiers such as "rare," "uncommon," "often," "sometimes," and "usually."

Clearly, none of these phrases are quantifiable;[2] they're simply the best of a variety of suboptimal ways to handle generalities. Different phrases will mean different things to different people. If you disagree with a qualifier, then you have my apologies in advance.

A Note on Nomenclature

As we'll discuss in the very first chapter, "content" can mean many different things, from HTML files to images to Word documents.

I will use the terms "content" and "CMS" loosely for convenience. However, understand that this is a book about *web* content management specifically, so I'm specifically talking about "web content" and "WCM" and "WCMSs."

In dropping the "web" and "W" qualifiers, I am not staking claim to content as purely a web asset or problem. Rather, I am merely bowing to convention and brevity.

A Note on Sidebars

Throughout the book, you will find a dozen sidebars from other professionals working in the CMS industry. I am grateful to these friends and colleagues for taking the time to share their experiences here.

For each sidebar, a draft copy of the chapter was provided, and the author was asked to express an opinion about something in it. They were free to disagree, call out something that was missed, or put a different angle on anything they read. No attempt was made to edit their opinions.

As I say many, many times in the following chapters, content management is as much art as science, and there are no doubt countless people who will disagree with one or more things I've written here. I'm grateful that my guest authors were willing to provide glimpses into how different experiences often lead to different conclusions.

A Note on Bias

As a consultant who has worked in this field for almost two decades, I assure you that I have many preferences. However, I also understand that even a system I loathe still

---

2 Though the CIA tried back in the 1960s. Turns out that "almost certain" is 93% and "probably" is 75%. See "Words of Estimative Probability" on the CIA website (*http://1.usa.gov/1KV5gtX*).

has fans. My preferences will no doubt show through, but I've done my best to be objective and provide adequate reasoning behind my conclusions.

I also understand that—like any consultant—my experience is likely biased toward one type of project or problem in ways that I might not even notice. Just like you can't walk a mile in another person's shoes, I can't completely relate to problems that I have never been tasked with solving. Systems I find enormously lacking for projects I have worked on might be entirely appropriate for the problem in front of you.

Finally, my experience with particular systems, paradigms, and methodologies has made it easier for me to draw examples and screen captures from those systems. For this, I apologize, but there are many negative practicalities involved with bootstrapping a system with which I'm unfamiliar to obtain an image or example. I thank those in the industry whom I bothered to share their experiences with some systems I felt were important to discuss, but to which I had had no exposure or access.

Conventions Used in This Book

The following typographical conventions are used in this book:

Italic
  Indicates new terms, URLs, email addresses, filenames, and file extensions.

`Constant width`
  Used for program listings, as well as within paragraphs to refer to program elements such as variable or function names, databases, datatypes, environment variables, statements, and keywords.

`Constant width bold`
  Shows commands or other text that should be typed literally by the user.

`Constant width italic`
  Shows text that should be replaced with user-supplied values or by values determined by context.

This element signifies a tip or suggestion.

This element signifies a general note.

This element indicates a warning or caution.

Safari® Books Online

 *Safari Books Online* is an on-demand digital library that delivers expert content in both book and video form from the world's leading authors in technology and business.

Technology professionals, software developers, web designers, and business and creative professionals use Safari Books Online as their primary resource for research, problem solving, learning, and certification training.

Safari Books Online offers a range of plans and pricing for enterprise, government, education, and individuals.

Members have access to thousands of books, training videos, and prepublication manuscripts in one fully searchable database from publishers like O'Reilly Media, Prentice Hall Professional, Addison-Wesley Professional, Microsoft Press, Sams, Que, Peachpit Press, Focal Press, Cisco Press, John Wiley & Sons, Syngress, Morgan Kaufmann, IBM Redbooks, Packt, Adobe Press, FT Press, Apress, Manning, New Riders, McGraw-Hill, Jones & Bartlett, Course Technology, and hundreds more. For more information about Safari Books Online, please visit us online.

How to Contact Us

Please address comments and questions concerning this book to the publisher:

> O'Reilly Media, Inc.
> 1005 Gravenstein Highway North
> Sebastopol, CA 95472
> 800-998-9938 (in the United States or Canada)
> 707-829-0515 (international or local)
> 707-829-0104 (fax)

We have a web page for this book, where we list errata, examples, and any additional information. You can access this page at *http://www.oreilly.com/catalog/0636920034186.do*.

To comment or ask technical questions about this book, send email to *bookquestions@oreilly.com*.

For more information about our books, courses, conferences, and news, see our website at *http://www.oreilly.com*.

Find us on Facebook: *http://facebook.com/oreilly*

Follow us on Twitter: *http://twitter.com/oreillymedia*

Watch us on YouTube: *http://www.youtube.com/oreillymedia*

Acknowledgments

Foremost, I'd like to thank this industry. Stepping back from this book as it came to a conclusion, I realized that nothing I wrote here is particularly original. What I'm doing is simply curating, collating, remixing, and elaborating on concepts and ideas put into practice every day by thousands of people around the world.

I've learned that, at the most basic level, this is what a writer does: we process information. Unless we're reporting on original research or writing a wholly original work of fiction, we simply consume information from other sources, collect it, filter it, analyze it, reorganize it, explain it, then distribute it. Considered from that perspective, this process is not unlike the content management process itself, which we'll spend the next 300 pages discussing.

However, some more specific acknowledgments are clearly necessary.

Thanks to my wife Annie, my children Alec, Gabrielle, and Isabella, and my goddaughter Brookelynne, for putting up with me while I was writing the initial draft, and especially after I swore it was "done"...but then kept writing anyway.

Thanks to my business partners, Joe Kepley, Karla Santi, and Dennis Breske, for giving me the time to write this.

Thanks to the unparalleled employees at Blend Interactive for helping build a business that gives me the opportunity to spend my days thinking about content management. I hope this book represents at least a vague shadow of the breadth of experience and knowledge that exists in the Blend office.

Thanks to my editor, Ally MacDonald, for taking a chance on some random guy who filled out O'Reilly's online submission form.

Thanks to the speaker crew from the Now What 2014 conference who sat around a table in Crawford's Bar and Grill in Sioux Falls, South Dakota, and talked me into writing this book in the first place: Karen McGrane, Kristina Halvorson, Jeff Eaton, Jarrod Gingras, Jeff Sauer, Corey Vilhauer, and Jeff Cram.

Thanks to my technical editors, Arild Henrichsen, Lynsey Struthers, Seth Gottlieb, and Corey Vilhauer. Any one of them could have ended this by simply telling me the book was no good. The fact that they didn't was the first hurdle I had to clear.

Thanks to my assistant Kerrie Vilhauer, who did the first copyedit on every chapter and spent far too much time changing "that" to "which" and crossing out my promiscuous hyphenation.[3] Her giddy determination at clarifying obscure rules of the English language was both appreciated and occasionally frightening.

Thanks to Tony Byrne, a close friend and mentor for many years who has helped me enormously by repeatedly putting this business and practice into context, and who did me the honor of writing the foreword.

Finally, thanks to Bob Boiko for writing *The Content Management Bible*. I finally finished it while on a plane that had been diverted to Kansas City back in 2006 or so. I still clearly remember closing the 1,122-page behemoth and flopping back in my seat to take it all in.

I think I might have actually been sweating.

---

[3] It's worth pointing out that the word "copyedit" in this sentence was hyphenated in the first draft of this preface.

PART I

The Basics

CHAPTER 1

What Content Management Is (and Isn't)

We tend to look at content management as a digital concept, but it's been around for as long as content. For as long as humans have been creating content, we've been searching for solutions to manage it.

The Library of Alexandria (300 BC to about AD 273) was an early attempt at managing content. It preserved content in the form of papyrus scrolls and codices, and presumably controlled access to them. Librarians were the first content managers.

Fast-forward a couple of thousand years, and the Industrial Revolution and the rise of technology increased the accumulation of information exponentially. The problem of managing it became more critical. The early 20th century was full of great thinkers who examined the problem of communicating and managing information: S.R. Raganathan, Vannevar Bush,[1] Paul Otlet, Claude Shannon, and even Melvil Dewey, the father of the venerable Dewey Decimal System.

So, the need for content management didn't begin with the World Wide Web, but simply shifted into fast-forward when the Web was born in the early '90s. At that moment, the ability to create and publish content tumbled down from its ivory tower and into the hands of the masses. Almost anyone could create a web page about virtually anything.

Content subsequently exploded. I was a college student at the time, and was slightly obsessed with James Bond. Suddenly, I could find reams and reams of information on

---

1 Bush wrote an incredibly influential essay in 1945 entitled "How We May Think" that lamented the lack of necessary information management tools and envisioned a future that turned out to be remarkably similar to what actually happened over the 70 years following its publication. Bush essentially described the World Wide Web about 50 years before Tim Berners-Lee made it happen.

007. The sheer amount of trivia was staggering. Of course, I attempted to print most of it, because if it wasn't on paper, how would I manage it?

It wasn't long before I was coediting a popular James Bond website—Mr. Kiss Kiss Bang Bang.[2] I learned that keeping track of content was a challenge. An article only existed as an HTML file in the web server's root directory at any given time. I wasn't an IT professional back then, so the only backup outside that file was the one on my local computer. There was no versioning or access control—one fat-finger mistake and the entire thing could be gone.

This struck me as dangerous. Even then, I knew that a website is essentially a content-based business, and with nothing more than a bunch of files lying around, I was effectively performing without a net. Content was our only business asset, and I remember thinking it was so brittle; one unforeseen problem and it could simply "blow away" like a dandelion in the wind.

Additionally, each HTML file was a mass of mid-'90s-era markup, complete with nested TABLE and FONT tags all over the place. There was no way to separate what was content from what was presentation, and each redesign of the site (there were many) involved manually reworking these files. Server Side Includes had helped to a certain extent, but each file was still a massive glob of mixed content and formatting code.

Some time later, I was working for The Microsoft Network as a forum manager for The World of James Bond. We were still writing HTML files in text editors, but Microsoft had introduced its content managers to the wonders of Visual Source Safe, a now long-since-deprecated source code management system. It provided backups, versioning, and file locking.

This clearly made us safer from a risk management perspective, but there was a mental shift too. We had a safety net now. The content we were creating had solidity to it. There was history and context. We were editing and grooming a continuing body of content, rather than just changing it in place. Content didn't exist only in simple files, but lived inside a larger system which provided a set of services to protect and safeguard it. We had gone from hiding money inside our mattresses to depositing it at an FDIC-insured financial institution.

Finally, at some crude level, my content was *managed*. It was still all mixed up with its presentation, and probably had a host of other problems, but I was at least a couple of steps safer than I had been before. Without me realizing it, Visual Source Safe effectively became my first content management system.

---

2 While now defunct, the site was at *http://ianfleming.org* for many years. There's an archive of screencaps in a public Facebook group (*https://www.facebook.com/groups/249445859356*), for those interested.

A lot has changed since then, but let's start at the beginning. Along the way, we'll hopefully answer all of the following questions:

- What is *content*?
- What is content *management*?
- What is a content management *system*?
- What are the different *types* of content management systems?
- What does a content management system *do*?
- What *doesn't* a content management system do?

What Is Content?

Many people have tried to draw a distinction between the fuzzy concepts of "data," "information," "content," and even "knowledge." Bob Boiko dedicated the entire first part of his seminal work *The Content Management Bible* (Wiley) to this question—some 5 chapters and 61 pages.

We're not going to go that far, but we'll summarize by simply differentiating between content and raw data, which is likely the highest-value return we can get out of the question. How is content management any different from managing any other type of data?

There are two key differences:

- Content is *created* differently.
- Content is *used* differently.

Created by Humans via Editorial Process

Content is created through "editorial process." This process is what humans do to prepare information for publication to an audience. It involves modeling, authoring, editing, reviewing, approving, versioning, comparing, and controlling.

The creation of a news article, for example, is highly subjective. Two editorial teams, given the same information, might develop two completely different news articles due to the human factors involved in the editorial process. Whereas a computational function seeks to deliver the same output from the same input every time, an editorial process never quite does.

The creation of content pivots largely on the opinions of human editors:

- What should the subject of the content be?
- Who is the intended audience of the content?
- From what angle should the subject be approached?
- How long should the content be?
- Does it need to be supported by media?

Despite significant advances in computing, these are not decisions a computer will make. These are messy, subjective, imperfect decisions that pour forth from the mind of a human editor sitting behind a keyboard. A small deviation in any of them (the proverbial flapping of a butterfly's wings (*https://en.wikipedia.org/wiki/Butterfly_effect*)) can spin a piece of content in an entirely different direction. Content is subjective and open for evaluation and interpretation. It has nuance. It is artisanal.

The editorial process is iterative—content is rarely created once, perfectly, and then never touched again. Rather, content is roughed in and refined over and over like clay on a potter's wheel, often even after being published. Content can change with the passage of time and the evolution of circumstance. What was relevant at one point might need to change or be withdrawn later.

Content is constantly in some state of flux and turnover. It's never "right." It's just "right now."

Compare this process to the creation of the record of a retail sale. There is no editorial process involved with swiping your credit card across a terminal. Furthermore, the data created is not subjected to any other process, will not be reviewed and approved. It is not subjective, it is deterministic. The transaction happened in an instant, a historical record was created, and that's that.

The sales transaction is designed to be as repeatable and devoid of subjective opinion as possible. It will never be edited (indeed, to do so would likely violate a policy or law). It is cold, sterile, and inert by design.

Consequently, management of these two types of information is quite different.

Intended for Human Consumption via Publication to an Audience

Content is data we create for a specific purpose: to distribute it with the intention of it ultimately being consumed by other humans. Sure, it might be scooped up by another computer via an API and rearranged and published somewhere else, but eventually the information is going to make its way to a human somewhere.

Bob Boiko writes:

> If you strip away all of the technology and terminology that we use to describe information systems, what do you have left? A simple and utterly commonplace idea: Information systems help you talk to people who are not in front of you.[3]

Our sales transaction from the prior section has no such destiny. It was created as a backward-looking record of a historical event. It will likely not be consumed by someone in the future, except in aggregate through reporting of some kind. It may be retrieved and reviewed individually, but only by necessity and likely on an exception basis.

Our news article, by contrast, was created as a forward-looking item to be published in the future and consumed by humans, through whatever channel (perhaps more than one). It might be repurposed, abbreviated, rearranged, and reformatted, but the ultimate goal for it is to be consumed and evaluated by another human being.

Our content has value in the future. It might be consumed for years (even centuries or millennia), and can continue providing value to the organization far into the future. Every time our article is read, or every time a new employee reads the payroll policy, there is a benefit attributed to the content creator.

Content is an investment in the future, not a record of the past.

A Definition of Content

Bringing these two concepts together, we arrive at our best attempt at a concise definition:

> Content is information produced through editorial process and ultimately intended for human consumption via publication.

This definition also points to a core dichotomy of content management: the difference between (1) management and (2) delivery. Content is created and managed, *then* it is published and delivered. The two disciplines require different skills and mindsets, and the state of current technology is creating more and more differences every day.

We'll revisit this two-sided approach to content management throughout this book.

What Is a Content Management System?

A content management system (CMS) is a software package that provides some level of automation for the tasks required to effectively manage content.

---

3 Bob Boiko, *Laughing at the CIO* (Medford: CyberAge Books, 2007), 99–100.

A CMS is usually server-based,[4] multiuser software that interacts with content stored in a repository. This repository might be located on the same server, as part of the same software package, or in a separate storage facility entirely.

A CMS allows editors to create new content, edit existing content, perform editorial processes on content, and ultimately make that content available to other people to consume it.

Logically, a CMS is comprised of many parts. The editing interface, repository, publishing mechanisms, etc., might all be separate, autonomous parts of the system behind the scenes. However, to a non-technical editor, all of these parts are generally viewed as a single, monolithic whole: "the CMS."

The Discipline Versus the Software

What's important to note is that a "content management system" is a specific manifestation of *software* designed to enable the *discipline* of content management. Just like a Ford Taurus is a specific manifestation of a device enabling personal transportation, Drupal, WordPress, and Episerver are specific manifestations of software enabling content management.

The discipline of content management—the accumulated theories, best practices, and accepted patterns of the field—transcends any specific system. In this sense, it's a Platonic ideal: an abstract, subjective representation of how content is to be managed.

The specifics of this ideal can be very different depending on the experiences, preferences, and needs of the observer. This means there's no single, accepted definition for content management as a discipline, just a set of debatable best practices. While people might try to lay claim to a Grand Unified Theory of Content Management, no such thing exists.

Thankfully, this means that skill with a particular content management system can be somewhat transferable. Even if System A differs from System B in extreme ways, they both still need to solve transcendent problems of the discipline, like workflow, versioning, publishing, etc. While specific technical skills might not transfer, working with a content management *system* requires the exercise and development of skills in the content management *discipline*.

---

4 Early CMSs were not server-based. Some of the first CMSs were client-side templating tools, such as City-Desk, MarsEdit, and Radio UserLand. These were installable software packages that allowed editors to work on content in a desktop interface. The systems then templated that content and transferred the resulting HTML to a server environment, usually via FTP. Today, these are often referred to as "desktop content management" tools. Few of these platforms are actively developed, but most still exist for purchase.

So, a CMS is a tool to assist in and enable the theoretical ideal of content management. How well any one CMS successfully brings that ideal to life is the subject of great debate and Internet flame wars.[5]

Types of Content Management Systems

We defined content as "information created through editorial process and intended for human consumption." Note that there was no mention of the Web in this definition (nor of the Internet itself, really).

However, given that this is a book about *web* content management, it's probably best that we define some different flavors of content management rather than lumping them into one big bucket.

The "big four" of content management might be identified as:

Web content management (WCM)
> The management of content primarily intended for mass delivery via a website. WCM excels at separating content from presentation and publishing to multiple channels.

Enterprise content management (ECM)
> The management of general business content, not necessarily intended for mass delivery or consumption (e.g., employee resumes, incident reports, memos, etc.). This flavor was more traditionally known as "document management," but the label has been generalized over the years. ECM excels in collaboration, access control, and file management.

Digital asset management (DAM)
> The management and manipulation of rich digital assets such as images, audio, and video for usage in other media. DAM excels at metadata and renditioning.

Records management (RM)
> The management of transactional information and other records that are created as a byproduct of business operations (e.g., sales records, access records, contracts, etc.). RM excels at retention and access control.

Clearly, the line blurs here quite a bit. A DAM[6] system is often used to provide content for a website through integration with a WCM. Furthermore, some ECM systems have systems by which they can publish some of their information to the Web.

---

5 "Flame" was the original term for two people hurling insults at each other in front of a virtual audience through the anonymous magic of the Internet. I think this is now called "Facebook."

6 An acronym that is the source of countless jokes, which, contrary to what some might say, just never seem to get old.

Software systems are known only through their *intended* use and their perception in the industry. Drupal is well known as a WCM system, but there are undoubtedly organizations using it to manage internal enterprise content. Conversely, Documentum is an ECM system, but some organizations might use it to deliver all or part of their websites.

DAM is interesting in that it is differentiated primarily on the basis of what it *does* to content. While almost any content management system can store video and image files, and ECM actually excels at it, DAM goes a step further by providing unique tools to render and transform digital assets. Images can be mass-resized and video can be spliced and edited directly inside the system, making a DAM system's point of differentiation one of processes that can be applied to content. Therefore, the core management features of a DAM system overlay quite closely those of an ECM system, with the DAM system layering a level of functionality on top. (Indeed, many DAM systems are sold simply as add-ons to ECM systems.)

There are other, even blurrier shades of gray. Some examples:

Component content management systems (CCMSs)
Used for management of extremely fine-grained content (paragraphs, sentences, and even individual words), often to assemble documentation or highly technical content.

Learning management systems (LMSs)
Used for management of learning resources and student interaction; most colleges and universities manage syllabi and the learning process via an LMS.

Portals
Used for management, presentation, and aggregation of multiple streams of information into a unified system.

Again, the lines here are very blurry.

Only some of what an LMS does is specific and unique to an LMS. Many different WCM systems, for instance, have add-ons and extensions that claim to turn them into an LMS, and many more are simply used as such out of the box.

In the end, a given software system is mentally classified among the public based on several factors:

- The market in which it promotes itself and in which it competes
- The use cases and examples that the user community creates and promotes
- The specific features designed to meet the needs of a particular user or type of content

CMS software is *targeted* at particular markets or usage scenarios. That has never stopped anyone from using it in ways outside of the one the vendor designed it for.

For the purposes of this book, we will concentrate on mainstream WCM—that software designed to manage a website intended for public delivery and consumption.

(And, at the risk of beating this subject to death, even this designation is blurry. Organizations commonly power social networking platforms from their WCM systems, managing content that ends up as Facebook updates, tweets, or even emails. While this is not technically "website content," our definition will have to suffice.)

What Does "Enterprise" Mean?

You see that word a lot, as part of phrases like "enterprise software" or "enterprise content." It has no precise definition, but it generally means "big" or "intended for large organizations."

It's a vague term, and there is no exact opposite—few CMSs would describes themselves as "provincial" or "boutique." And nothing is stopping the world's smallest CMS from describing itself as "enterprise," either. It's highly subjective—what's big to one person is small to another.

CMS vendors use the term to indicate that their systems can handle large amounts of content, or fit into a very distributed, sophisticated environment (multiple load-balanced servers across multiple data centers, for instance). It's also often used to set expectations on pricing—"enterprise" usually means "expensive."

"Enterprise content" is often used to refer to internal content that is not published outside the organization. Using this definition, a news article release is not "enterprise content," whereas the internal minutes of an executive meeting would be.

An "enterprise content management system" is vaguely accepted to mean a system that is designed to manage this type of internal organizational content. They are consequently heavy on management tools and light on publication tools.

What a CMS Does

Let's break down the core functions of a CMS. In broad terms, what is the value proposition? Why are we better off with a CMS than without?

Control Content

A CMS allows us to get control of our content, which is something you'll understand well if your content is out of control. A CMS keeps track of content. It "knows" where our content is, what condition it's in, who can access it, and how it relates to other content. Furthermore, it seeks to prevent bad things from happening to our content.

Specifically, a CMS provides core control functions, such as:

Permissions
> Who can see this content? Who can change it? Who can delete it?

State management and workflow
> Is this content published? Is it in draft? Has it been archived and removed from the public?

Versioning
> How many times has this content changed? What did it look like three months ago? How does that version differ from the current version? Can I restore or republish an older version?

Dependency management
> What content is being used by what other content? If I delete this content, how does that affect other content? What content is currently "orphaned" and unused?

Search and organization
> How do I find a specific piece of content? How do I find all content that refers to X? How do I group and relate content so it's easier to manage?

Each of these items increases our level of control over our content and reduces risk—there is less chance that the shareholder report will be released early, or that the only copy of our procedures manual will be deleted accidentally.

Allow Content Reuse

Using content in more than one place and in more than one way increases its value. Some examples:

- A news article appears on its own page, but also as a teaser on a category page and in multiple "Related Article" sidebars.
- An author's bio appears at the bottom of all articles written by that person.
- A privacy statement appears at the bottom of every page on a website.

In these situations, this information is not created every time in every location, but simply retrieved and displayed from a common location.

This reuse of content was one of the original problems that vexed early web developers. Remember the James Bond site I discussed earlier? One of the great frustrations was creating an article, and then adding it to all the index pages where it was supposed to appear. If we ever deleted the article or changed the title, we'd have to go find all the references and remove or change them.

This problem was mitigated somewhat by Server Side Includes, which allowed page editors to insert a snippet of HTML by simply referring to a separate file—the files were combined on the server prior to delivery. Later platforms tried to automate this even further; Microsoft FrontPage, for example, had a feature it explicitly called "Shared Borders."

The ability to reuse content is highly dependent on the structure of that content. Your ability to structure your content accurately for optimal reuse is highly dependent on the features your CMS provides for you.

Allow Content Automation and Aggregation

Having all of our content in a single location makes it easier to query and manipulate it. If we want to find all news articles that were written last week and mention the word "SPECTRE," we can do that because there is one system that "knows" all about our content.

If our content is structured correctly, we can manipulate it to display in different formats, publish it to different locations, and rearrange it on the fly to serve the needs of our visitors more effectively:

- We can allow users to consume content in other formats, such as PDF or other ebook formats.
- We can automatically create lists and navigation (more generally, "content aggregations"—see Chapter 7) for our website.
- We can create multiple translations of content to ensure we deliver the language most appropriate to the current user.
- We can alter the content we publish in real time based on the specific behaviors and conditions exhibited by our visitors.

A CMS enables this by structuring, storing, examining, and providing query facilities around our content. It becomes the single source of information about our content; the thing that has its arms around the entire repository; the oracle we can consult to find information about our content.

Increase Editorial Efficiency

The ability of editors to create and edit content quickly and accurately is enormously affected by the platform used. It's rare to find an editor who has unconditional love for a CMS, but the alternative, editing a website manually, is clearly much less desirable.

Editor efficiency is increased by a system that controls what type of content editors can and can't add, what formatting tools are available to them, how their content is structured in the editing interface, how the editorial workflow and collaboration are managed, and what happens to their content after they publish.

A good CMS enables editors to publish more content in a shorter time frame (it increases "editorial throughput"), and to control and manage the published content with a lower amount of friction or drag on their process.

Editorial efficiency has a huge impact on morale, which is intangible but critical. Many editors have a historically antagonistic relationship with their CMSs, and nothing destroys editorial efficiency more quickly than a clunky editorial interface and flow.

What a CMS Doesn't Do

Now for the bad news: there are things a CMS doesn't do. More specifically, there are things that a CMS doesn't do *but that people mistakenly assume it does,* which leads to problems and unfulfilled expectations.

Create Content

A CMS simply *manages* content, it doesn't *create* content. It doesn't write your news articles, procedure documents, or blog posts. You must still provide the editorial horsepower to generate the content that it's supposed to be managing.

Many times, a CMS implementation has ended with a group of people looking at each other and thinking, "So...now what?" Every web development shop in the country can tell you stories about the shiny new CMS that was never once used by the client because they never changed their site after the day it launched. Occasionally, my company has taken calls from clients *years* after their sites launched wanting to know how to log in to their CMS for the first time.

Related to this, a CMS won't ensure that your content is any good, either. Although a CMS might offer several tools to minimize poor-quality content from a technical standpoint (ensuring that hyperlinks are valid, or that all images have ALT tags, for instance), a CMS cannot edit your content to be sure it makes sense and meets the needs of your audience.

The best-laid plans to create massive amounts of quality content often fall through when confronted with the hard reality of schedule pressure and business deadlines. You need to ensure that your content creation process exists apart from your CMS.

Create Marketing Plans

Even assuming your content is created consistently and managed well, that doesn't mean it actually provides your organization with any value.

A CMS doesn't "know" anything about marketing. While some systems have marketing tools built into them, they still depend on human beings for direction. Effective marketing is a uniquely human practice involving a combination of aesthetics, sociology, psychology, experience, and intuition. A CMS can make executing your marketing plans easier and more efficient, but those plans still need to be conceived, created, and analyzed by a competent human.

A CMS doesn't take the place of a creative team that understands your marketplace, your customers, your competitors, and what you need to do to differentiate yourself. No software can take the place of a good digital marketing strategy or team.

Effectively Format Content

While a CMS can structure content and automatically format it during publication, there is still an unfortunate amount of room for a human editor to screw it up. Most CMSs have a rich text editor or some other interface element that allows editors to format text and images. This can lead to things like:

- Too much use of **bold** and *italics*
- Inconsistent alignment of content
- Random and inconsistent hyperlinking
- Poor image placement

Editors have never seen a button on an editing interface that they didn't want to press. The only way to limit this seems to be to remove as many editing options as possible, then try to withstand the hailstorm of editor complaints that will inevitably follow.

Provide Governance

"Governance" describes the access to and processes around your content: who has access to what, and what processes/steps they follow to make changes to it. For example:

- If Bob adds a news article, who needs to approve this, and what does that approval look like? Does someone copyedit and someone else edit for quality, voice, and tone? Can you diagram this process out on a piece of paper?
- If John wants to change how the news archives are organized, and the CMS allows him to do this…can he? What process does he have to go through to do this?
- If Jennifer wants an account on the CMS to start creating content, how does she get that? Who decides who is allowed to become an editor?

Every CMS has some method to limit the actions a user can take, but these limits have to be defined in advance. The CMS will simply carry out what your organization directs it to do. These plans have to be created through human interaction and judgment, then converted into the permissions and access limits the CMS can enforce.

Governance is primarily a human discipline. You are determining the processes and policies that humans will abide by when working with your content. The CMS is just a framework for enforcement.

A Homebuilding Analogy

The home you live in is a rough combination of three things:

- The raw building materials (wood, nails, glass)
- The tools and building equipment (hammers, saws)
- The human power to make it all go (Ted, your contractor)

None of those things builds a house by itself. A pile of wood is just a pile of wood until Ted takes his hammer and makes something happen. Ted is the key here. The materials and tools are inanimate. Ted is the prime mover.

In terms of content management:

- Raw materials = your content
- Tools and equipment = your CMS
- Ted = *you*

All the content in the world doesn't do much if it's not managed. And all the management in the world doesn't do much if there's no content. Neither of them does anything without human processes and effort to make them work together, just like a pile of wood and a hammer don't magically build a house.

You are the thing that ties it all together. You are the one that makes it all go. A CMS is just a tool.

CHAPTER 2

Points of Comparison

In medicine, certain conditions are known as "spectrum disorders" because they're not simple binary conditions from which you suffer or don't suffer. Rather, these conditions exist along a spectrum of severity. One can suffer from a condition slightly or severely, and the difference might manifest as entirely different symptoms and require entirely different treatments.

Web content management can be the same way.

To demonstrate this, it might help to examine the aspects of content management as a series of comparisons or dichotomies. By understanding the range of available options along a particular axis and what the boundaries are on either side, we can begin to understand the full breadth of options.

There are numerous facets to systems, implementations, and practices that are simply not black and white. In fact, there are few absolutes in content management. What's correct in one situation is clearly wrong in another. What's right for one organization would be a disaster at another. The key to making a CMS work is making the right decisions for *your* situation, which often makes it seem like more art than science.

Furthermore, the fundamental differences we're going to explore here make it difficult to compare CMSs accurately. Instead of apples to apples, you end up with apples to pot roast. For example:

- Drupal Gardens is a hosted service built in PHP using a coupled model, offering few marketing tools and little in the way of customization or implementation.
- Ingenuix is an installed system built in ASP.NET using a decoupled model, offering marketing automation and deep customization and requiring significant implementation.

Technical comparisons of those two systems are difficult because they lie at opposite ends of multiple axes of comparison:

- One is hosted, the other is installed.
- One is built in PHP, the other is in .NET (and since one is hosted, often users simply won't care that it's built in any particular language).
- One is coupled, the other is decoupled.
- One is commercial, the other is open source.

The correct solution for any particular aspect of your situation will fall somewhere between two ends of the scale. Therefore, we need to understand what each end of that scale looks like.

Target Site Type

Different CMSs are targeted at different types of sites. The range in intended end results is vast. A "website" could be any one of the following:

- A small, static marketing site for a dental office
- A multinational newspaper publishing hundreds of articles a day
- A single-author blog for a technology writer
- An intranet for a medium-sized accounting firm
- An extranet for the dealers of a farm implement manufacturer
- The product documentation library for a software developer
- The course materials and syllabi for a small university
- An online community and social network for owners of Porsches

There's just no easy way to draw hard boundaries around what we mean when we say "website." Content management is a problem for all of the examples given here, and CMSs exist that specialize in each of them. The CMS used for the dental office could conceivably be used to power the newspaper's website, though it likely wouldn't work very well.

A CMS is very rarely promoted as a general system to solve all problems of every type of site. A particular CMS is usually targeted at a particular type of problem. Some problems might be broad, some might be narrow, but the architects behind a CMS are pursuing a target problem to be solved. It's usually in your best interest to match the intention of your CMS as closely to your problem as possible.

Systems Versus Implementations

It's important to separate a content management *system* from a CMS *implementation*. An implementation is the process by which a CMS is installed, configured, templated, and extended to deliver the website you want.

Unless you build your CMS from scratch, you are not the only one using it. Other organizations are using the same software to solve different problems and deliver different types of websites, so it's not going to be preconfigured to do any one thing particularly well. This means a necessary step is the initial effort of adapting the CMS to do exactly what your organization and circumstances require from it.

 "Initial effort" is a gross oversimplification. The fact is, CMS projects never seem to end. When you launch, you usually already have a list of changes. Websites are constantly in flux. The idea that you'll launch your website and never have to do any further development is hopelessly naïve.

To revisit our homebuilding analogy from the first chapter, a pile of wood and a set of tools are not the house you want. Ted the Contractor exerts effort to use the tools to build the house. This is a one-time effort, and the final product is a completed house. Furthermore, Mike the Contractor might use the same materials to build an entirely different house.

An implementation is a significant programming project. The skillsets required are not unlike those for other development efforts: you need designers, developers, frontend specialists, project managers, and experts in the CMS itself. Organizations sometimes do their own implementations, but it's often contracted out to a development firm that specializes in the CMS being implemented.

The expense of the implementation is usually the largest expense in the budget, far eclipsing even the license fees for a commercial CMS. The rule of thumb differs depending on who states it, but implementation fees are usually some multiple of the licensing cost of the software.

 A friend, when asked if an organization should "buy or build," responded, "There's no such thing as buy *or* build. It's always buy *and* build."

The implementation should be considered at least as important to the success of the project as the CMS software itself. There are many decisions to make during an implementation, and two different implementations of the same website using the

---

same CMS might bear little resemblance. Any of these decision points can be implemented well or poorly, and those results will have a huge impact on the final result.

The most perfect CMS in the world can be rendered all but useless by a poor implementation. And while I concede there are some CMSs that are irredeemably poor or inappropriate for a given situation, I've seen many stellar implementations that were able to make mediocre CMSs work for a particular project.

Platform Versus Product

If we consider a CMS a range of functional "completeness," the extremes might look like this:

- No CMS functionality at all, just a raw programming platform
- A fully functional CMS ready to go out of the box, complete with prebuilt features to solve all your content problems with no changes

 "Out of the box" is a phrase used often in the CMS world. It means functionality that theoretically works with no implementation necessary. It's commonly used to oversell software of all types. Be skeptical whenever you encounter it.

In between these two extremes, we can insert a third option:

- A programming framework providing flexible API access to common content management features and functions that can be used to develop your own solution, along with a default user interface and configuration to support common needs

Tony Byrne from Real Story Group has referred to this type of CMS as a "platform," and the opposite prebuilt extreme as a "product."[1]

Platform-style[2] systems are designed to be rearranged and customized during implementation. Product style systems are designed to solve specific problems quickly and without significant effort.

---

1 "How the New Platforms vs. Products Debate Impacts Your Success," (*http://www.realstorygroup.com/Library/Download/43/How-the-New-Platforms-vs.-Products-Debate-Impacts-Your-Success*) February 23, 2010.

2 Note the intentional use of "platform-style" as a qualifier. It's hard to definitively say if something is a platform or not. Refer back to the comment about spectrum disorders at the start of the chapter. Some systems are "platform-y" in some aspects, but not in others, and some systems are more "platform-y" than others overall. Being a platform as opposed to a product is very much a matter of degree.

Platform-style systems are flexible but effort-intensive. Product-style systems are rigid but supposedly easy to implement.

It's a natural trade-off. With a product, you trade reduced implementation costs for agreeing to accept how the system works. With a platform, you trade increased implementation costs for more flexibility and control.

Many vendors market their systems as products that are ready to solve all content problems out of the box with very little effort. The inverse is more rare: very few vendors want to be known as providing systems that require heroic customization and programming in order to build a website. While this may appeal to hardcore developers, they're not usually the people making purchasing decisions.

The platform orientation of a system can be used to explain the extent and expectation of the system's extensibility and customizability. Some CMSs are highly customizable, and this is absolutely expected in every implementation. Other CMSs are designed to go in as purchased and provide few options for customization.

This is simply due to the fact that every CMS vendor or development community has use cases (literally, "cases for use") in mind when their system is developed. Whether these use cases are explicitly recorded somewhere or not, every CMS is created to solve a set of theoretical problems. One system might be designed to manage a blog, another might be designed to manage an intranet.

Your ability to use a product-style CMS to solve *your* problems depends highly on how closely your situation resembles these theoretical problems. If they don't match up, then your ability to use this CMS for a purpose outside its original designed intention depends highly on the extensibility of the CMS.

Often, a product-style system will provide prebuilt functionality that gets very close to the desired solution of one of your problems. In situations where 90% isn't enough, the product will have to be customized to bridge the gap. Some systems are designed to allow this, and others are not.

Actual Versus Theoretical Benefits

When discussing the benefits of any type of software, it's important to differentiate between actual and theoretical benefits:

- *Actual benefits* are benefits your organization uses and derives value from.
- *Theoretical benefits* are benefits that exist and could theoretically provide value to your organization, but that you do not actually implement or use.

Software is largely sold on theoretical benefits. Those in sales know how to paint a positive picture in your head of how you would use all the functionality they offer, and a negative picture of what might happen to your organization (and you, professionally) if you were caught without this theoretical benefit.

More than one CMS has been selected based solely on features that the organization had no immediate plans to use (and usually never does). The idea of wanting a feature-rich product is not inherently wrong, but it becomes problematic when the desire for a particular feature causes the abandonment or minimization of a more relevant feature.

I call this "Ferrari Syndrome," in honor of the car buyer who will never drive over 80 mph but nevertheless loves the idea that he could go 200 if he really wanted to, and gives up a much-needed backseat in pursuit of this idea. The excitement of benefits "possible but never realized" has been driving purchasing decisions since the beginning of commerce.

As consumers, we like the vision of ourselves as competent, skilled professionals who solve complicated problems. We're naturally drawn to powerful tools that promise to help us tackle challenging issues because they reinforce this vision.

Be realistic about the features you will actually use. Identify those core features that you absolutely cannot function without (the "must-haves") and make sure those are well served before moving on to features you think might work well for you and merely hope to use one day (the "nice-to-haves").

Be sure to evaluate what you *think* is a "must-have" against this criterion: if you find a system that does everything perfectly *except* this one thing, will you reject it because of this single omission? If not, then this is not a "must-have."

Open Source Versus Commercial

With most software, both commercial (paid license) and open source options exist. This is probably more true of content management than any other genre. Literally thousands of options exist, and extremely common open source CMS platforms like WordPress and Drupal power a significant percentage of websites worldwide.

Given the installed base and depth of use, open source CMSs are generally well tested, feature rich, and have a large volume of contributed code and modules. The availability, responsiveness, and accuracy of community support is usually quite high, but varies widely.

An open source CMS project can usually trace its roots back to a developer champion who originally created it to solve a specific personal or professional problem. Very few systems are "clean sheet" designs built from scratch with the intention to be distributed. Rather, they begin as small, internal projects and grow until reaching critical mass and being contributed to the open source community for continued development.

This results in a fair amount of developer-centrism—some of them are written *by* developers, *for* developers. Most open source projects subconsciously evolve to be interesting and desirable for developers first, then everyone else second. Editors and marketers are often the second-class citizens in these cases.

This results in a common pattern—an "open source syndrome," if you will—characterized by:

- Platform-style systems with highly extensible APIs
- Emphasis on the database-like features of a CMS, such as content modeling and aggregation
- An assumption that a developer will always be available for implementation and management
- Average to below-average user interfaces with some rough edges
- A tendency to overwhelm editors with numerous options
- An emphasis on generalization, configurability, and elegance of code
- Lack of higher-end marketing or delivery tools

Open source systems normally go through large amounts of teardown and reconstruction over time. For many developers, the code and process of solving content problems is an end goal in itself. Rearchitecting the system to be more elegant, efficient, or generalizable is held to be a worthwhile effort.

Over a decade ago, Joel Spolsky of Fog Creek Software was complaining about this exact problem:

> We're programmers. Programmers are, in their hearts, architects, and the first thing they want to do when they get to a site is to bulldoze the place flat and build something grand. We're not excited by incremental renovation: tinkering, improving, planting flower beds.[3]

Commercial systems, on the other hand, have a built-in limitation—they need license fees, *so the end goal is selling the software, not architecting it*. Clearly, this can result in some bad decisions and wallpapering over of genuine technical problems, but it also results in more end-user-focused development, because features for the end user is what sells licenses. At the end of the day, commercial software *has to ship* for the company to stay in business.

New open source systems are quite common, though as the market is more crowded now, it's harder and harder for any new system to gain any traction and achieve a sig-

---

3 "Things You Should Never Do, Part I," (*http://www.joelonsoftware.com/articles/fog0000000069.html*) April 6, 2000.

nificant installed base. Consequently, the most successful open source CMSs are also some of the oldest.

PHP-based systems form the lion's share of the open source CMS landscape. The three most common CMSs of any license style in popular use (WordPress, Drupal, and Joomla![4]) are all PHP systems.

Systems lose traction and developer support primarily due to the inability of their underlying technology stack to attract new developers—there are dozens of systems from the mid-'90s written in Perl, ColdFusion, and (occasionally) C++ that are slowly dying off. New Java-based open source systems are also becoming more and more rare as Java becomes a less popular web framework.

Using an open source CMS provides numerous benefits:

- The software is free.
- Community support is often plentiful.
- Contributed code is often available to solve common problems.
- Developers and contractors are usually highly available.

But some drawbacks exist too:

- The "open source syndrome" we discussed tends to make these systems less attractive to non-editors.
- Ubiquitous usage results in large amounts of malware, penetration attempts, and security patches (the sheer number of WordPress installations makes it an attractive target for hackers).
- Community support for especially complicated problems will often run short.
- Professional service-level support may not be available.
- Usage of open source software may violate an organization's IT policies.
- Open source software (not just CMSs) is heavily weighted toward the PHP and Java technology stacks.

We'll discuss some of these points in greater depth in Chapter 3.

---

4 I'm not an excitable person by nature. The exclamation point is actually an official part of the name of the CMS (*http://issuu.com/joomladocs/docs/20150308_joomla_brandmanual_basic_d/1*).

While many open source CMSs start out as engineer hobbyist projects, the successful ones have evolved to put user experience front and center. The "Big 3" in particular (Drupal, WordPress, and Joomla!) put a great deal of effort into making the inherently complex world of structured content more approachable for end users.

In addition, as they tend to be more engineer-heavy, OSS projects don't suffer from "commercial software syndrome"; many proprietary CMSs have very polished demos, but that polish is only skin deep. The slick UI hides a lack of underlying power and flexibility—crucial power and flexibility that open source developers find interesting to work on.

As a result, leading OSS projects often have much stronger functionality than their proprietary counterparts, even if it may take a bit more training and documentation to leverage it. And that's while remaining free to use, which can often be a major benefit.

Larry Garfield is a Senior Architect and Community Lead at Palantir.net, a full-service digital agency in Chicago, and one of the lead developers of Drupal 8.

Technology Stack

All software runs on a "stack" of supporting software, databases, and languages. A CMS is always implemented in a specific language and storage framework (which may or may not be "swappable"). This language and storage framework strongly influence what hosting environment the CMS needs to run.

The stack includes the following:

- The CMS itself
- A programming framework
- A programming language
- A database server
- A web server
- An operating system

You can envision that as a pile of technologies, with the CMS sitting on top of it all and requiring everything below it to run properly. Table 2-1 shows an example stack comparison for two very different systems: Episerver and eZ Platform.

Table 2-1. Comparison of the technology stacks of Episerver and eZ Platform

Stack item	Episerver	eZ Platform
Programming framework	ASP.NET MVC	Symfony
Programming language	C#	PHP
Database server	SQL Server	Multiple (usually MySQL)
Web server	Internet Information Server (IIS)	Multiple (usually Apache)
Operating system	Windows	Multiple (usually Linux)

The crudest categorization of CMSs might be by technology stack.[5] The most common stacks are:

- LAMP (Linux, Apache, MySQL, and PHP/Python/Perl; although almost always PHP)
- ASP.NET (Windows)
- Java/J2EE (Linux or Windows)

Less common stacks include:

- Ruby on Rails
- Python (usually the Django framework)
- Node.js

Systems cannot be swapped into different runtime languages, but hosting environments can vary slightly. For instance, while PHP normally runs on Apache and Linux, it can run reasonably well on Windows. ASP.NET almost always runs on Windows, but can sometimes run on Linux via the Mono framework.

This matters primarily if your organization limits the technology stacks it will support. While it would be ideal to select a CMS based solely on features and its fitness for your particular situation, the CMS still has to be installed and hosted somewhere. If your organization is hosting it, they might dictate all or parts of the stack. The same limitation applies if your organization is going to implement in-house—if your devel-

---

5 To developers, of course, this is usually the defining characteristic. When developers describe a CMS, they'll invariably lead with a stack descriptor: "Well, that's a PHP system…" or "It's built in .NET…"

opment group is full of Java programmers, then there's a good chance you're going to be limited to that stack.

It's quite common for an IT department to only support specific combinations of technologies. Windows servers are a common requirement in corporate IT, as are specific database frameworks. Some companies dictate Oracle as their only officially supported database, while others might be more liberal. If these limitations exist in your organization, they will necessarily pare down the pool of possible CMSs you are able to implement.

The desirability of any particular stack is the subject of great debate and far beyond the scope of this book. The important point is that technology stack limitations—if they exist—are usually very rigid. If your organization dictates that only Windows servers can run in its data center, *this is something you absolutely need to know before picking a CMS.*

 Of course, hosting your CMS outside the reach of your organization's IT policy is a commonly used tactic to make an end run around imposed limits. Many a marketing department has added hosting services to an RFP with the goal of not having to abide by the limitations the IT department dictates.

Management Versus Delivery

While almost everything a CMS does is lumped under the umbrella of "management" by default, the lifecycle of a piece of content can effectively be split at a hypothetical "Publish" button.

Everything that happens to content from the moment it's created until the moment it dies is "management." The subset of everything that happens to the *published* version of that content from the moment it's published is "delivery." The two disciplines are quite different.

Management is about security, control, and efficiency. It's composed of functionalities like content modeling, permissions, versioning, and workflow. These are features that ease the creation of content, enable editorial collaboration, and keep content secure.

Delivery is about optimization and performance. The features involved in delivery depend highly on the capabilities of the CMS. These capabilities are currently evolving quickly in the marketplace. Until recently, delivery simply meant making content available at a public location. Today, the modern CMS is highly concerned with the performance and optimization of the content it delivers.

In the commercial space we've seen a plethora of tools that enable advanced marketing during delivery. Features like personalization, A/B testing, and analytics have proliferated as different vendors try to set their systems apart. These features used to be provided by separate "marketing automation" software packages that operated solely in the delivery environment. More and more, these tools are being built into the CMS.

The unintended result is that core management tools have changed little in the last half-decade. These tools have reached maturity in many cases, and the focus is currently clearly on marketing and optimization tools during delivery. Management is generally considered "good enough."

Coupled Versus Decoupled

The "management vs. delivery" dichotomy manifests itself technically when considering the coupling level of a CMS. What hosting relationship does the management environment of a CMS have to the delivery environment?

In a coupled system, management and delivery occur on the same server (or farm of servers). Editors manage content on the same system where visitors consume it. Management and delivery are simply two sides of the same software.

This is an extremely common paradigm. Many developers and editors know of nothing else.

In a decoupled system, management and delivery are (wait for it) *decoupled* from one another. Content is managed in one environment (one server or farm) and then published to a separate environment (another server or farm). In these situations, the management functions are sometimes referred to as the "repository server," and the delivery of the content takes place on a "publishing server" or "delivery server." In these cases, published content is transported to an entirely separate environment, which may or may not have any knowledge of how the content was created or how it is managed.

Fewer and fewer systems support this paradigm, and it's normally seen in high-availability or distributed publishing environments, such as when a website is delivered from multiple servers spread across multiple data centers (though this may be changing, as we'll discuss at the end of the book). It has the perceived benefits of security, stability, and some editorial advantage, as editors can make large-scale changes to content without affecting the publishing environment, only to "push" all changes as a single batch when the content is ready (though this advantage is steadily finding its way into more and more coupled systems).

Actual technical benefits of decoupling include the ability to publish to multiple servers without the need to install the CMS on each (which lowers license fees, in the case of commercial CMSs), and the ability to publish to highly distributed environments (multiple data centers on multiple continents, for example). Additionally, the delivery environment could be running on an entirely different technology stack than the management environment, as some systems publish "inert" assets such as simple HTML files or database records, which have few environment restrictions.

The primary drawback to decoupling is that published content is separated from the repository, which makes "live" features like personalization and user-generated content more complicated. For example, accepting user comments is more difficult when those comments have to be transported "backward" from the delivery server to the repository server, and then the blog post on which they appear has to be republished (with the new comments displayed) "forward" to the delivery server.

To counter this, decoupled CMSs are moving toward publishing content directly into companion software running on the delivery servers that has some level of knowledge of the management CMS and can enable content delivery features. The result is a CMS that's split in half, with management features running in one environment, and delivery features running in another.

Decoupled systems tend to be clustered on the Java technology stack. Some ASP.NET systems exist, but virtually no PHP systems use this paradigm.

We'll discuss the differences between the two publishing models in Chapter 9.

Installed Versus Software-as-a-Service (SaaS)

More and more IT infrastructure is moving to "the cloud," and CMSs are no different. While the norm used to be installation and configuration on your server infrastructure, vendors are now offering hosted or SaaS solutions more often. It's not uncommon to have software rented from the vendor and hosted in its environment.

The benefit purports to be a CMS that is hosted and supported by the vendor that developed it. Whether or not this provides actual benefit is up for debate. For many, "hosted" or "SaaS" just means "someone else's headache," and there are multiple other ways to achieve this outside of the vendors themselves.

Closely related to the installed vs. SaaS debate is whether or not the CMS supports multiple, isolated users in the same environment. So-called "single-tenant" vs. "multitenant" systems are much like living in a house vs. an apartment building. Users of a multitenant system exist in the same shared runtime environment, isolated only by login. They occupy a crowded room, but each appears to be the only one there.

The purported benefit here is a "hands off" approach to technology. These systems are promoted as giving you instant access and allowing you to concentrate on your content, not on the technology running it. The trade-off is limits on your ability to customize, since you're sharing the system with other clients.

We'll discuss this dichotomy in greater detail in Chapter 3.

Code Versus Content

The implementation of a CMS will almost always involve two types of programming code at some level. The system will have (1) customizations that are developed in the native code of the system (PHP, Java, or C#, for example), and (2) custom templating and the associated HTML, CSS, and JavaScript.

This code is usually managed in a source code management system such as Git or Team Foundation Server. It's usually tested in a separate environment (a test or integration server) prior to launch. Launching new code is usually a scheduled event. Depending on your IT policy, new code might have to have approved test and change plans, as well as failure and backout plans in the event that something goes wrong.

With code under source control, there's always "another place" where it lives. The CMS installation where it's executing and providing value is not its home; it's just deployed there for the moment. If that copy was ever destroyed for some reason, it could be redeployed from source control.

Content, on the other hand, is developed by editors and *lives in the CMS*. In coupled systems, it's often developed in the production CMS and just kept unpublished until it's ready to launch. It might be reviewed via a formal or informal workflow process, but often isn't otherwise "tested." If an editor has sufficient permissions, it's possible to make a content change, review it, and publish it all within the span of a few minutes with no oversight.

Content will almost always change vastly more often than code. An organization might publish and modify content several dozen times a day, but only adjust the programming code behind the website every few months. When this happens, it's to fix a bug or fundamentally change how something on the website functions, not simply to change the information presented to visitors.

Code and content are sometimes confused because of the legacy of static HTML websites. For an organization that built its website with static HTML, an HTML file had to be modified for a single word to change. Thus, *a code change and a content change were the same thing*.

Decoupled content management can also blur the line between code and content. In a decoupled system, modified content is often published to a test sandbox where it's reviewed for accuracy, then published to the production environment. The existence of an entirely separate environment is similar to how code is managed. Content starts to act like code.

In these situations, it's sometimes mentally hard to separate the test environment for *content* from the test environment for *code*. You have two different testing paradigms, each with its own environment, each pushing changes into the production environment.

This changes with a CMS, especially a coupled CMS. Under this paradigm, content changes without code changing at all. The verbiage of a press release might be completely rearranged, but the template that renders it is the same.

Organizations moving from static websites or decoupled systems sometimes have trouble adjusting to the idea of a "virtual" test/staging environment—unpublished content is created on the production server, and just not visible while it's awaiting publication.

Their past correlation with code tempts them to treat content the same way and intermix the two concepts.

Code Versus Configuration

Many features in a CMS can be implemented through (1) developers writing code—either core code or templating code—or (2) editors and administrators working from the interface.

Developers have complete freedom, up to the limits of the system itself. There's generally no functionality that is not available from code, as code itself is the core underpinning of the system. The only limitation on a developer is how well the API is architected to allow access and manipulation. But even with a poorly implemented API, a developer has the full capabilities of a programming language to get around shortcomings.

Editors, on the other hand, have access to only a subset of what a developer can do from code. They are limited to the functionality that has been exposed from the interface, which varies greatly depending on the system. Some systems allow minor configuration options to be set, while others have elaborate module and plug-in architectures that allow new functionality to be created from the interface on a running, production system.

Why wouldn't a system expose *all* functionality from the interface? Sometimes it's because a particular setting or piece of functionality is changed too infrequently to justify the effort of building an interface for it. Other times it's because the person using it is more likely to be a developer who would like to change it from code, to ensure it gets versioned as source code and deployed like other code changes.

However, the most common reason is that the feature is simply too complicated to be managed by an interface. The ability to write code allows for the clear expression of extremely complex concepts. Developers are used to thinking abstractly about information and codifying it in code.[6] Some features are simply too complex to easily build a management interface around them.

While building features from configuration sounds enticing, it can be a problem for management and maintenance. When editors are able to inject new modules and functionality in the production environment, this can make developing new code difficult for developers. Two groups are now developing the website together—one via code and one via configuration. The two groups are subject to different testing and deployment paradigms, and they might not be communicating about what they're doing. Mysterious and sometimes catastrophic problems can result.

Uni- Versus Bidirectional Publishing

Some CMSs are like printed newspapers—they're intended for a small group of editors to create and publish content to a large group of visitors who can't directly respond. If an article in your local newspaper angers you over breakfast, there isn't much you can do about it except throw your eggs, then write a letter to the editor that might get published weeks later.

Other CMSs are like town hall meetings—you are allowed and expected to participate. If a political candidate says something that annoys you, you can stand up, shake your fist, and yell your input directly into the conversation.

Before social media was a thing, and before user participation in websites was expected,[7] most CMSs were very one-way. Editors published content that visitors consumed, blindly. Visitors didn't have accounts on websites. They couldn't create "profiles" or have "discussions."

As one of my technical reviewers noted, "If user content showed up on your site, you had been hacked."

Times have changed, and publishing can now go in both directions.

- Unidirectional (one-way) publishing means your organization is always pushing content "outward" to the consumer, often blindly (meaning the user is anonymous, and not logged in or otherwise identified).
- Bidirectional (two-way) publishing means the consumer can sometimes push content "backward" to the organization (by posting a comment, for instance).

Content coming back from the user is known as *user-generated content* (UGC). Some systems are designed for limited UGC, while others are built around it. Some might

---

6 That wasn't an intentional attempt at alliteration—the root of the word "codify" is "code."

7 Commenting wasn't even common until the "blog revolution," circa 2002 or so.

---

primarily be frameworks for managing UGC, more so than managing editor-created content.

This has all changed over the last decade, and such tools are common and expected these days. This means that older CMSs (those dating from the '90s) have had to backport this functionality, while newer CMSs have it built in.

Handling UGC requires some different tools than unidirectional publishing. If your CMS doesn't provide these, then they need to be developed, or handled by other services (Disqus or Facebook for commenting, for instance).

Additionally, UGC blurs the line between editors and other users who can provide content—if visitors can create blogs on your site and publish blog posts, are they editors? What differentiates them from "real" editors, from inside your organization? If your entire website is built around UGC, then do you need a CMS, or do you really need a social network or a community-building tool? What about software that provides both?

UGC provides additional technical challenges for decoupled CMSs, as we discussed in the prior section. In effect, content can now be created from both directions, which makes concepts like the repository hard to isolate. In some cases, UGC like comments is actually stored directly in the delivery environment, rather than the repository, as it's considered "lesser" content than that created by internal editors, and less likely to require editorial process or management.

There are several CMSs that position themselves in this space and promote feature-rich community tools. Other systems that don't have these features are having to play catch-up, either tacking them on through extensions and add-on software, or integrating with other services.

When I first encountered Drupal in about 2005, I thought, "This isn't a content management system at all. This is a *community* management system." The presence of community management tools was a bit disorienting.

In his October 2004 article "Making a Better Open Source CMS," (*http://www.veen.com/jeff/archives/000622.html*) Jeffrey Veen was almost incredulous when he said this: "Users of a public web site should never—*never*—be presented with a way to log into the CMS."

The migration from one-way to two-way publishing caught many of us off guard, and it took some time to realize it was a natural progression. Content can now be expected to come from any direction, and systems are designed around this reality.

Practicality Versus Elegance, and the Problem of Technical Debt

This final comparison isn't specific to CMSs, but applies to software development in general. Still, it's important to understand when discussing the context of the development of a CMS over time, and the implementation of your CMS specifically.

When considering new functionality, there's a constant battle between (1) "just getting it done" and (2) taking a step back and rationally considering the best way to fit this functionality into the bigger picture. The former is faster and gets new features out the door, but the latter is more sustainable over time.

Just jamming new features into software creates what's become known as *technical debt* (*https://en.wikipedia.org/wiki/Technical_debt*). These are small problems and incompatibilities that accumulate over time. You pay "interest" on this debt in the form of workarounds, hacks, and extra work you have to do in the future to account for the poor choices made when the features were implemented. Eventually, you have to stop and "pay off" this debt by reimplementing the features, or the interest expense will crush you.

Extending our discussion about UGC from earlier, consider the need to add a commenting feature to an existing CMS. An eager developer might look at this and think, "Well, this is easy. I'll just make a new system to handle comments, with its own storage and API calls, etc."

This is a practical, quick solution. The developer might implement it in an afternoon.

However, somewhere down the road, suppose the editors get concerned about inflammatory comments, and decide they want the ability to hide certain comments. Okay, our intrepid developer says, that can be added.

Then, later, the editors want to go a step further and have the ability to edit comments. This brings up larger architectural issues of permissions and versioning. Our developer swallows hard, and declares that can also be added to the commenting system.

Finally, the editors have had it with flame wars in comment threads, and decide they want to implement full-blown workflow and approval on comments.

It's at this point that our developer realizes that *comments are content too*, and perhaps they should have been implemented that way. It would have taken a little more work and thought, but the long-term sustainability and stability of the feature would have been improved. By treating comments as actual content—rather than a separate conceptual system—a lot of core functionality that the editors are asking for would be built in.

Now, this is just an illustration, and there are clearly situations where a separate commenting system might be appropriate. But the larger point is that sometimes the quick fix is not the right way to do something, and developing software is a constant battle between appeasing users who want something *right now* and making sure that they stay happy over the long term.

You can see this dichotomy in different CMS platforms. Some are a hacked together mishmash of programming paradigms and architectures, while others are well thought out and centrally planned to work in harmony long term. The former develop quickly, while the latter are slower but more stable and easier to learn because there tend to be core principles and philosophies, with fewer exceptions and one-off workarounds.

While "analysis by paralysis" can cause the development of a platform to grind to a halt, slower and more thoughtful development is generally healthier for a platform over time. All that glitters is not gold, and just because you got a feature quickly doesn't mean it was done *correctly*. If it wasn't, the best scenario is that you recognize this early, before you're too deeply invested in it.

CHAPTER 3

Acquiring a CMS

Before we discuss features and get into the specifics of CMS architecture, let's take a brief detour into the software business. In order to start working with a CMS, you need to get your hands on one.

Your search will usually begin from one of three starting points:

Software

> If you begin your search by looking for CMS software first, vendors will likely introduce you to one of their "partners" to assist in scoping the implementation, or they might offer their own professional services group for that (assuming they have one).

Integrator

> If you begin your search by looking for a CMS integrator (a developer or firm that installs and configures CMSs), they will usually specialize in one or more CMSs and will invariably attempt to steer you toward those systems. They would obviously like to implement a system with which they're comfortable, and/or for which they'll receive a markup, discount, or kickback from the vendor.[1]

Selection consultant

> If you begin your search by using an independent CMS selection consultant, they will help you select a system based on your requirements and desired features, presumably free from influence or bias. The drawback is additional expense and likely additional time, but as a participant in many formal CMS selection processes, I can validate that it's money and time well spent.

---

1 Or for another reason no one talks about: implementing expensive software is often seen as a mark of significance among industry peers. People like being taken seriously at conferences, and system name-dropping happens more than anyone will admit.

Those three types of searches should identify one or more CMS vendors, each representing one of the following paradigms of acquisition:

Open source
> You download and install.

Commercial
> You license (purchase) and install.

Software-as-a-Service (SaaS)
> You "rent" and use.

Build your own
> You develop from scratch, within your organization.

Any of these will provide you with a working CMS with which to begin implementation. However, lurking within each of these seemingly straightforward options are countless variations, idiosyncrasies, and paradigms.

Open Source CMSs

There are likely more open source options available in CMSs than in any other genre of software. The most commonly used platforms in the world—systems like Word-Press, Drupal, and Joomla!—are all open source. (In fact, almost all LAMP-stack systems are open source, demonstrating the close relationship between that technology stack and the open source philosophy.)

An examination of the intricacies of open source is beyond the scope of this book,[2] but a key point is that open source CMSs are typically free to use without paying a license fee. These systems all have a website where you can download the software, and you can then install it in your own environment and use it.

That said, remember that the license cost is not the sum total of your expenses. You will still need to:

1. Host the software.

2. Integrate the software.

Some open source CMSs are very easy to host on commodity shared hosting accounts costing less than $20/month. Other systems require more libraries, computational power, and permissions than the average hosting account offers, and therefore require a self-hosted environment with complete control.

---

2 For an examination of the philosophy of open source software, I highly recommend *The Cathedral & the Bazaar* (*http://shop.oreilly.com/product/9780596001087.do?*) by Eric Raymond (O'Reilly).

Open Source vs. Commercial vs. Proprietary vs. Closed Source

When discussing open source software, figuring out what to call *non*-open source software can be tricky. Some call it "commercial," but others claim it's more accurate to say "proprietary" or "closed source."

For the purposes of this chapter, we'll trade hair-splitting accuracy for simplicity and simply use the descriptor of "commercial" to mean software that is not free to use. The rights over a commercial CMS are owned by a for-profit organization that is in business to sell licenses.

Additionally, we're not going to quibble over the different varieties of open source licensing. There are several ways to license open source software, the most popular being GPL (GNU General Public License). Discussion of open source in this book will assume GPL licensing.

When it comes to ease of integration, open source software also varies greatly. Some projects are mature enough to have significant documentation and bootstrapping installers to get you up and running quickly. But these features are often developed late in the lifecycle of open source software, so many younger systems fall quite short in these areas. Additionally, there's often a clear developer bias in open source software ("written *by* developers, *for* developers," as mentioned in Chapter 2), and a general feeling that since no one is paying for it, users can just figure it out.

Given the lack of a license fee, open source systems are used quite often in smaller projects that don't have the budgets to pay for a license. This means that applicability to much larger projects might be questionable. For every Drupal, there are a hundred other systems that have never been asked to scale much larger than a small to mid-sized marketing site or blog.

Ubiquitous use does present enormous advantages in community support. Many open source systems have thriving user communities that are available to answer questions quickly and accurately. However, this can be offset by the lack of professional support (which is sometimes available at cost—see the next section), and the lack of a community's ability or willingness to solve more intricate questions.

And, as mentioned previously, open source CMSs are tilted heavily by platform. LAMP systems are almost always open source, while there are comparatively fewer .NET and Java systems.

Business Models of Open Source Companies

Many open source CMS products have full-fledged companies behind them, which either actively develop the software internally (for example, eZ and its eZ Platform

CMS), or guide and manage the community development (for example, the Drupal Association). Additionally, many open source systems have commercial companies lurking around the edges of the community to provide paid services for those systems (for example, Acquia is a company that provides enterprise Drupal hosting, and which was founded by Dries Buytaert, the creator of Drupal itself).

To pay the bills, companies behind open source software operate on one or more of the following models:

Consulting and integration

No one knows the CMS better than the company that built it, and it's quite common for vendors to integrate their own software from start to finish, or to at least provide some higher-level consulting services with which to assist customers in integrating it themselves.

Freemium

The basic software is free, but a paid option exists that allows access to more functionality, a larger volume of managed content, or scaling options, such as the ability to load-balance. Sometimes the free product is quite capable, and sometimes it's just a watered-down trial version meant to steer users toward paying for the full product.[3]

Hosting

Many vendors offer "managed hosting" platforms for the open source systems they develop. The purported benefit is a hosting environment designed specifically for that system, and/or system experts standing by in the event of hosting problems. Note that the actual value here is a bit questionable, as there's rarely secret information known only to the vendor that allows it to tailor a hosting platform to one CMS over another. Any available performance enhancements or configuration tweaks could just as easily be implemented by a savvy customer. The value is often just peace of mind that an "expert" is in charge.

Training and documentation

Open source software often lacks in documentation, and developer bias can lead to idiosyncratic, API-heavy systems. For these reasons, professional training can be helpful. Many vendors will offer paid training options, either remote or in-person. Less commonly, some offer paid access to higher-quality documentation.

---

3 This raises the question of whether these companies are open source or commercial entities. eZ distributes eZ Platform, which is an open source content management framework. It also *sells* eZ Studio, which is a commercial interface and editorial management system—an add-on that makes eZ Platform work better. Does this make eZ a commercial or open source company?

Commercial licensing

Depending on the exact license, changes to open source software might have to be publicly released back to the community. Some vendors will offer paid commercial licenses for their open source systems to allow organizations to ignore this requirement, close the source, and keep their changes to themselves.[4]

Support

When community support falls short, professional support can be helpful, and some vendors will provide a paid support option, either on an annual subscription or a per-incident basis.

Additional testing and QA

Some vendors offer a paid version of the software that is subjected to a higher "enterprise" level of testing and QA. In these cases, the free or "community" version is presented as lightly tested and nonsupported, while the enterprise (paid) version is marketed as the only one suitable for more demanding implementations.

Many of the paid advantages offered by open source vendors are an attempt to address the largest fear companies traditionally have of open source: lack of accountability. Companies want a "neck to choke" if something goes wrong. A CIO wants a phone number to call, product documentation to download, a trainer to fly on-site, and a single point to hold accountable for any problems.

Many open source companies have entire business models built around addressing this need. In most cases, these advantages are never actually invoked or acted upon, but exist to provide informal peace of mind, or to meet formal audit or regulatory requirements.

Commercial CMSs

Like with any other genre of software, numerous commercial CMS vendors are available and eager to sell you a license to use their systems.

After our discussion of open source, you may be wondering why anyone bothers purchasing when so many options are available for free. First, a commercial company presents itself as a more formal business entity than an open source community, which is important to some organizations (we'll discuss this further shortly). Second, commercial vendors generally adhere to a higher standard of quality and functional-

---

4 In reality, however, open source enhancements are rarely released, and most organizations simply keep their source code private in quiet violation of the open source license and philosophy. Therefore, this option is usually only attractive for companies with strict policies governing the release of open source changes.

ity, as they have to keep paying customers happy and they have incoming revenue from license fees to fund professional development.

Like any generalization, this is not always true, as some open source systems are mature and well-used enough to compete against any commercial offering. Conversely, some commercial vendors are terrible at QA and sell products riddled with bugs. But as a general rule, it holds.

Additionally, in the last five years, there has been a distinct separation between open source and commercial CMSs along the lines of marketing features. While the open source development community is obsessed with solving problems of content *management*, the commercial world has moved on to content *marketing*, which is the tools and features that help enhance your content once it's published.

It's been said that open source CMSs are made for the CIO (chief information officer), while commercial CMSs are made for the CMO (chief marketing officer). This largely holds true in how the systems are marketed, with the commercial sector concentrating their selling solely on the marketing departments of their customers, while open source providers are more interested in trying to capture the hearts and minds of the IT staff.

Like with the open source offerings, platform distinctions are clear. Very few LAMP systems are commercial, while many of the .NET and Java systems come with price tags.

Finally, remember that the numbers under discussion in this section apply only to the license costs. Buying a commercial CMS doesn't liberate you from the costs of implementing it—you will still need to find (and pay) someone to install, configure, and template your system. In some cases, the commercial vendors provide an option for this (so-called "professional services"), and in other cases they have a "partner network" of integration firms who are experts in their systems and willing to integrate for a fee.

Licensing Models

Commercial systems rarely come with a single, simple price tag. Vendors usually have a byzantine system of formulas and tables to determine your final price, with the overall goal of forcing well-heeled customers to pay more, while not losing smaller sales to customers with more modest budgets.

At this writing, the "mid-market" is roughly defined as systems with a list price (the stated "official" price) between $20,000 and $80,000, and most everything is valued in relation to this—vendors are categorized as being either above or below the mid-market.

The range of commercial pricing is vast—Perch (*https://grabaperch.com*)[5] sells for $79, while Adobe CQ can't be had for less than $250,000 and large installations will easily cross into the seven figures.

Here are the more common ways of determining pricing:

By editor/user

The system is priced by the number of editing users, either per seat or concurrent. More rarely, the system is priced by the number of registered public users, but this usually only applies to community or intranet/extranet systems where it's expected that visitors will be registered.

By server

The system is priced by the number of servers on which it runs (or, less commonly, on the number of CPU cores). This is quite common as larger installations will require more servers, thus extracting a higher price tag. With decoupled systems where the delivery environment is separated from the repository environment, this can get confusing: Do you pay for repository servers or delivery servers? Or both?

By site

The system is priced by the number of distinct websites running on it. This can be blurred by the vagueness of what constitutes a "website." If we move our content from "microsite.domain.com" to "domain.com/microsite," are we still under the same website and license fee? What about websites with different domain names that serve the same content (branded affinity sites, for instance)? What about alternate domains for different languages ("en.domain.com" for English and "de.domain.com" for German)?

By feature

The system is priced by add-on packages installed in addition to the core. Almost every commercial vendor has multiple features or packages that can be added on to the base system in order to increase value and price. These range from ecommerce subsystems to marketing tools. Note that each one of these features might *also* be licensed by user, server, or site, making their prices variable as well.

By content volume

The system is priced by the amount of content under management. This is less common than other models, as the number of content objects managed is highly dependent on the implementation. For example, should you manage your blog comments? Or can you move them to a companion database (or external service, like Disqus) and reduce content volume by 80% or more?

---

5 Actually advertised as "The really little CMS."

Most systems are priced on multiple axes—for instance, by a combination of editors, servers, *and* sites. Final pricing can often be impossible to determine without considerable consultation with the vendor's sales department.

Vendors attempt to price for the value provided and the customer's ability to pay. The methods listed here are essentially all proxy models for what a vendor might really prefer: to have inside information on how much a customer is able to pay, and price their product at that number. Since no customer would ever allow that, vendors use metrics like number of editors or sites to provide some rough estimation.

When to Buy a CMS

The realities of business dictate that the end of a quarter is usually a very good time to negotiate a license sale. Vendors have to report their quarterly numbers to Wall Street or their board of directors at those times, and they're therefore highly incentivized to discount in order to pump up their revenues.

Given that the marginal cost of production is essentially static with software (it costs no more to "create" 100,000 copies than it does to create 1), the only disincentive they have to discounting is that by doing so, they increase the expectation among future customers that the list price is up for negotiation.

Software Subscription

One thing you can always count on with commercial vendors is the need to pay for software subscription, which is a continuing annual fee based on the purchase price. This is not at all unique to CMSs—almost all enterprise software is priced similarly.

Subscription is usually a percentage of the purchase price—typically 18% to 22%. The first year is often built into the purchase, but the customer will be invoiced on the purchase anniversary date every year after.

At an average of 20% per year, this adds up quickly. Simple math will tell you that you will effectively "rebuy" your CMS every 4–6 years.

Whether or not you *have* to pay this fee varies by vendor. With most, you can simply stop paying the subscription at any time and continue to use the product, but you will lose all the value-added benefits that your subscription fee grants. With most vendors, those benefits are some combination of the following:

- On-demand support
- Upgrades and patches as they are released
- Free licenses for development or test servers

- License management, in the event you need to license new servers or sites

The fear that keeps customers paying subscription fees is that they might be stranded in some situation with a problem they can't solve or a critical security bug they can't patch. Vendors play on this fear by forcing customers to "catch up" on their subscriptions if they stop paying and then want to restart, in order to prevent customers from only paying for subscription when they need it.

For example, if a customer stops paying the subscription fee after year 1, and has a problem in year 3, the vendor will require retroactive payment for years 2 and 3 in order to restart the subscription (and sometimes with an added penalty). In some cases, vendors will force customers to repurchase the entire system from scratch.

Software subscription has become so ingrained in the enterprise software industry that few customers question it. Vendors simply require it in the sale of their systems, and customers expect to pay it.

Subscription revenue is the engine that keeps many vendors in business. If their new license sales ever slow down or stop completely, they still have a large cushion of subscription-paying customers to keep the lights on. This continuing revenue is critical to their viability and valuation, and subscription is sometimes more important to them than the initial license sale itself.

The Lure of Recurring Revenue

Another reality of the software business is that companies are often in the process of acquiring another company or being acquired themselves. Continuing/recurring revenue is absolutely critical to their valuation—the price they're going to pay or be paid.

How much of this type of revenue a company has is one of the first questions it's going to be asked by a potential suitor. A one-time payment of $10 might not be worth as much as a continuing payment of $2 every year.

For these reasons, commercial software companies will often try to steer customers into some type of recurring revenue stream. Single license sales with no recurring component are not what they're looking for.

Perspective: IT Is Only One Stakeholder

by Cathy McKnight

Content and its perceived value have changed drastically over the past few years, with simple online content now being viewed as a valuable digital asset with many uses and purposes. Accordingly, content-related technology has also evolved, with new solution and subset solution types being introduced to the market every year. So before starting down the path of deciding what type of CMS—open source (OSS), commercial, Software-as-a-Service (SaaS), or homegrown—to acquire, you first have to answer the question, "Is a new CMS the right solution to the business problems being solved for?"

For many organizations the decision of whether to buy a CMS (or any other enterprise technology), and which one, is often deferred to the technology team—after all, they are the ones who understand the company's systems and technology landscape best. Right? Perhaps. But this is a surefire way of finding a technology that fits IT's needs, not the organization's. IT should be involved, but only as one of many stakeholders. Left to just them, their myopic view typically leads to end user and business needs—current and future—not being met (or even considered), thus ultimately leaving the business problem at hand unresolved.

Absolutely, attention has to be given to technical considerations (hosted versus on-premise, interoperability with implicated existing systems, in-house skillsets), as well as the associated technology and implementation costs (implementation partner/team, licensing/subscription, maintenance, and overall total cost of ownership). But equally as important, if not more so, is identifying and understanding the current and foreseeable future content management needs of the content's owners and stakeholders.

In order to ensure that the technology acquired addresses the needs of the organization, representatives of impacted stakeholders need to be involved in the process from the get-go—from confirming the need for a CMS to defining the requirements upon which the CMS will be selected. Focusing on business needs (planned CMS-supported channels' business purposes and goals) instead of features will help determine not only what type of CMS (OSS, SaaS, commercial, or homegrown) is the best approach, but also what the solution needs to offer in order to ensure the organization's content is able to be managed successfully as it, and the organization, evolves and matures.

If the answer is "yes" to needing a CMS, then a CMS selection project can begin in earnest and should start with thorough (not IT-driven) requirements gathering.

Cathy McKnight, Vice President of Consulting and Operations and founding partner at Digital Clarity Group, helps clients navigate their digital transformation via strategic advisory and consulting engagements, including technology selections.

Software-as-a-Service

Software-as-a-Service (SaaS; pronounced "sass") used to be quite a clear and simple proposition: rather than purchase and install a CMS, you simply paid a monthly fee and ran your website inside a larger system managed by the vendor. You became one of many customers running their websites inside this same system.

This is known as "multitenant" software. Whereas purchased and installed software is "single tenant"—you are the sole occupant, much like in a single-family home you built yourself—multitenant software is like an apartment building in which many people live.

The purported benefits are quick ramp-up time and no hosting issues. Indeed, the system is already running and just waiting for you, and since it runs on the vendor's servers, you don't need to worry about any of the headaches that go along with infrastructure management.[6] SaaS was "cloud" before that term became common.

Another claimed benefit is to always be on the leading edge of versions. Since the vendor runs the hosting environment, when they release a new version, the customer gets it right away. Indeed, "releasing a new version" is synonymous with upgrading their customers, since that's what has to happen to constitute a "release."

CMS companies were early entrants into the cloud paradigm, and when vendors like Clickability and CrownPeak came on the scene in about 2000, this model was new and original and provided clear benefits for customers who didn't want to install and manage the software themselves. What happened in the intervening years is that the market changed, and the difference between true multitenant SaaS and everything else has gotten very blurry.

Today, "purchase and install" (often referred to as "on-premise" or "on-prem" when comparing to SaaS) is just one way of getting open source or commercial (non-SaaS) software. If you want either of those options but don't want to host yourself, there is a large ecosystem of vendors willing to install and host anything for you. In effect, many vendors will *become* SaaS vendors if that's what you want.

---

6 With the exception of "decoupled SaaS" models. In these architectures (which are not common), the management portion of the CMS is owned and hosted by the vendor, but it publishes content remotely into a delivery environment owned by the customer, via FTP, rsync, web services, or other methods.

The "instant on" feature of SaaS was further marginalized with the advent of server virtualization and computing grids like Amazon's EC2 and Microsoft Azure. You can now get an installation of almost any CMS in less than an hour. These systems aren't multitenant, but offer the same benefits of minimal ramp-up time and third-party hosting.

This raises the question: just what is SaaS? Is SaaS defined simply as when a vendor can give you an instance immediately and also provide the hosting environment? If so, then almost any CMS can be purchased and managed in such a way that it fulfills these criteria.

Or does SaaS refer only to the true multitenant systems we discussed previously? If so, then these systems are becoming less common at the higher edges of the market (in terms of price, capabilities, and complexity of integration), and more common at the lower edges. Vendors like WordPress.com, Drupal Gardens, and Squarespace offer "unattended" multitenant CMSs where you can get a fully content-managed platform in minutes with nothing but a credit card and without any human interaction. If you can live within the functional restrictions and don't need much customization, these systems might be exactly what you need.

However, at the enterprise level, where customers require significant customization, SaaS CMS vendors are struggling. Some still exist, but their value proposition has dwindled precipitously. Many enterprise SaaS vendors are offering a lower monthly fee and comparing that to the six- and seven-figure licensing costs of purchased systems. Traditional commercial vendors have responded by offering to "rent" licenses, where customers pay a monthly fee for the license and lose it when they stop paying. (This is also valuable for customers who might need to bring up extra sites or servers for a limited time, in response to temporary load.)

If you're considering multitenant SaaS, several questions become important:

- *Is it appropriate for your industry?* SaaS systems tend to group by the vertical in which they serve. For instance, OmniUpdate traditionally services higher education and HubSpot specializes in smaller, marketing-heavy websites. This enables these vendors to develop features common to those industries that will be used by multiple tenants of their systems.

- *How much control do you have over the system?* To what extent can you integrate with other systems or inject your own business logic? Since these systems are multitenant, vendors are leery of allowing significant customization, lest this destabilize the larger system for other clients. Some vendors will offer a dedicated, "sandboxed" environment in which you have more control, but this raises the question of how you're now any better off than you would be if you installed a CMS yourself.

- *Who can develop the website?* Some vendors might require that template development or other integration be performed by their own professional services groups. This is common in SaaS systems that grew out of the in-house CMS of a development shop. In some cases, the subscription fee to use the system is simply a minimal gateway to enable the vendor to generate professional services income.

- *If you part ways with the vendor, what happens to your content?* Can you export it? In what format? What about your templates, which contain all of your presentation logic? Can you get that information out? Vendors in all software genres are notorious for lock-in, in order to prevent customers from leaving. Wise customers will evaluate the process for leaving a vendor as a system feature like any other.

- *Are you considering the CMS on its merits, or just because it's SaaS?* Don't engage with a SaaS vendor solely because they offer their software as a service, *especially* if you're not particularly fond of the software itself. If SaaS if what you want, there are numerous options to get a SaaS-like experience from software you might like much more.

In the end, what once was a clear market for SaaS vendors has now been muddied considerably through changes in technology and business models. If the idea and benefits of SaaS are attractive to you, understand that almost any CMS vendor is now willing to engage in a model that effectively emulates the SaaS model that used to be unique to a handful of vendors.

Build Your Own

Like any other software, a CMS can be built inside your organization by your own development team. In some senses, a CMS resembles any other data-driven application, and it's not difficult to build a simple CMS fairly quickly.

There are several common justifications for this, including:

- An in-house CMS doesn't require a license fee (clearly, this is rendered moot by open source options, but it's still quite common in project justifications).

- You'll be experts in the usage of the resulting system and will not have to suffer the learning curve for an existing system.

- You will only build the needed functionality, avoiding software bloat and unnecessary complication.

On deeper analysis, few of these reasons withstand scrutiny. Often, the project is justified based on a very superficial understanding of the needs of the organization or the overall discipline of content management. While it's possible to generate quick wins, the initial thrill of progress wears off too quickly, and the organization eventually finds itself rebuilding large pieces of core CMS functionality that other systems have long since solved.

From the outside, a CMS looks like a simple exercise in editing and publishing content. But get deeper into the project, and editors begin asking for features like versioning, multiple languages, workflow, multisite management, etc. These functions can be deceptively complex to develop—even more so when they have to be backported into a running system.

CMS development tends to "hockey stick" over time. It starts very quickly and development teams make huge strides early, often having a simple, workable proof of concept in a matter of weeks or even days. Simple CRUD operations (CReate, Update, Delete) are very quick to implement, especially with modern development frameworks.

Other features, however, such as content aggregation, editorial usability, and especially advanced marketing features, will cause development time to shoot skyward and forward progress to drop to a snail's pace. It wouldn't be surprising to spend as much time implementing a minor marketing feature as you did building the entire content editing interface.

 Years ago, when building a CMS from scratch with my business partner, I remarked that the work we were doing that week seemed much more tedious and slow-going than what we'd done the prior week.

His response spoke volumes: "Well, I think we solved all of the easy problems last week."

A subtlety is that many of the problems involved with building a CMS are logical and behavioral, rather than technical. Vendors working in this space have the benefit of years of experience with editors and how they work with content. There's often an "entry fee" of implementing a feature wrong two or three times before finally getting it right. If you build something from scratch, you're often going to pay this fee every time you expand the system.

Over years of work, the developers of existing CMSs have learned how editors think and what things they want to do. This is critical, because knowing *how* to accomplish something technically is often not the real problem. Rather, the problem is knowing *why* the editor wants to do it. The underlying reasons for this can drive development decisions in ways that only experience will reveal.

Additionally, in-house CMS efforts are often developer-led, and developers tend to treat content as data, not as a business asset. To a developer, a page of content is simply a database record like any other, not a marketing asset designed to generate revenue. As such, marketing, optimization, and enhancement features often take a backseat to developer-centric features like data management.

Eventually, developing the CMS itself begins to take more time than solving the organization's core content problems, which the CMS was originally needed to remedy. Additionally, the organization realizes it has invested far more time developing the CMS than it would have ever spent becoming an expert in an existing CMS.

The resulting software can be idiosyncratic and unstable. It's also unknown outside the organization, resulting in an inability to find outside contractors and creating a significant training curve for new hires.

Finally, the system is "locked in," meaning it has been developed to service the stated requirements and nothing more. While this sounds like a sound development practice, some additional features beyond what the editors immediately need are often helpful for experimentation and understanding the scope of what's possible.

Typically, most organizations cross a "line of regret" where they'd like to rewind and choose a prebuilt option. It's not common to see a positive result from an in-house effort over the long term.

However, there are situations where it might be the right choice:

- When the content model—more on that in Chapter 6—is *very* specific to the organization. (If all you publish is cat videos, building a management platform might not be difficult.)
- When the management needs are very simple and future development plans are absolutely known to be limited
- When the CMS is built by heavily leveraging existing frameworks to avoid as much rework as possible (e.g., Symfony for PHP, Django for Python, Entity Framework and MVC for ASP.NET)

If your organization is pushing for an in-house CMS, don't begin until you've carefully reviewed the open source options available. Ask yourself this critical question: if we spent as much time developing expertise in Platform X as we would building a CMS from scratch, would we be better or worse off?

There are very few situations where an honest answer to that question would indicate that you should build your own CMS.

Questions to Ask

When considering the acquisition of a CMS, the combination of variables make your options almost limitless. The following questions might help give you some perspective:

- Where will the final CMS reside? Are we hosting it ourselves, or having someone else host it?

- If we're hosting it ourselves, does our IT department have platform limitations we must abide by?

- What is our capacity for a license fee? How much of the project budget can we carve out for this? Do we need to consider a lower fee, payable over time rather than all at once?

- Have we budgeted for continuing subscription costs in the years after launch?

- Are we going to integrate the CMS in-house, or do we need to find a partner firm to do this?

- Do we have the skill and capacity to build a CMS in-house? Can we manage maintenance and feature upgrades along with our other workload?

Finally, it's important to note that none of these questions is perhaps the most important of all: *will the system under consideration meet the functional needs of our organization?*

Do not invest in a system just because the method of acquisition seems easy. An open source system that's free but doesn't offer marketers the tools they want isn't good value—you will save on a license fee, but invest money in an implementation that will not provide the result you want. Along the same lines, a commercial vendor offering a good deal on tools you will never use is simply helping you throw money away.

The method by which you acquire a CMS is but one aspect of a much larger question of matching need to platform. This is the topic we'll discuss in Chapter 5.

The CMS Selection Process and Unknown Unknowns

The selection of the appropriate CMS for your specific set of problems can be very complex. Getting the decision right is critical, and it's especially problematic because you often "don't know what you don't know."

I'll quote a former Secretary of Defense talking about the search for hidden weapons in Iraq back in 2002:

> There are known knowns; there are things that we know that we know. We also know there are known unknowns; that is to say we know there are some things we do not know. But there are also unknown unknowns, the ones we don't know we don't know.
>
> —Donald Rumsfeld

Obtuse as this seems, Rumsfeld makes a critical point: unless you understand the entire breadth of possible scenarios, there might be unanswered questions that you don't even know to ask. It's hard to pick the right option when you don't even know a set of options exists.

For example, I don't know the chemical symbol for boron offhand. Neither does my young daughter. The key difference: *I know that this thing exists*, whereas she does not. If I need the answer, I know to go look for it, whereas she doesn't. To me, the symbol for boron is a *known* unknown; to her it's an *unknown* unknown.

Because of this, it's generally a best practice to break off the CMS selection process into its own project, managed by someone who knows what questions to ask.

There are consultants that specialize in this exact type of decision. Large technology analyst firms like Forrester and Gartner provide general analysis and assistance in this area, and small, CMS-specific firms such as Real Story Group and Digital Clarity Group do CMS selection process consulting as a large segment of their business.

CHAPTER 4

The Content Management Team

From inception through launch and ongoing usage, a content management project might impact many people throughout your organization, all with different roles and responsibilities.

While a comprehensive look at web operations and governance is beyond the scope of this book,[1] it will be helpful to discuss these roles before digging into CMS features so we can have some clarity about exactly which people a particular aspect of the CMS might affect.

Primarily, members of the content management team can be divided into:

- Editors
- Site planners
- Developers
- Administrators
- Stakeholders

Note that these labels are *roles*, not *people*. It might be discouraging to look at this list —you may think that your project is somehow deficient because you don't have all these people milling about. However, understand that the lines between the roles are not absolute, and it would be rare to see a project where every single role described here was staffed by a separate person.

---

1 For more on this subject, I recommend the aptly titled *Managing Chaos: Digital Governance by Design* by Lisa Welchman (Rosenfeld Media).

Members of the team usually fill multiple roles, and commonly overlapping roles will be noted in each section. In the meantime, just know that for a very small project, the entire team might consist of a single developer and a single editor (and a developer hobby project might be an entirely one-person show).

That said, the content management team is usually comprised of some combination of the following.

Editors

Editors are responsible for creating, editing, and managing the content inside the CMS. We'll talk about editors a lot throughout this book, as this is the role that will interact with the CMS most intimately after launch.

Editors tend to get lumped into a single group, but the "editor" role is a crude generalization: all editors are not created equal, and they might have a wide variety of capabilities.

What characterizes a "normal" or "mainstream" editor is project-specific. Therefore, it might be helpful to discuss how editors can be limited in their capabilities to refine their subroles:

By section/branch/location
> Editors might be able to edit only a specific subset of content on the website, whether that be a section, a branch on the content tree (we'll talk about trees in Chapter 7), or some other method of localization. They might have full control over content in that area (the press section, or the English department, for example), but no control over content in other areas.

By content type
> Editors might be able to edit only specific types of content (we'll talk much more about content types in Chapter 6). They might manage the employee profiles, which appear in multiple department sites, or manage company news articles, regardless of location. In fact, some editors might be better defined by what content types they are *not* allowed to create—some editors, for instance, might not be allowed to create advanced content like aggregations or image carousels.

By editing interface
> Editors might be limited by the interface they're allowed to use. In larger installations, it's not uncommon to channel certain editors through specialized, custom-built interfaces designed to allow them to manage only the content under their control. For instance, if the receptionist at your company is responsible for updating the lunch menu on the intranet and nothing else, then he doesn't need an understanding of the larger CMS interface and all the intricacies that go with

it. Instead, it might be appropriate to build that person a special editing interface to manage the lunch menu and nothing else.

In contrast to these limitations is the so-called "power editor," who can perform all content operations across the website. This person sometimes performs multiple duties as a site administrator, trainer, subject matter expect, and all-around CMS champion inside the organization.

Several other specific editorial roles are common:

Approvers

> This role is responsible for reviewing submitted content, ensuring it's valid, accurate, and of acceptable quality, and then publishing that content. That is, approvers perform steps in one or more workflows. Many editors are also approvers, responsible for vetting content submitted by more junior editors. These editors may also have the right to approve their own content. Some approvers might have the ability to edit submitted content prior to publication (an editor-in-chief, for example), while other approvers might only have the ability to approve or reject (those in the legal or compliance department, for example). This role might only need to understand the content approval features of the CMS.

Marketers

> This role is responsible for reviewing content for marketing impact, and managing the marketing value of the entire website. It requires an understanding of the marketing and analytics features of the CMS. For some sites, this is the dominant role because new content isn't created nearly as often as existing content needs to be optimized, promoted, and analyzed.

UGC/community managers

> This role is responsible for verifying the appropriateness of content submitted by users (user-generated content, or UGC), such as user profile information and blog comments. These managers are similar to approvers, but they only have control over UGC, rather than core editorial content (in some cases, this might be the majority of the content on the site). Additionally, given that the submission volume of UGC is often high, it's commonly managed post-publication—inappropriate content is reviewed and removed after publication (or after a complaint is received), rather than holding it from publication until review. This role will only need to understand the CMS to the extent that allows them to moderate UGC. In some cases, the CMS provides separate tools for this, while in others this is handled as normal content.

Translators

> This role is responsible for the translation of content from one language to another. Translators only need to understand the editorial functionality of the CMS to the extent required to add translations of specific content objects (per-

haps even of only specific content attributes, in the event that content objects are only partially translated). We will talk about localization issues much more in Chapter 10.

Not all roles in this list will be filled. Sites without UGC will not require a role to manage it. Organizations managing product documentation or library content might not have a marketing/optimization role. An editorial team of one has no need for approvers. Content presented in a single language will not need translators.

Some roles might also be filled externally. UGC/community managers might not be employed by the organization. In community sites, it's common to depend on the community itself to self-monitor, empowering specific members to moderate content. In these situations, site users will hold a quasi-editorial role, usually enforced with permissions or perhaps a completely separate user and management system.

Content translation is often handled by third-party organizations. In these cases, the translator will be remote and might not work with the CMS at all, instead moving content in and out via a translation-specific workflow and exchange format, such as XLIFF.[2]

Site Planners

Site planners are responsible for designing the website the CMS will manage. Most of their involvement will be prior to launch, with sporadic further involvement as the site develops and changes over time.

Several subroles exist:

Content strategists
   This role is responsible for designing content, both holistically and tactically. As a byproduct of the content planning process, content strategists define the content types and interactions the website must support. This role will require knowledge of how the CMS models and aggregates content in order to understand any limitations on the design. Additional knowledge of the marketing features will be necessary if the content strategist is responsible for optimizing the marketing value of the site prior to launch.

User experience (UX) designers and information architects
   These roles are responsible for organizing content and designing the users' interaction with the website. They will need to understand how the CMS organizes content, and what facilities are available to aggregate and present content to end users.

---

2 XML Localisation Interchange File Format, a language standard for automated import/export for content translation. XLIFF is discussed further in Chapter 10.

Visual designers

This role is responsible for the final, high-fidelity design of the website (as opposed to lower-fidelity prototypes and user flows provided by previous roles). Visual designers don't need intimate knowledge of the CMS, as CMS-related limitations will have guided the process up to their involvement. (In some cases, this role overlaps with template development, which we'll discuss in the next section.)

Developers

Developers are responsible for installing, configuring, integrating, and templating the CMS to match the requirements of the project.

How much development effort this takes is specific to the complexity of the requirements and how well matched the CMS is to those requirements out of the box. Deploying a simple blog powered by WordPress will take very little development (perhaps none at all), while an enterprise intranet built from scratch is a huge undertaking.

Like editors, not all developers are created equal. Under the umbrella of development, there are multiple categories of tasks that define different roles:

CMS configuration

This role is responsible for the installation and configuration of the CMS itself, including the establishment of the content model, creation of workflows and other editorial tools, creation of user groups, roles, and permissions, etc. This work is done at a fairly high level, through facilities and interfaces provided by the CMS.

Backend (server) development

This role is responsible for more low-level development performed in a traditional programming language (PHP, C#, Java, etc.) to accomplish more complex content management tasks, or to integrate the CMS with other systems. This developer should have experience in (1) the required programming language and (2) the API of the CMS.

Frontend (client) development or templating

This role is responsible for the creation of HTML, CSS, JavaScript, template logic, and other code required to present managed content in a browser. This developer needs only to know the templating language and architecture provided by the CMS, and how it integrates with HTML, CSS, and JavaScript. (Different template architectures and paradigms can vastly change the responsibilities of this role, as we'll see in Chapter 9.)

In many cases, all three of these development roles are performed by the same person. Alternatively, a very common split is to have the frontend development performed by one developer, and the CMS and backend development performed by another developer. In these cases, the frontend developer is responsible for templating content that the backend developer has configured the CMS to manage and provide.

It's becoming increasingly common for visual designers to code their own frontend implementations. Thus, the same person might design a complete interface from a wireframe, then ultimately template the CMS to reflect that design.

The split between CMS and backend development depends on the CMS. Some systems allow an enormous amount of development to be performed from the interface, and writing programming code is considered the exception, rather than the rule[3] (and remember that in multitenant SaaS environments, the option to write programming code might not be available).

Other systems are designed primarily as programming platforms, which means that most of the configuration consists mainly of writing, compiling, and deploying programming code. In these cases, CMS configuration and backend development are largely the same thing.

Administrators

Administrators are responsible for the continued operation of the CMS and the associated infrastructure. Within this group are several subroles:

- **CMS administrator:** This role is responsible for managing the CMS itself, which includes user and permission management, workflow creation and management, licensing management, and all other tasks not related to content creation.

- **Server administrator:** This role is responsible for the maintenance and support of the server(s) on which the CMS runs and/or deploys content. This is a traditional IT role, and the server administrator often has no understanding of the CMS itself other than the basic architecture required for it to run without error (operating system, runtime framework, web server, etc.). This role provides support when there's an underlying server issue that prevents the CMS from functioning correctly.

- **Database/storage administrator:** This role is responsible for managing the database server and storage networks that hold the CMS content. This administrator

---

3 Drupal is famous for this. You can implement a significant amount of functionality in that CMS without ever writing a line of code. Thus, some Drupal sites can be delivered without needing a backend developer at all—though, as we discussed in "Code Versus Configuration" on page 29, this can lead to other complications.

needs very little understanding of the CMS, other than the file types, sizes, and aggregate volumes that will need to be stored and backed up.

The CMS administrator role is often staffed by a power editor.

It's very common to see the server administrator and database/storage administrator roles combined in the same person (sometimes a developer even stands in for both of these roles). However, many larger organizations have separate groups of data administrators responsible for managing storage and nothing else.

Stakeholders

The stakeholders of a CMS project are an amorphous group representing the people responsible for the results that the CMS is intended to bring about. Stakeholders are normally business or marketing staff (as opposed to editorial or IT staff) who look at the CMS simply as a means to an end.

In general, stakeholders are looking to a CMS to do one of two things:

- Increase revenue.
- Reduce costs and/or risk.

These goals can be achieved in a number of different ways, a CMS simply being one of them. Stakeholders often have no direct contact with the CMS, and they might not care about the specific features the CMS enables—their only goal is the result the CMS can manifest.

For example:

- The chief marketing officer is dissatisfied with the percentage of visitors who complete the "Get a Quote" form after browsing the website. She is convinced that a personalization strategy—varying site content to target each visitor specifically—will increase this conversion rate and therefore increase revenue.

- The manager of the support department feels that the company is taking too many support calls because of the sorry state of the online product documentation. Attempts to improve the documentation have been thwarted by technical limitations, which a new CMS might solve, hopefully resulting in a lower volume of incoming support calls and therefore reducing costs.

- The editor-in-chief is trying to increase article volume, but the current CMS forces hours of editorial overhead and rework to get an article published. The editor is hoping to increase content throughput with a CMS that has a streamlined editorial workflow. The goal here is to push more content, which increases revenues, and do it more efficiently with less editorial labor, which reduces costs.

Note that, in each case, the end goal was not to install a new CMS. The CMS is simply the means to achieving a larger stated business goal.

In each of these three examples we have someone who (1) is not directly going to use the CMS, and (2) is not going to develop or integrate the CMS. So, why are the stakeholders important? *Because they are usually the decision makers on a CMS purchase who control the budget from which the project will be funded.*

They are included in this discussion of the CMS team because sometimes it's easy to lose sight of the forest for the trees. The closer you get to a CMS project—as an editor, administrator, site planner, or developer—the easier it is to obsess over small details.

Never lose sight of the fact that stakeholders have little regard for anything beyond the critical question: will this expense bring about the business goal we are seeking? The specifics of exactly *how* the CMS does this are simply details.

Perspective: Content Management Is One Part of a Much Larger Puzzle

by Jeff Cram

The role of content management has changed considerably over the years. What was once a relatively separate piece of enterprise software used to manage a website has become an integral part of an organization's digital business. Content management systems now act as a central hub in delivering digital experiences that are more than marketing—experiences that are the essential connections between a business and its customers.

This reality fundamentally changes the way organizations invest in digital capabilities, organize teams, and rely on external partners.

Unfortunately, many organizations still look at the CMS from the inside out—as a piece of software to install and configure before moving on to the next IT project on the road map. You may have been able to get by with this approach 3–5 years ago. Not today.

The elements required for success with a CMS can't be stuffed into a single project Gantt chart. And yet over and over we see organizations try, and then blame the technology or an external partner when it falls short.

There are plenty of organizations that get CMSs right, though.

These are organizations that realize the path to sustainable success means investing in new internal competencies, establishing a more customer-centric culture, and aligning the organization around meaningful change.

These are organizations that put in place ongoing practices for content strategy, governance, customer insight, and measurement—and actively work on them independently of putting in a new CMS.

These are organizations that hire external partners not just for their technology skills, but for their ability to bring the connected expertise necessary to make the technology successful.

These are organizations that understand that a CMS sits within a much larger (and expanding) marketing technology ecosystem, and work to understand how it needs to integrate, support, and often get out of the way of other systems.

Be one of these organizations. It's a lot more work, but also a lot more fun than the alternative.

Jeff Cram is the cofounder of and Chief Strategy Officer at Connective DX.

PART II

The Components of Content Management Systems

CHAPTER 5

CMS Feature Analysis

This section of the book is devoted to describing the component features of common content management systems. I'll start with a warning to set your expectations, then give you an overview of what's to come.

Without wanting to seem overly pessimistic, this chapter is intended to set your expectations for a feature-level evaluation of content management. Understand that this isn't an exact science, and if the border around a particular feature feels fuzzy and vague, that's likely accurate.

The Difficulties of Feature Analysis

Before we embark on a detailed analysis of content management features, we need to make an important point: *feature-by-feature analysis and comparison is hard*. As much as we want this to be a clear science, it's messy and imperfect.

Mathematics is a very objective science. You're not going to get much argument about the answer to two plus two. There is a Grand Unified Theory of Basic Math that has been accepted and perfected over millennia about how math works. This truth is something that mathematicians can remove from debate.

Content management is not like this. There is no Grand Unified Theory of Content Management. You can pose an architectural question to five different bona fide experts and get five different answers (maybe six), all of which would serve to solve the problem posed by the question and can thus be considered "correct" to some extent.[1]

Why is this?

"Fitness to Purpose"

In evaluating anything, we tend to think in terms of relativity.

If we say that some thing is "on the left side," we're implying that some other thing is to the right of it. You can't be on the left side of nothing, after all, so the concept of leftness only exists because something else is on the right.

Likewise, content management systems exist only in clear relation to a problem they need to solve. Their competence can only be evaluated in terms of their distance from what is needed for *your particular situation.*

The correct answer for a content management question lies in an intersection of dozens of factors, including:

- The type and goals of the website
- The shape of the content being managed (see Chapter 6)
- The output and publishing requirements (see Chapter 9)
- The sophistication of the editors (see Chapter 8)
- The business environment, decision-making process, and budget

These are just five factors. There are likely hundreds more, and the weighting of the individual factors will be different for every organization.

When comparing systems, it's easy to look at two features and say, "This one is better." In doing this, the unspoken end to that sentence is "for the particular requirements I'm thinking about right now." What's right for one set of requirements could be clearly wrong for another.

Furthermore, some applications simply don't need certain features. If you're the only editor of your web content and you know for certain there won't be any other editors in the future (this is more common than you might think), then concepts of work-

---

1 The same is somewhat true of economics, a field in which much is left to interpretation and theory. Economist Dani Rodrik has said: "The point is not to reach a consensus about which model is right...but to figure out which model applies best in a given setting. And doing that will always remain a craft, not a science, especially when the choice has to be made in real time." On this same topic, Paul Romer has coined the term "mathiness" to describe the irrational and potentially destructive desire to forcibly quantify a fuzzy discipline. See Rodrik's article "Economists vs. Economics" (*http://www.project-syndicate.org/commentary/economists-versus-economics-by-dani-rodrik-2015-09*) for more.

flow, collaboration, and permissions become largely meaningless. Noting that a system is bad at those things might be an accurate observation, but it's not relevant.

A content management expert once declared that the single criterion for CMS selection should be "fitness to purpose." That phrase describes an intersection between:

- The capabilities of a system ("fitness")
- The requirements under consideration ("purpose")

I doubt a better standard of evaluation exists.

"Do Everything" Syndrome

Content management systems, like other software, tend to try to include as much functionality in one package as possible. No vendor (or open source community) wants to say, "We don't offer that feature," so they're motivated to handle every possible situation or eventuality. If an editor has to go outside the system, that's considered a failure.[2]

As a result, content management systems are getting more and more complex every year. The industry has steadily crept outward from the clearly defined core of 15 years ago. We've already discussed the drift from content into community management, and now we have systems managing social media, offering powerful marketing suites, and even trying to act as general application development frameworks.

The price we pay for this is complexity. The list of features you're going to ignore and try to find ways to disable can easily be longer than the list of features you're actually going to use.

As systems become more complex, they tend to become more generic. Developers working on any system for too long drift into larger architectural concepts and frameworks. They become what Joel Spolsky has called "architecture astronauts":

> When you go too far up, abstraction-wise, you run out of oxygen. Sometimes smart thinkers just don't know when to stop, and they create these absurd, all-encompassing, high-level pictures of the universe that are all good and fine, but don't actually mean anything at all.[3]

---

2 In contrast, Basecamp (formerly 37 Signals) has famously said of its popular project management tool, "Our default answer to every feature request is *No*." Features have to earn their way into the product. There's a significantly high bar for inclusion, and the developers actually pride themselves on what their software *doesn't* do.

3 "Don't Let Architecture Astronauts Scare You" (*http://www.joelonsoftware.com/articles/fog0000000018.html*), April 21, 2001.

Hypothetical conversations like this actually happen when discussing content management:

> If we can manage web pages, then we can manage general content too! In fact, let's just manage random strings of text—if the user wants to make a web page out of them, she can do that! And why even text? Everything is comprised of bytes in the end, so let's just manage sequences of bytes and let editors select an optional text encoding or file type! How elegant is that?!

Remember: a system designed to do everything tends to do nothing well, and you should only evaluate the features you actually need.

When extended features outside core content management are added, they're often added poorly. In many cases, the vendor is trying to "check a box" that it's seen on customer requirements lists. Just because a feature exists doesn't mean it's done well.

Form-building tools are a classic example (more on this in Chapter 10). Many systems have them, as they've become a de facto requirement to compete in the marketplace. However, I've never evaluated a form-building system that was developed at the same level as the core content management tools. In almost all cases, this was an add-on feature that had to survive only as long as a sales demo.

We have a natural desire to think that one system can solve all of our problems. However, the solution might lie in multiple disconnected systems and how you use them together. Do you love the collaboration features of Google Docs? Why can't you use that to work on content, then just paste the result into your CMS for delivery? Clearly, this is a bit rough around the edges and has some disadvantages, but many organizations would be better served by this plan than by a full-blown CMS implementation to solve a single problem.

But we often look down at simplicity. We like to think that we're burdened with very difficult problems that require intricate solutions, and that the complexity of the solution is a direct reflection of the sophistication of the underlying problem. Breaking this habit is difficult.

Going outside of your shiny new CMS is not necessarily a failure. It might be exactly the right decision, rather than suffering through using a poorly implemented feature out of nothing but a desire for one product to "do everything."

The Whole Is Greater than the Sum of Its Parts

Content management systems are complex and full of moving parts. The effect of all these parts working together forms a whole that might not be representative of the parts that make it up.

It's understandably hard for a system made up of poorly designed features to rise above them, but sadly it's not uncommon to have a portfolio of features that are stellar when evaluated individually, but just don't quite come together as a whole.

This can be caused by poor usability in the intersections between features—a workflow system that offers a stunning array of functionality but simply doesn't interact well with editors when they're creating content is not much use to anyone.

Another problem can be misplacement of priorities, when one feature is over-developed compared to others. The perfect templating system in service of content that can't be modeled accurately won't help you much, and the end result is like a Ferrari in a traffic jam—lots of power with no place to go.

The only way to effectively evaluate the whole is by subjecting it to as long a use case as possible. Don't just pick small snippets of functionality to compare ("Can we select an approver when starting a workflow?"), but rather complete a full cycle of interaction ("Let's publish a news release from initial conception all the way through distribution"). Scenarios like this can poke unexpected holes in systems that seemed sound from the feature level.

Implementation Details Matter

The value of a CMS feature is not just in the final result. It also matters how you get there. Just because different systems can check a box on a feature list doesn't mean that the feature was implemented equally well in both systems.

Usability matters. Many features are conceived, designed, and built by developers, and this may result in interfaces and user models that make little sense to editors. Developers tend to be more forgiving of rough edges, and more concerned with ultimate flexibility rather than usability.

Beyond just the interface, does the mental model of the feature make sense? When an editor is working with it, is it easy to describe how it works and theorize ways in which it can be used? Simple features can be made obscure by idiosyncratic philosophies and ideas that made sense to the person who designed them, but no one else.

Some features can be hopelessly complex, either through poor design or just because they are, in fact, very complex. Consider the Drupal Views module—this is a system designed to let editors build aggregations of content. That seemingly simple goal is extremely complex in practice, and even though the interface has been labored over for years and refined to an extremely high degree, it's still going to be somewhat overwhelming (see Figure 7-10 in Chapter 7).

Other features might be built specifically for developers. A workflow system might be very powerful, but if it has to be configured in code, then compiled and deployed, this drastically limits its utility for anyone other than a developer or teams that have developers on hand for future changes. Similarly, templating systems that are not extractable from the core code of the system limit their utility to only people who have access to that code.

Some features might require additional software. It's very common for vendors to "partner" with other firms to provide plug-in functionality. This functionality looks great in a sales demo, but requires extra expense and often a separate purchase and license from the third-party company.[4]

The lesson here is that just because a feature exists, that doesn't mean it's any good. When you have a list of boxes you're trying to check—either an actual list, or a mental list—there's seldom room to say, "Yes this feature exists, but it doesn't work very well." In most feature-matrix spreadsheets, there's a column for "yes" and a column for "no," and nothing in between.

It's a very cynical observation, but vendors know this. They realize that someone evaluating their software is wondering about functionality and just assuming it works well. It's very hard to dive deep enough into a software demo to uncover all the warts. The vendor might be counting on this, which is why you'll often hear: "Sure, we do that. Now, lemme show you this other thing we do…"

Do not evaluate features based merely on their existence or on a cursory examination of the result. Find out exactly how the feature is implemented and ensure that you'll be able to use it to achieve the same result.

Does a Feature Solve the Right Problem?

Of greater importance than discussions about how well a feature works is the unspoken question of whether or not a certain feature is what you actually need to solve your underlying problem.

Referring back to the "unknown unknowns" quote from Donald Rumsfeld in Chapter 3, it's common to not truly understand the underlying issue, and instead jump to a solution that might be in service of the wrong problem.

For example, many CMS customers look for systems capable of supporting complicated workflows. Deeper analysis of their situation, however, indicates that their real problem is simply one of permissions—if they could separate "edit" and "publish" permissions and isolate editors to subsections of the content repository, then this would solve all the problems they're convinced are in need of advanced workflow.

At an even more basic level, some problems a customer seeks to solve actually have non-technical origins. Many editorial process issues have been solved by the implementation of offline governance policies or organizational changes. A faulty org chart is often the source of more problems than a faulty CMS.

---

4 I remember seeing a great workflow demo from an ECM company about 20 years ago. The workflow developer could simply drag boxes around and connect them with arrows to represent states and transitions. It was elegant and simple. They forgot to mention that it was also a $15,000 add-on (and this was in 1997 dollars).

It's sadly common to find CMS customers who are absolutely convinced they need feature X, and that it's the panacea that will solve all that ails them. They complete a large, expensive, disruptive project that gives them feature X. Unfortunately, they then find that they just chased the problem backward, peeling off an outer layer or two and the real problem was something larger and more foundational. In the end, feature X just put a bandage over one of the *symptoms*.

Former CIA analyst Philip Mudd has promoted what he calls "thinking backward," meaning we should start by thinking about the underlying problem or question rather than the set of facts (features, in our case) at our disposal:

> When we're working on how to analyze a problem, we shouldn't start with the data or information that we know and then build a case from there. Instead, we should begin with the question of what we need to know...to solve a problem.[5]

Start with the problem. Examine that problem and work backward through potential solutions. There are likely multiple options, and by starting at the problem and working back, you have a better chance of viable options spreading out before you rather than you getting stuck in the mindset that feature X is the only path to solving your underlying problem.

An Overview of CMS Features

We'll start by covering the Big Four of content management. These are the four features that are required in some form to manage content at the most basic level. They are:

Content modeling
> You need to describe the structure of content and store your content as a faithful representation of this structure.

Content aggregation
> You need to logically organize content into groups and in relation to other content.

Editorial workflow and usability
> You need to enable and assist the creation, editing, and management of content within defined boundaries.

Publishing and output management
> You need to transform content in various ways for publication, and deliver the prepared content to publishing channels.

---

5 Philip Mudd, *The HEAD Game: High Efficiency Analytic Decision-Making the Art of Solving Complex Problems Quickly* (Liveright Publishing Corporation, 2015).

These are the core pillars of content management. If a system fails at one or more of these four, it's hard to manage any content effectively.

From there, we'll review extended functionality:

- Multiple language handling
- Personalization, analytics, and marketing optimization
- Form building
- Content file management
- Image processing
- URL management
- Multisite management
- APIs and extensibility
- Plug-in architectures
- Reporting tools and dashboards
- Content search
- User and developer community support (yes, this is a feature too)

Perspective: The Truth About Buying a CMS

by David Maffei

You're in the market to buy a WCM solution. You've just sat through four vendor demonstrations. It seems like you're on a path to a decision on selecting the digital experience platform that's going to take your business to the next level. Things are progressing just as you planned.

What you don't know is that better than 50% of what you just saw is all fake. That's right. The solution you are going to buy can do maybe half of what you just saw—the rest was a combination of imaginative code-writing and "strategic" visioning by a really good presales team. Vendor demonstrations toe the not-so-bold line between "demo world" and "reality" in terms of showcasing their solutions to you.

The question is: how do you sort through what's real and what's not, and which solutions get you as close to your final solution as possible?

The reality is that 100% of the tools available in the market do 80% of what every single end user needs. As an organization looking to select and implement the right WCM tool, you need to focus on the other 20%: your unique needs.

This might sound both logical and simple—it is neither. The success of a WCM implementation hinges on the selection of the tool—not based on the tool itself, but based on your specific and unique requirements. Hidden in that 20% is where you'll find the intricacies and the details that make or break the adoption and actual production use of your tool. That 20% is the difference between a solution that provides operational efficiency, stability, and reliability and one that ends up as cursed-off shelfware. What's worse? The unique percentage that defines you was more often than not demonstrated to you through the lens of "demo world" and not reality.

Organizations always focus on the 80%. They create thousand-row RFPs and view demos of hundreds of tools—each one showing its strengths and limiting the visibility of its weaknesses. To be a successful end user, you should spend less time talking with analysts about vendors, less time viewing demos, and less time reading RFP responses, and take all that saved time and put it into understanding two things: what your strategic goals are (and the tactics required to achieve them), and whether the product you want to buy can excel at the 20% that differentiates your needs from everyone else's. The 80% is a given—everyone does it.

David Maffei is the Chief Revenue Officer at Akumina, an enterprise software provider delivering compelling digital web experiences for mid-sized and large enterprises.

CHAPTER 6

Content Modeling

At the risk of triggering bad memories, consider the form you have to complete at the local Department of Motor Vehicles when renewing your driver's license. You're envisioning a sheet of paper with tiny boxes, aren't you?

But what if it wasn't like that? Imagine that instead of a form, you just got a blank sheet of paper on which you're expected to write a free-form essay identifying yourself and providing all the information you can think of. Then someone at the DMV sits down to read your essay and extract all the particular information the DMV needs. If the information isn't there—for instance, you forgot to include your birthdate because no one told you to put it in your essay—they send you back to try again.

You might have thought it impossible to make the experience of renewing your driver's license worse, but I'd wager that this process might accomplish just that.

Thankfully, the DMV has forms with separate boxes for you to input different information: your name, your birthdate, etc. These boxes even have labels describing them and prompts to ensure you enter the information in the correct format: there might be "mm/dd/yyyy" in the birthdate field, two dashes in the Social Security number field, and checkboxes for "male" or "female."

The people who designed this form considered the range of information they needed from people, and then structured it. They broke it into separate boxes on the form, and took steps to ensure it was entered correctly.

Put another way, someone "modeled" the information the DMV requires. They extracted an explicit structure from the amorphous chunk of information the DMV needs, broke it down into smaller pieces, and provided an interface for managing it (the form itself).

Similarly, a core goal of any CMS is to accurately represent and manage your content. To do that, it has to know what your content is. Just as you can't build a box for something without knowing the dimensions of that thing, your CMS needs to know the dimensions of your content to accurately store and manage it.

In most cases, you start with a *logical idea* of the content you need to manage in order to fulfill the project requirements. For instance, you know that you need to display a news release. This is a general notion of content. But what is a news release? What does it look like? How is it structured? Ask five different people and you might get five different answers.

A CMS can't read your mind (much less the minds of five different people) and therefore has no idea what *you* think a news release is. So, this logical notion of a news release needs to be translated into a concrete form that your CMS can actually manage.

To do this, you need to explain to the CMS what a news release is—what bits of information make up a news release, and what are the rules and restrictions around that information? Only by knowing this will your CMS know how to store, manage, search, and provide editing tools appropriate for this content.

This process is called *content modeling*. The result is a description of all of the content your CMS is expected to manage. This is your *content model*.

Content modeling is often done poorly, either through mistakes in judgment or because of the built-in limitations of a particular CMS. The stakes can be unfortunately high. Content modeling is the foundation on which a CMS implementation is built. Mistakes made here breed multiple future problems that can be tough to recover from.

 Warning: Theory Ahead

This chapter (and the next) might seem a bit abstract or technical, depending on your experience. We're going to discuss the core characteristics of content in general, separated from concrete representations like the interface in which editors create content or the web pages that the CMS generates.

Even if some of this seems theoretical, please try to stick with it. The foundation laid in these chapters will make it easier for you to understand more specific topics later in the book.

Data Modeling 101

Modeling is not unique to content management. "Data modeling" has been around as long as databases. For decades, database designers have needed to translate logical ideas of information into database representations that are in an optimally searchable, storable, and manipulatable format.

The similarities between traditional databases and content management are obvious: both are systems to manage information at some level. In fact, CMSs are usually built *on top* of a relational database. Almost every CMS has a database underneath it where it stores much of its information.

In this sense, a CMS might be considered a "super database," by which we mean a database extended to offer functionality specific to managing content. In fact, a friend once referred to a CMS as a "relational database management system *management system*" to reflect the idea that the CMS wraps the basic data management features of a database in another layer of functionality. As such, many of the same concepts, paradigms, benefits, and drawbacks of relational databases also apply to content management systems in varying degrees.[1]

Another word for the process of transforming logical ideas into concrete data structures is *reification*, which is from the Latin prefix *res*, which means "thing." To reify something is literally "to make it a thing."

Computers don't understand vagueness. They want hard, concrete data that's restricted so they know exactly what they're working with. Reification is a process of moving from an abstract and unrestricted idea of something to a concrete representation of it, complete with the limitations and restrictions this brings along with it.

A classic example of a modeling problem is a street address:

123 Main Street
Suite 1
New York, NY 10001

This is quite simple to store as a big lump of text, but doing so limits your ability to ask questions of it:

- What city are you in?
- What floor of the building are you on?
- What other businesses are nearby?
- What side of the street are you on?

---

1 If you're thinking that perhaps a background in database design would be helpful, you're absolutely correct. To this end, I recommend *Database Design for Mere Mortals* by Michael Hernandez (Addion-Wesley). Even if you never have to design a traditional database, the ability to separate a data model from the information stored within it is a key professional skill.

To answer these questions, you would have to parse—or break apart—this address to get at the smaller pieces. These smaller pieces only have meaning when they're properly labeled so a machine knows what they represent. For example, the "1" in the second line makes perfect sense when it refers to a unit number, but doesn't work as a zip code.

Consider this alternative model of the preceding address:

- *Street number*: 123
- *Street direction*: [none]
- *Street name*: Main
- *Street suffix*: Street
- *Unit label*: Suite
- *Unit number*: 1
- *City*: New York
- *State*: NY
- *Postal Code*: 10001

By storing this information in smaller chunks and giving those chunks labels, we can manipulate and query large groups of addresses at once. What we've done here is reify the general idea of an address into a concrete representation that our CMS can work with.

Couldn't you just parse the address every time you wanted to work with it? Sure. But it's much more efficient to do it once when the content is created, rather than every time you want to read something from it. Common sense says that you'll read content far more often than you'll create or change it. Additionally, when it's created, a human editor can make proactive decisions about what goes where instead of a parsing algorithm taking its best guess.

It's worth noting that by creating a model for the address, we've actually made it *less* flexible. As inefficient as storing the big lump of text may be, it's certainly flexible. A big lump of text with no rules around it can store anything, even an address like this:

123 Main Street South
Suite 200
Mail Stop 456
c/o Bob Johnson
New York, NY 10001-0001
APO AP 12345-1234

This address wouldn't fit into the model we created earlier. To make that model work for this content, we'd need to expand our model to fit. For instance, we'd need to create a space for APO/FPO/DPO numbers.[2]

Addresses in this format might be relatively rare, but when creating a content model, your judgment is an unavoidable part of the process. Is this situation common enough to justify complicating the model to account for it? Does the exception become the rule? Only your specific requirements can answer that.

While most problems seen in poor implementations involve understructured content, know that you can go in the other direction as well. Structuring content too much can damage the editorial experience.

Former CMS architect and current UX author[3] Josh Clark had this to say about the decision of how much to structure a particular content type:

> The big advantage to structuring content, of course, is that it lets you repackage it and present it in different forms and contexts. The downside is that it forces editors to approach their content like machines, thinking in terms of abstract fields that might be mixed and matched down the road. The benefits often outweigh this usability cost if you're going to present the content elements in multiple contexts and/or offer various sorting options with a large number of elements. If not, then I typically go with [less structure].[4]

The key, as always, is a balance driven by a solid understanding of your content, your requirements, and your editors.

Edge Cases

In software design, our complicated address is called an "edge case," since it's a usage case at the edges of the mainstream.

Software design is littered with these situations, and you can't possibly account for them all. Trying to handle *everything* will lead to bloated software that has become so generic and complicated that it even fails at its original purpose.

Only experience and knowledge of your users and requirements can help you decide which edge cases to accommodate.

---

2 These are methods to send mail to military and government personnel serving in remote locations. They're acronyms for Air Post Office, Fleet Post Office, and Diplomatic Post Office.

3 Josh developed the Big Medium CMS for many years, and recently authored *Designing for Touch* (*http://aboo kapart.com/products/designing-for-touch*) (A Book Apart).

4 Personal communication with the author, December 2007.

Data Modeling and Content Management

Every CMS has a content model. Even the simplest CMS has an internal, concrete representation of how it defines content.

The simplest model might be a wiki, where you have nothing but a title and a body of text. Simplistic and rigid as this is, it's clearly a predefined content model.

The original blogging platforms—the early WordPress, Movable Type, Blogger, etc.—worked largely the same way: everything you put into the system had a title, a body, an excerpt, and a date. Since the only thing they needed to manage was a series of blog posts, this was effectively a built-in content model designed specifically to fit the requirements of that content.

In most cases, you need more flexibility than this. You need to store information beyond what's offered by default. When this happens, you're limited by the content modeling features of your CMS.

Some systems offer a limited number of "custom fields" in addition to the built-in model (blogging platforms like WordPress have moved in this direction; see Figure 6-1), while other systems assume nothing and depend on you to create a content model from the ground up. To this end, they can offer a dizzying array of tools to assist in content model definition.

Figure 6-1. A free-form custom fields interface in WordPress

The unspoken standard that most CMSs are chasing is that of a custom relational database, which has been the traditional way to model data and information since the early 1970s.[5] CMSs have varying levels of fidelity to this ideal—some force you to

---

5 See "A Relational Model of Data for Large Shared Data Banks," (*https://www.seas.upenn.edu/~zives/03f/cis550/ codd.pdf*) by E. F. Codd.

simplify more than you'd like, while others are essentially thin wrappers around your own custom relational database.[6]

Why aren't all CMSs like this? Because it's often more than you need. The CMS industry has evolved around common content problems, and has created patterns for dealing with situations that are seen over and over again. Most web content management problems will fall within the range covered by these patterns—the exceptions are…wait for it…*edge cases*—so they're enough to function well under most requirements.

Where a particular CMS falls in the range of modeling capabilities has a huge impact on the success or failure of your project. Some projects have complex content models and absolutely hinge on the ability of the CMS to represent them accurately. In these cases, content modeling limitations can be hard to work around.

Separating Content and Presentation

It's tempting to look at some form of your content—your news release rendered in a browser, for instance—and say, "This is my content."

But is it? In a pure sense, your actual content is the structure and words that make up the news release. The information in your browser is just a web page. So, are you managing content or are you managing web pages?

I argue that it's the former. Your content is as close to pure information as possible. The web page is actually a piece of media created by your content. Put another way, it's simply a *representation* of your content.

Your content has been combined with presentational information—in this case, converted to HTML tags—and published to a specific location. Ideally, you could take those same words and use them to create a PDF, or, after publishing your web page, you could use the title of your press release and the URL to create a Facebook update.

These publication locations (email, web, Facebook, etc.) are often called *channels*. The media that is published to a channel might be referred to as a *rendition* or a *presentation* of content in a particular channel.

The relationship of content to published media is one to many: one piece of content can result in many presentations. In that sense, a presentation is *applied* to content in order to get some piece of published media.

We can only do this if we separate our content and our presentation, which means modeling our core content as "purely" as possible. Ideally, we do this without regard

---

6 A select few systems are *literally* thin wrappers around a custom database. Some CMSs just add a few fields and tables to a database of your own creation to add the extended functionality of a CMS.

to any particular presentation format. (We might need to add some extra information to ease the application of a particular presentation, but this information won't be used in other presentation contexts.)

This concept is not new. Gideon Burton, an English professor at Brigham Young University, has traced this all the way back to the ancient Greeks.

> Aristotle phrased this as the difference between logos (the logical content of a speech) and lexis (the style and delivery of a speech). Roman authors such as Quintilian would make the same distinction by dividing consideration of things or substance, *res*, from consideration of verbal expression, *verba*.[7]

Our content is *logos*, and the presentation method is *lexis*.

Binding your content to a specific presentation drastically limits what you can do with that content. If your requirements are simple and won't change, then perhaps this isn't a great disadvantage. But when content is structured well, its utility increases:

Templating is easier
Having content in smaller chunks allows you to use it in more specific ways when templating. Want to display an author's last name first on the bio page? This is much easier to do if the last name is stored separately from the first name.

Mass presentation changes are possible
Should author headshots and bios appear in the left sidebar now, rather than at the bottom of the article? If this information is separable from the main body of content, this is a simple templating change, whether you have 10 or 10,000 articles.

Content can be easily presented in other contexts
When your pages have isolated summaries, these can be posted in other contexts with shorter length requirements, or content can be shortened for environmental limitations such as mobile devices.

Editorial usability is improved
Granular content models often allow you to customize the editorial interface with specific elements to allow editors to accurately work with specific pieces of information that make up your content. Should you limit the HTML tags that editors can use when writing their article summaries? If Summary is its own attribute, this is easier to do.

---

7 Gideon Burton, "Silva Rhetoricae." (*http://rhetoric.byu.edu/Encompassing%20Terms/Content%20and %20Form.htm*)

Going back to Burton's Aristotelian example, Aristotle might have a theory about man's position in the universe. This theory is his content. He can "render" this content into an essay, a play, a speech, even a drawing. Those items are the media generated from his content. They're just presentations—the core concepts of Aristotle's theory underlie them all.

Much Ado About Nothing: The Content Versus the Presentation

Recently, I read *Much Ado About Nothing*, a play written by William Shakespeare sometime toward the end of the 16th century. It's one of his most popular works, and it's been performed, reprinted, and adapted thousands of times since.

I track all of my reading in a service called Goodreads (*http://goodreads.com*), and I went there to jot down my thoughts on it. However, I was bit frustrated by the fact that Goodreads is presentation-centric, not content-centric. When I tried to look up *Much Ado About Nothing* to add it to my list, I was confronted with 222 different published works.

My copy was printed in 2007 by Modern Library. But that wasn't what I wanted to review. I wanted to review *the play itself*. I wanted to discuss the concepts and ideas Shakespeare wrote about 400 years ago, not the trade paperback I was holding in my hand.

My book was just the medium through which the play was communicated in this particular instance. The play was the *content*. My paperback was one possible *presentation*.

For that matter, it was actually a specific instance of a *type* of presentation. *Much Ado About Nothing* has been printed in many books; this was just one of them. It's been a film too, in 1993 and 2011. Those are specific instances of different types of presentation.

Within each instance, the details changed, but the core of Shakespeare's play stayed the same. The play itself has been depicted in settings from British Colonial India to Cuba of the 1950s. Joss Whedon's 2011 film even moves it to the present day. All these different presentations were working from the same script, presenting the same Shakespearean content, and often using the exact same dialogue.

Content/presentation confusion is sometimes apparent when reading negative product reviews of creative works. Some reviewers aren't discussing the work itself, but rather *the medium it was presented in*. They don't have an issue with the concepts in the book they read, but they're upset that the font size was too small. The movie on the DVD they watched was actually great, but they're giving it one star because the title menu was confusing. I've even seen poor reviews given for the package something was shipped in, which is really just the medium of the presentation—a wrapper around a wrapper around the content.

Your content is an abstract ideal. It has to be wrapped in some presentation, but in this world of digital manipulation, that presentation is *not* an integral part of the work.

A few days after my Goodreads experience, I watched the 1993 movie adaptation of *Much Ado About Nothing* starring Denzel Washington and Kenneth Branagh. It gave me the same goosebumps as the play. The ideas that Shakespeare explored were just as good on screen as they were on paper. Regardless of the specific presentation, the content was universal.

The "Page-Based" CMS

A core question is whether your CMS is managing *content* or *pages*. Does your CMS assume every piece of content in the repository should result in a web page? Or are they pure content objects that can then be embedded into pages?

The conflation of *content object* and *page* has resulted in the phrase "page-based CMS" being used to describes CMS that explicitly manages web pages, over more abstract notions of content without presentation. The phrase normally pops up when comparing two systems and is usually meant pejoratively, with the assumption that managing simple pages is less noble and sophisticated than managing pure content.

This is a fair point, but it might be misplaced, for a couple of reasons.

First, while multichannel publishing and content reuse is very valuable, not all instances need it. In many cases, 99% of content views will be page views in a browser, so managing the page is of utmost importance.

Second, just because a CMS manages pages doesn't mean the content in those pages can't be used in other ways. Even if your CMS offers you a content type called News Article Page, that doesn't mean that content can't be extracted and repurposed into things like RSS feeds and web APIs.

While a true page-based CMS will likely bake in some web-page-specific properties—META tags, menu labels, template selection, etc.—it will also include more neutral, presentation-free information that can be used in other ways.

In the end, the difference between a "page" and a more generic "content element" seems to be one of URL addressability. Pages get URLs and are intended to be viewed in isolation, as the main content object resulting from a single web request. Content elements (non-pages) are meant to exist in support of other content through referencing or embedding (see "Content Embedding" on page 97), and will not be individually URL addressable.

At what point does a tweet about a news article become content in itself? To generate a tweet from our CMS, we can simply add some attributes to the News Article content type—"Twitter Text," for example. This means that the tweet "piggybacks" on the same content model as the news article itself.

But at what point would it make sense to break off the information required for a tweet and publish it as a separate content object? We could create another content type, "Tweet." It would have a attribute for text, and perhaps another attribute to link to the article we're promoting with it.

In this form, it would have its own life in our CMS. It would be an object with its own content lifecycle, permissions, workflow, and even editing interface. Whether or not this is necessary or advantageous depends on your requirements.

Defining a Content Model

A content model is defined by three things:

- Types
- Attributes
- Relationships

These three things, used in combination, can define an almost infinite variety of content.

Content Types

A content type is the logical division of content by structure and purpose. Each type serves a different role in the model and is comprised of different information.

Humans think in terms of types every day. You label specific things based on what type of thing they are—in terms of "is a":

- This three-bedroom, two-bath Colonial *is a* building.
- This 2015 Colnago AC-R Ultegra Complete *is a* bicycle.
- This Footlong Firebreather *is a* burrito.

In thinking this way, we're mentally identifying types. We understand that there are multiple bicycles and burritos and buildings in the world, and they're all concrete representations of some type of thing. We've mentally separated the type of thing from a specific instance of the thing.

Editors working with content think the same way. An editor wants to create a new News Release or a new Employee Bio.[8] Or, this existing content *is a* News Release or *is an* Employee Bio. In your editor's head, the idea of a generic Page is separate from actual representations of the "About Us" or "Products" pages.

Whether explicitly acknowledged or not, whenever you work with content you have some mental conception of the type of content you want to manage. You mentally put your content into boxes based on what that content is.

A content type is defined to your CMS in advance. Most CMSs allow multiple types of content, but they differ highly in terms of how granular and specific they allow the definitions of these types to be.

All content stored by a CMS will have a type. This type will almost always be selected when the content is created—indeed, most CMSs won't know what editing interface to show an editor unless they know what content type the editor is trying to work with. It is usually difficult to change the type of a content object once it's created (more on this in the next section).

It's important to draw a clear line between a content type and a content *object*. A content type is a pattern for an object—bicycle, burrito, or building, from the previous example. You might have a single content type from which thousands of content objects are created.

Consider making Christmas cookies. You have a cookie cutter in the shape of a Christmas tree, candy cane, snowman, or whatever. Using this, you cut cookie dough. You have *one* cookie cutter, which you use to create *dozens* of cookies. The cookie cutter is your content *type*. The actual cookies are the content *objects*.

A content type can be considered the "pattern" for a piece of content, or the definition of the information a particular type of content requires to be considered valid. An Employee Bio, for example, might require the following information:

- First Name
- Last Name
- Job Title
- Hire Date

---

8 For the remainder of the book, I will capitalize the names of content *types* as proper nouns. I will lowercase content *objects* (e.g., a particular article is an object of the type Article).

- Bio
- Manager
- Image

(These are attributes, which we'll talk about shortly.)

You must create this definition in advance so that your CMS knows what information you'll be putting into what spaces.

There are multiple benefits to organizing your content into types:

Structure
Different content types require different information to be considered valid. A Person requires a First Name. This doesn't make sense for a Page.

Usability
Most CMSs will automatically create an editing interface specific to the type of content you're working with. When editing the Hire Date in an Employee Bio, for example, the CMS might render a date selection drop-down.

Search
Finding all blog posts is quite simple when they all occupy the same type.

Templating
Our Employee Bio pages will be clearly different from our News Release pages. Since the two types store different information, they obviously have different methods of outputting that information.

Permissions
Perhaps only the Human Resources department can edit Employee Bios. Depending on the CMS, you might be able to limit permissions based on type.

In these ways, the content types in a CMS implementation form boundaries around logically different types of content, allowing you to apply functionality and management features to just the types for which they apply.

Switching types

Switching the underlying content type after a content object has been created from it can be logically problematic.

Let's assume that we created a piece of content from our Employee Bio content type. Now, for whatever reason, we want to convert this to a News Release. We have a problem because we have information specific to the Employee Bio type that doesn't exist in the News Release type (First Name, for example), which means that when we switch types, this information has nowhere to go. What happens to it?

Because of this, switching content types after content has been created is often not allowed. If it is, you have to make hard decisions about what happens to information that has no logical place in the future type (Figure 6-2).

Figure 6-2. Converting content types in Episerver—when the new type doesn't contain matching attributes for everything defined on the old type, hard questions result

Oftentimes, you must swallow hard and give the system permission to simply throw that information away. As such, switching types is not for the faint of heart, especially when you have hundreds or even thousands of content objects based on a specific type.

Attributes and Datatypes

Content types are wrappers around smaller pieces of information. Refer back to our previous definition of an Employee Bio. An Employee Bio is simply a collection of smaller pieces of information (First Name, Last Name, etc.).

Nomenclature differs, but these smaller pieces of information are commonly referred to as attributes, fields, or properties (we'll use "attribute"). An attribute is the smallest unit of information in your content model, and it represents a single piece of information about a content object.

Each attribute will be assigned a datatype, which limits the information that can be stored within it. Common basic datatypes are:

- Text (of varying length)
- Number
- Date
- Image or file
- Reference to other content

Depending on the CMS, there might be dozens of possible datatypes you can use to describe your content types, and you might even be able to create your own datatypes, which are specific to your content model and no other. Figure 6-3 shows some of the options available in the eZ Platform CMS.

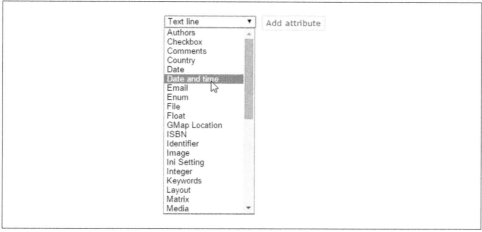

Figure 6-3. Predefined types of attributes available for eZ Platform

Referring back to our previous model, we can apply the following datatypes:

- First Name: short text
- Last Name: short text
- Job Title: short text
- Hire Date: date
- Bio: rich text
- Manager: reference to another Employee Bio object
- Image: reference to an image file

By specifying datatypes, you allow your CMS to do several things:

Validation
> The CMS can ensure that the information you enter is valid. For instance, Manager must be a valid reference to another Employee Bio object. Additionally, the CMS may warn you against deleting that other object while there are still outstanding references to it.

Editing interface generation

The CMS can render different interface elements to enable you to easily work with different attributes. You might allow rich text[9] in your Bio attribute, which means displaying a WYSIWYG[10] editor with editing controls.

Sorting and filtering

The CMS understands how to use different datatypes to sort and filter content. By filtering and sorting by Hire Date, you could locate all employees hired between two dates, and order them by seniority.

Some CMSs do not allow the datatyping of attributes, but this is rare. In these cases, the CMS normally allows you to simply declare "custom fields," which it stores as simple text. The utility of these fields is extremely limited, as you must ensure editors enter the values correctly (enforcing a date format in a simple text field is tricky) and you must jump through hoops to use these values when sorting and filtering.

Built-in Attributes

Most CMSs will have a handful of built-in attributes that automatically exist in every content type and don't have to be explicitly added to the content model. These include:

ID

Without exception, every content object has some type of identifier that uniquely identifies that content, not unlike the primary key in a database table (in fact, behind the scenes, this *is* often the primary key of a database table). Most systems have numeric, incremental IDs. Some others use GUIDs,[11] which is helpful when moving content between installations since they're guaranteed to be globally unique.

Title or Name

Most systems will have some way to name a content object. Usually this is an explicit Title field, which either is used only as an internal title or is dual-purposed as the displayed title of the object (the headline of a News Release, for

---

9 "Rich text" is often used to refer to any text that allows embedded formatting, such as bold, italics, etc. In most cases, this means HTML. A "rich text editor" is therefore assumed to be a visual editor that generates HTML in the background. However, some systems use the term "rich text" to refer to plain text fields that allow the manual insertion of HTML tags, or even shorthand formats such as Markdown.

10 "What You See Is What You Get." A WYSIWYG editor is a rich text editing interface that generates HTML but allows you to edit the text visually, instead of using tags or other markup.

11 Globally unique identifiers. A GUID is a sequence of random numbers and characters long enough to virtually ensure uniqueness. A common length is 32 digits, which is long enough to ensure that if each person on Earth possessed 600 million different GUIDs, the probability of a new GUID already existing would still only be 50%.

---

example). In some cases, the system will allow you to derive this value from other attributes using tokens which are replaced with values. For example, specifying the Name of an Employee Bio as `$LastName, $FirstName` will always set the Name to something like "Jones, Bob" whenever the object is saved.

Body

It's very common to have a rich text field automatically available for the "body" of the object, whatever that might mean for the particular type. This assumes that most objects will have a free-form Body field, which is valid in many cases. Some types will not, and these systems usually have a way to hide the field for those types when necessary.

Teaser or Summary

While less common than the body field, some systems will provide a smaller Summary field. This is quite common with systems that have blog roots, such as WordPress.

These built-in attributes, where available, are automatically present in all types, and your content model is composed of the attributes that exist *in addition* to these.

Attribute Validation

To ensure information is entered correctly, it needs to be validated, which means rejecting it unless it exhibits the correct format or value for its purpose.

Basic validation is enforced via the datatype. If something is meant to be a number, then it has to be entered as a valid number. Additionally, the editing interface might enforce this by only displaying a small text box that only allows entry of numeric characters.

However, the datatype doesn't tell the entire story. What if our number is only a number in *format*, but our intention for this number is for it to be a year? Then we potentially need to validate it in other ways: against the value, the pattern, or via some custom method.

We can validate values through ranges. In our year example, it most likely needs to be a four-digit, positive integer (depending on whether or not we're allowing dates BC, or dates after AD 9999), and it most likely needs to be within a specific range. For instance, we may require that it be in the past, or that it be within a particular defined period (e.g., from 100 years in the past to the current year). Figure 6-4 shows an example of specifying an allowable range for a field in Drupal.

Figure 6-4. Numeric validation options in Drupal

Alternatively, perhaps we're storing a product stock-keeping unit (SKU), and we know that this must always be a pattern of three letters, followed by a dash and four numbers. A regular expression (discussed more in Chapter 8) of "[A-Z]{3}-[0-9]{4}" can ensure we only accept data matching this pattern.

Beyond simple validation, occasionally it becomes necessary to validate input through custom integration. Perhaps our product SKU needs to be cross-checked against our product database to ensure it exists. In this case, when an editor saves a content object, the CMS performs a query against the product database to ensure the product SKU exists, and rejects the content if it doesn't. Querying *your* product database is a requirement that is needed by no other customer of your CMS, so it will clearly not support this out of the box. The best a system can do is provide you with the ability to program around it using the API.

Value, pattern, and custom validation capabilities differ widely. If appropriate methods are not available, then the only solution is to train editors well, and provide graceful error handling if they enter something incorrectly.

Using Attributes for Editorial Metadata

Attributes usually store information that is either displayed to the information consumer or used to directly affect the presentation of content. However, there is a valid case for using attributes to store administrative or "housekeeping" information.

Metadata means "data about data," which means data that isn't the primary purpose of the content object, but serves some secondary purpose. The idea of metadata in web content management is a little abstract—systems don't usually call anything metadata and instead just treat all attributes the same—but it can be accurately used to refer to data that isn't related to the content object directly, but rather is about the *management* of that object.

For example:

- A text attribute called To Do might be used to keep running notes, wiki-style, of things that need to be done with that content. A report could generate all content with some value in this attribute, which represents all content that needs some attention.

- A user selection called Content Owner could indicate what person in the organization is ultimately responsible for that content.

- A date attribute called Review By could indicate when the content needs to be reviewed for accuracy. Combined with the Content Owner attribute, a report could show a user all the content for which that user is responsible that needs to be reviewed.[12]

Content Type Inheritance

If content types are simply wrappers around sets of attributes, then it follows that we must create a new content type for every possible combination of attributes in our content model. This makes sense, since a News Release uses a fundamentally different set of information than an Employee Bio.

But what if two content types are very similar? Many times, you'll have a content type that is exactly like another type, except for the addition of one or two extra attributes.

Consider a basic Page content type that represents the simplest content we can come up with—a basic page of rich text with a title. It consists of nothing but:

- Title
- Body

As mentioned previously, these will often be simply built-in attributes.

For our blog, we need another type for Blog Post. It needs:

- Title
- Body
- Summary
- Published Date

Do you see the similarity? A Blog Post is simply a Page with two extra attributes. You could do this for many different types of content. A Help Topic, for example, could be

---

12 I read once about an intranet that used attributes such as these to "shame" content owners. When a page was rendered with a Review By date more than 30 days in the past, a notice was displayed at the top of the page: "Bob Jones is responsible for this content but has not reviewed it in 14 months. Contact Bob at extension 1234 to check if this content is still accurate."

a Page with the addition of Software Version and Keywords. An Event could be a Page with the addition of Start Date and Location.

Now suppose that sometime after your site launches, your marketing manager asks you to add an SEO Description to all the pages on the website. You're faced with the prospect of adding another attribute to *all* the types in your content model (and then deleting it when the marketing manager decides he doesn't want it anymore).

Wouldn't it be helpful if you could *inherit* the attribute definition of Page and simply specify what attributes are available beyond that?

So, the definition of a Blog Post would be "everything a Page has, plus Summary and Published Date." By doing this, you would ensure that whenever the Page content type changed (via the addition of SEO Description, in this case), the Blog Post type— and all other types inheriting from Page—would change as well. Figure 6-5 shows how this would work for our example content types.

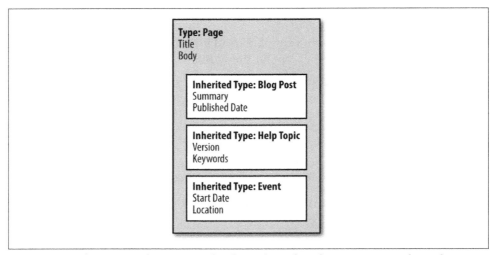

Figure 6-5. A base type of Page provides the Title and Body to every type that inherits it: Blog Post, Event, and Help Topic get Title and Body, and then add to them with specific attributes of their own

 To an object-oriented programmer, this is not a new concept. Class inheritance has been a paradigm of this type of programming for decades. The same values of conciseness and manageability apply equally well to content management. By being able to extend one type into another, you gain increased control over your model as it changes in response to future requirements.

Sadly, content type inheritance is not common in CMSs. Few systems currently offer it, though it seems to become slightly more common every year.

Partial type composition

What's even rarer than simple inheritance is the ability to combine multiple types (or *partial* types) to create a new type. For instance, we could define a Content Header type as:

- Title
- Subtitle

Does this make sense as a standalone type? Probably not—what content just has a Title and a Subtitle? However, when defined as a part of a larger type, this makes more sense. Many types might use a Title and a Subtitle as part of their definition.

To this end, we might define an Article Body as:

- Body
- Image
- Image Caption

And we might define an Author Bio as:

- Author Name
- Author Bio
- Author Image

We might then define an Article type as simply the combination of all three:

- Title
- Subtitle
- Body
- Image
- Image Caption
- Author Name
- Author Bio
- Author Image

Figure 6-6 illustrates this idea of partial type composition.

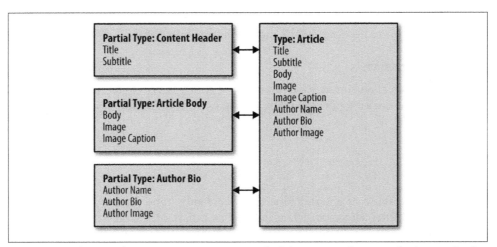

Figure 6-6. The Article content type is composed of three partial types, which can also be used to compose other types; any changes to a partial type are reflected in any type that uses it

How are we any better off in this situation? Because we can reuse the parts to define other types. For example, we could use our Content Header type in an Image Gallery type, since Title and Subtitle are common to both that *and* an Article. Then, if we added something to Content Header, it would be added to all types that use that type.[13]

Again, this ability is rare, but where available it vastly increases the manageability of a complicated content model. Figure 6-7 shows how partial type composition can be achieved in the Sitecore CMS.

---

13 Note the usage of "use" rather than "inherit." You can "inherit" from one other type. You "use" multiple types. When composing types, the relationship is one of composition, not parentage.

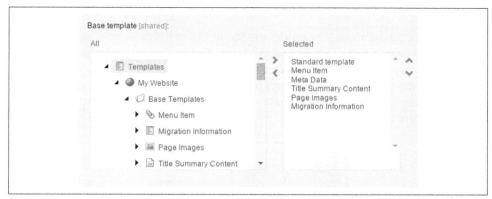

Figure 6-7. Multiple type composition in Sitecore—partial types (called "templates" in this system) can be browsed and selected in the left pane, and then added to the right pane to form a type composed of multiple partial types

Content Embedding

Some systems allow for the embedding of one content item into another item, either within rich text content or in data structures that render lists of referenced content. The embedded content is often called "blocks" or "widgets."[14]

 If the following sounds very vague, it is. This is a highly variable type of functionality with few universal implementations. The best we can do here is provide multiple examples of similar functionality in an attempt to tie it together.

Rich text embedding

Consider a project that requires a Photo Gallery page. You can easily model a Photo Gallery type with a Title, perhaps an introductory paragraph of text at the top (Description), and the images for the gallery underneath that.

Then suppose the editors say, "Well, we'd like to have another paragraph of text at the bottom of the page, underneath the gallery." You can handle this by changing the Description attribute to Upper Description and Lower Description, then altering the templating to display both, above and below the gallery.

Back to the editors: "Now we have some situations where we want more than one gallery on a page."

---

14 Note that blocks or widgets often reference managed content, but they don't have to. They may just render non-content-related functionality on the page, such as a weather forecast, for example.

Now what?

Perhaps the better solution is to model the Photo Gallery type as an element that can be embedded in rich text. This means the Photo Gallery might no longer be a URL-addressable page, but rather an embeddable content element (again, a "block" or "widget" in many cases) that gets wrapped in a page. Using this, the editors could write their page of content as rich text, and embed an object of this type of content within it (Figure 6-8).

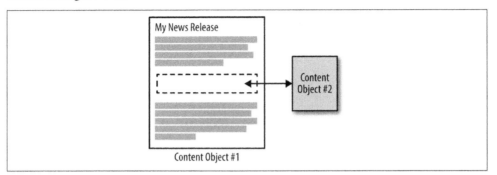

Figure 6-8. Content is embedded in rich text by placing a reference or token that identifies the embedded object; during templating, this token is detected and replaced by some templated view of the embedded object

Beyond enabling what the editors require for this specific instance, this has two other advantages:

- Photo Gallery objects can be used on multiple pages. One gallery could be embedded on 100 pages across the site.

- Photo Galleries can be embedded into objects based on other types, assuming they also allow for embedding. A gallery of Bob's karaoke performance at the Christmas party can be added to the rich text on his Employee Bio page, for instance.

The actual process of embedding ranges from simple text shorthand to sophisticated drag-and-drop interfaces.

WordPress, for instance, has something it calls "Shortcodes," which are text snippets that are processed during output. For example:

```
[photo_gallery folder="images/2015-christmas-party"]
```

This code might be mapped to a PHP function that renders all images from the specified directory. Clearly, this is not a managed content object; it's just a PHP function mapped to a text string. The "content" is just a directory of images on the filesystem.

If you wanted tighter control over the gallery, you might model it as a content type, then use a Shortcode to refer to the ID of that content:

```
[photo_gallery id="1234"]
```

The corresponding PHP function would retrieve content object #1234 and use the data to render a photo gallery.

Some systems go so far as to create HTML-like syntax that allows editors to write markup inline. The Articles Anywhere plug-in for Joomla! (*https://www.nonumber.nl/extensions/articlesanywhere*), for instance, provides syntax like this for embedding the most recent three articles from a specific category (category #9, in this example):

```
{articles cat:1-3:9}
  {title}
  {text:20words:strip}
  {readmore:More...|readon}
{/articles}
```

This markup is detected and processed during output.

 Clearly, this level of markup introduces training issues. Editors will need to understand all the options available to them, and will likely need access to some type of reference material.

eZ Platform uses a framework called Custom Tags, which allows for the embedding of data through a validated form. See Figure 6-9 for an example of embedding social media icons between two paragraphs in a body of rich text. While this embedding doesn't use any content, consider the content modeling we might *avoid* by having this functionality. If not for this method, the content type might have to be modeled with attributes for Show Twitter Icon, Show YouTube Icon, etc. And, even then, how would the author indicate where on the page they should be embedded?

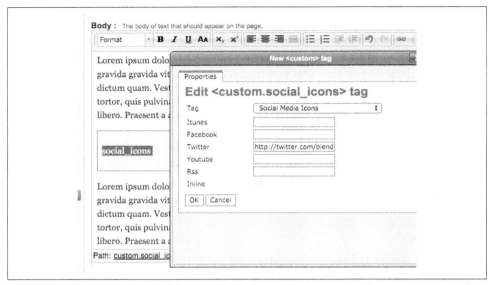

Figure 6-9. Custom tag embedding in eZ Platform: the data from the form is encapsulated in the custom tag embedded between two paragraphs

A smaller number of systems provide graphical interfaces for embedding content (see Figure 6-10). Content can be created, then dragged into rich text editors for placement.

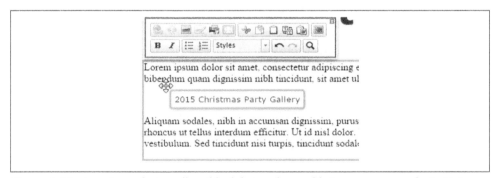

Figure 6-10. A custom photo gallery block being dragged between paragraphs in Episerver's WYSIWYG editor—this is a managed content object, and will be rendered as a photo gallery during content output

Blocks, widgets, and regions

Blocks or widgets can sometimes be stacked into structures we'll call *lists*. These lists hold one or more elements, which are rendered individually from the top down at designated locations on a template.

Content types might have element lists as attributes, or a template might have "regions" or "dropzones" into which elements can be added or dropped. These regions might be content-specific ("Right Sidebar for Content #1234") or global (the sitewide footer).

For example, Episerver will allow an attribute type of Content Area (see Figure 7-6 in Chapter 7). This allows the "stacking" of content elements inside of it. So, an attribute called Right Sidebar Content might allow editors to add miscellaneous content elements, which are then rendered in a specified location on the content type's template.

Drupal has extensive functionality for "blocks," which can be added to regions on a template. Likewise, WordPress offers "widgets" that can be stacked into specific regions on the template (see Figure 6-11).

Figure 6-11. A list of widgets stacked into a template region called "Sidebar" in Word-Press—the widgets can be reordered as desired

Implications for page composition

Both methods of embedding enable a form of dynamic page composition. One imagines editors as artists, painting on a canvas from a palette of element options.

The idea is seductive. Think back to our Photo Gallery example from earlier—we vastly increased the utility of this content by turning it into an embeddable object. Instead of it being a "destination," it became content that now supports and enriches other content.

So why shouldn't we do this for everything? We could create a single master type of Page, and all other content types could be embeddable types that go into regions on it —either lists, or rich text.

Systems like this do exist. They often have simple URL-addressable pages that are nothing but collections of lists or dropzones to which blocks or widgets are added.

Other systems treat pages almost as folders that contain individual content elements which are assigned to areas on a template—a page is simply a container of individual content items that are looped over, which each item rendered individually to form a page.

While this seems ultimately flexible on the surface, it never seems to work as well at a large scale as one might hope.

First, this paradigm introduces more steps into the editorial process. If you want to publish a blog post, now you have to create a Page, then find the Blog Post content type and place it into the page. To get around this, some of these systems implement templates or even macros that automatically provide commonly used combinations of page and widgets.

Regardless of how the page started, this model also lets editors have aesthetic control over the page that they might not have been intended to have. If our macro or template has put a Related Content widget in the sidebar by default, can an editor delete this?

The fact is that a lot of content was simply designed to be templated. If you have 10,000 technical notes on your website, you likely don't want editors to have any control over presentation. Allowing editors to change the page layout for one of them on a whim is a governance problem just waiting to happen.

Additionally, embedded content isn't as easily available as other content, due to the lack of URL addressability, among other things. What if we wanted to send a link to our photo gallery? It's not a page, remember, it's just embedded in a page. And remember too that it might be embedded in 100 pages, so which one is the canonical page for it? You might say that we'll just put it on one page and indicate that this is the one and only page on which it appears, but that then calls into question whether it's a separate content object at all. When a widget is irrevocably bound to a single container, is it really a widget, or is it just part of the model for that type?

This also complicates APIs and content migration. Content is now buried one or more levels deep in another construct. The relationship of widgets to regions (and their ordinal position) and then finally to pages is something that has to be accounted for whenever manipulating content from code.

Finally, it introduces some interesting logical questions about the relationship between content and presentation. If an editor drags a particular widget onto a page, does this widget have anything to do with the content itself, or is it related to *the page on which the content is embedded*? Does the News Article object "contain" that widget, or is the page itself a higher-level object that contains both the News Article and the widget?

A widget that tells me the current temperature might be handy, but does it have any relationship to the news article on the same page introducing the new CEO? Does it need to be managed in the same logical "space" as the news article? If I delete the article, what happens to the widget? Does one need to care about or even be aware of the other? Is their appearance on the same page simply incidental?

Contrast this with a widget that lists additional content about the new CEO. It could be argued that this has a logical relationship to the news article, so should be somehow tied or connected to it. Thus, our Related Content widget is associated with the *content*, not the *page*.

In practice, artisanal page composition is less necessary than you might think, and not nearly the panacea you might hope. If the idea appeals to you, the correct solution is likely to find a system that offers the ability to compose pages on an exception basis when necessary, but supports solid content modeling and templating as its core, intended architecture.

Horizontal vs. Vertical Stacking

Web pages naturally flow from top to bottom. There is rarely a hard limit on the height of a web page, and two decades of experience with the Web has taught us that elements—paragraphs, images, tables, whatever—can be stacked vertically without limit.

Horizontal stacking isn't the same. Horizontally stacked elements usually need to be grouped in a container where the width or number of elements is constrained—"half width" or "3-wide" or "60/40." The width of the elements within the container might need to be specified too—whether they take up one column or two columns, for example—or else they'll wrap incorrectly.

As a general rule, vertical stacking is simple and free from complication. Horizontal stacking is much less so.

Relationships

Modeling content is of two basic varieties:

Discrete
Describing a type of content internal to itself

Relational
Describing a type of content by how it relates to other content

In our Employee Bio example, we have both varieties. Attributes like First Name and Last Name are specific to a single content object only. The fact that one person's name is "Joe Smith" has no bearing on any other content. This is the discrete, self-contained data of that content.

However, the Manager attribute is a reference to another content object, which means it is relational, or it defines how a content object "relates" to another content object.

Figure 6-12 shows an example of relational modeling in Episerver, where a property entitled "Link to Page" allows editors to select another page in the CMS as its target.

Figure 6-12. An attribute can be a reference to another content object

Relational content modeling opens up a number of new challenges. Considering the Manager attribute again:

- You must ensure that the content object to which this attribute refers is another Employee Bio, and not, for example, the "Contact Us" page.

- Can an employee have more than one manager? This is an edge case, certainly, but if it happens, you either have to ignore it or modify the model to accommodate it. This means your Manager attribute must be able to store multiple values.

- How do you ensure the reference is valid? What if someone deletes the Manager object? Are you prepared to handle an employee with no manager?

- How do you allow editors to work with this attribute? Since this is a reference, your editors will likely need to go search for another employee to specify, which can make for a complicated interface.

Highly relational content models can get very complicated and are enormously dependent on the capabilities of the CMS. The range of capabilities in this regard is wide. A small subset of CMSs handle relational modeling well, and the relational sophistication of your planned content model can and should have a significant influence on your CMS selection.

We will discuss relational modeling more extensively in Chapter 7.

Content Composition

Some content isn't simple, and is best modeled as a group of content objects working together in a structure. Thus, a logical piece of content is *composed* of multiple content objects.

A classic example might be a magazine. We have a content type for Issue, but this is composed of the following:

- One featured Article
- Multiple other Articles

We might support this by giving our Issue content type these attributes:

- Featured Article (reference to an Article)
- Articles (reference to multiple Articles)

We can create our Articles as their own content objects, and an Issue is essentially just a collection (an "aggregation") of Articles in a specific structure. Our Issue has very little information of its own (it might have a single attribute for Published Date, for example, and maybe one more for Cover Image), and exists solely to organize multiple Articles into a larger whole.

This is a contrived example. A much more common example requires aggregating content in a "geographic" structure, which we'll talk about in Chapter 7.

Content Model Manageability

Any content model is a balancing act between complexity, flexibility, and completeness. You might be tempted to account for every possible situation, but this will almost always have the side effect of limiting flexibility or increasing complexity.

For example, when working with content types, editors need to be able to understand the different types available, how they differ, and when to use one over another. In some situations, it might make sense to combine two types for the sake of simplicity and just account for the differences in presentation.

Could a Page content type double as a Blog Post? If a Page also has fields for Summary, Author, and Published Date, is it easier to simply display those in the template only when they're filled in? If a Page is created within a Blog Post content type, then can we treat that Page as a Blog Post and give editors one less type to have to understand?

Whether this makes things easier or harder depends on the situation and the editors. If they work with the CMS often to create very demanding content, then they might be well served with two separate types. If they create content so rarely that they almost have to be retrained each time, then a single type might be the way to go.

If you don't have the ability to inherit content types, then it's to your benefit to limit content types as much as is reasonable. Having a content model with 50 different types becomes very hard to manage when someone wants to make model-wide changes.

It's hard to place general rules around manageability, but limiting content types to the bare minimum needed is usually a good idea. More types means more training for editors, more templating, and an increased likelihood of having to switch types after creation (which, as we saw earlier, is problematic).

The best you can do is to keep manageability in mind when creating or adjusting your model. Examine every request and requirement from the perspective of how this will affect the model over time. Almost every change will increase the complexity of the model, and is the benefit worth it?

Perspective: Content Modeling Is an Editorial Issue

by Sara Wachter-Boettcher

My love for content modeling started back in 2009, when I was leading the content strategy practice at an agency working on Arizona's state-run tourism website. Only, I didn't know to call it that at first. I just wanted the content to work for real people.

If you were planning to go hiking on your visit to Flagstaff, you wouldn't want to just learn about hiking or just learn about Flagstaff. You'd want to learn about hiking near Flagstaff. If you were spending a weekend in Tucson, you wouldn't want to wade through thousands of event listings from across the state. You'd want to know what was happening where and when you'd be visiting. But none of that was possible. Despite having thousands of articles, guides, listings, events, and other kinds of content—much of that content really good—everything on the site was disconnected, each item an island of information.

Before this project, I hadn't been too involved in the content management systems powering our sites. Sure, I knew how to use them—I knew how to format text properly and strip out any cruft; I knew how to handle versioning and talk about workflow. But deciding how to structure and map out the CMS itself? I'd always assumed that was our developers' job.

What I realized as I sifted through all that content, clustering like items and drawing arrows and establishing taxonomies, is that no developer can create the best content models alone. It takes editorial skill to recognize patterns and ensure content chunks are meaningful, not just modular. It takes UX expertise to identify which connections between content will be most valuable to users, and when. And it takes a strategic lens to decide which content structures and relationships will help your organization reach its goals.

Today, I see content modeling as a core skillset for all kinds of practitioners. Because the more a team thinks deeply about what its content is made of, and why, the better decisions we'll make at every stage: design, CMS development, migration, and beyond.

Sara Wachter-Boettcher runs a content strategy consultancy and is the author of Content Everywhere *(Rosenfeld Media) and the coauthor of* Design for Real Life *(A Book Apart).*

A Summary of Content Modeling Features

Since this chapter has been largely about the theory of content modeling, it can be hard to draw out specific features or methods of system evaluation. Here's a list of questions to ask with regard to a system's content modeling features:

- What is the built-in or default content model? How closely does this match your requirements?
- To what extent can this model be customized?
- Does the system allow multiple types?
- Does the system allow content type inheritance? Does it allow multiple inheritance?
- Does the system allow for the datatyping of attributes?
- What datatypes are available to add attributes to types?
- What value, pattern, and custom validation methods are available?
- Can you add custom datatypes to the system based on your specific requirements?
- Does the system allow multiple values for attributes?
- What editorial interfaces are available for each datatype?
- Does the system allow an attribute to be a reference to another content object? Can the reference be to multiple objects? Can it be limited to only those objects of a certain type?
- What options are available for content embedding and page composition?
- Does the system allow for permissions based on types?
- Does the system allow for templating based on types?
- How close can this system get to the (usually unreachable) ideal of a custom relational database?

A Note About Feature Lists

We discussed this in Chapter 5, but it bears repeating:

When evaluating this list (and any other feature list in this book), please remember that the objective is not simply to check every box on the list, for three reasons:

- It's doubtful that any system will provide every feature.
- It's not only important that the feature exists, but also *how well it works.*
- Some features aren't binary; rather, they exist on a range of functionality. Note that several questions in the preceding list relate to degree or extent of availability. These will not have yes/no answers.

Finally, always remember that features only have value in comparison to your own requirements. As such, evaluate them in that context only.

CHAPTER 7

Content Aggregation

In his book *Why Information Grows: The Evolution of Order, from Atoms to Econo-mies*,[1] César Hidalgo discusses a super car: the Bugatti Veyron.

The author calculates that the Bugatti—which has a sticker price of $2.5 million—is worth $600 per pound. This is quite a bit more than the $10 per pound of a Hyundai or even the $60 per pound of a BMW.

Now imagine that you ran the Bugatti into a wall at 100 mph. Assuming you survived the crash and then gathered up every last piece of the car, it would still weigh the same as the instant before it hit the wall. But it wouldn't be worth nearly $600 per pound any longer. It's the same steel, rubber, and glass it was, it's just not in the same form.

Here's the key:

> The dollar value of the car evaporated in the seconds it took you to crash it against that wall, but its weight did not. So where did the value go? The car's dollar value evapora-ted in the crash not because the crash destroyed the atoms that made up the Bugatti but because the crash changed the way in which these parts were arranged. As the parts that made the Bugatti were pulled apart and twisted, the information that was embod-ied in the Bugatti was largely destroyed.

The last sentence is key: the value of the Bugatti wasn't in the raw materials of the car, but rather in how these materials were arranged and ordered. Value is created by putting smaller pieces together to work as a whole. The selection, combination, and ordering of the parts *is more valuable than the parts themselves.*

---

1 *Why Information Grows: The Evolution of Order, from Atoms to Economies* (*http://www.amazon.com/Why-Information-Grows-Evolution-Economies/dp/0465048994*) by César Hidalgo (Basic Books).

Likewise, content often becomes more valuable when combined with other content. These combinations are called aggregations. In some senses, an aggregation of content becomes content itself. The "content," in this case, is in the selection, combination, and ordering of smaller content items to come together to form a new whole.

Content aggregation is the ability of a CMS to group content together. Note that we're not being too specific here—there are many types of aggregations and many ways a CMS might accomplish this. Furthermore, this ability is so obvious as to be taken for granted. We tend to simply assume every CMS does this to whatever degree we need.

For example:

- Displaying navigation links is aggregation. At some point, you need to tell your CMS to display a series of pages in a specific order to form the top menu of every page (a *static* aggregation that is *manually* ordered).

- Index pages are aggregations. The page that lists your latest press releases (Figure 7-1) is often simply a canned search of a specific content type, limited to the top 10 or so, and displayed in descending order chronologically (a *dynamic* aggregation with *derived* ordering).

- Search is aggregation. When a user enters a search term and gets results back, this is a grouping of specific content (a *dynamic*, *variable* aggregation).

Latest news releases	
Date	Title
18 Dec 2014	IBM Radically Simplifies Cloud Computing Contracts
17 Dec 2014	IBM Cloud Helps Diabetizer Improve the Accuracy and Flexibility of Diabetes Treatment
17 Dec 2014	IBM Adds Cloud Centers in Europe, Asia and the Americas
17 Dec 2014	Equinix and IBM Accelerate Adoption of Hybrid Cloud Computing Initiatives
17 Dec 2014	IBM Transforms National Express Customer Experience
17 Dec 2014	German Startup Protects Highly-Sensitive Patient Data in the IBM Cloud
17 Dec 2014	IBM Research Scientists Investigate Use of Cognitive Computing-Based Visual Analytics for Skin Cancer Image Analysis
16 Dec 2014	U.S. Department of Veterans Affairs Taps IBM Watson to Help Accelerate and Enhance Care Delivery
12 Dec 2014	Korea's Hancom Selects IBM Cloud to Securely Deploy SaaS Services Overseas
10 Dec 2014	Apple and IBM Deliver First Wave of IBM MobileFirst for iOS Apps

Figure 7-1. An aggregation of news releases on IBM's website as of December 2014

Aggregation is such a core part of most systems that it's assumed and often isn't even identified as a separate subsystem or discipline. But the range of functionality in this regard is wide, and breakdowns in this area are enormously frustrating.

Few things are more annoying than having the content you want, but being unable to retrieve it in the format you need. I've been in numerous situations working with multiple systems where editors threw up their hands in frustration and said, "All I want is to make *this* content appear in *that* place! Why is this so hard!?"

The answer to that question lies in a complex intersection of content shape, aggregation functionality, and usability.

The Shape of Content

The *shape* of content refers to the general characteristics of a content model when taken in aggregate and when considered against the usage patterns of your content consumers. Different usage patterns and models result in clear differences between content and its aggregation requirements. Content may be:

Serial

> This type of content is organized in a serial "line," ordered by some parameter. An obvious example is a blog, which is a reverse-chronological aggregation of posts. Very similar to that are social media updates—a tweet stream, for instance —or a news feed. This content doesn't need to be organized in any larger construct beyond where it falls in chronological order relative to other content. A glossary might be considered serial as well—it's a simple list of terms, ordered alphabetically by title.

Hierarchical

> This type of content is organized into a tree. There is a root content object in the tree that has multiple children, each of which may itself have one or more children, and so on. Sibling content items (those items under the same parent) can have an arbitrary order. Trees can be broad (lots of children under each parent) or narrow (fewer children) and shallow (fewer levels) or deep (more levels). An example of this is the core pages of many simple informational websites. Websites are generally organized into trees—there is primary navigation (Products, About Us, Contact Us), which leads to secondary navigation (Product A, Product B, etc.). Navigational aggregations for these sites can often be derived from the position of content objects in the tree.

Tabular[2]

> This type of content has a clearly defined structure of a single, dominant type, and is usually optimized for searching, not browsing. Imagine a large Excel spreadsheet with labeled header columns and thousands of rows. An example would be a company locations database. There might be 1,000 locations, all clearly organized into columns (address, city, state, phone number, hours, etc.). Users are not going to browse this information. Rather, they search it based on parameters.

Network

> This type of content has no larger structure beyond the links between individual content objects. All content is equal, flat, and unordered in relation to other content, with nothing but links between the content to tie it together. An obvious example of this is a wiki. Wikis have no structure (some allow hierarchical organization of pages, but most do not), and the entire body of content is held together only by the links between pages. A social network—if managed as content—would be another example. Content ("people") is equal in the network, and arbitrarily connected ("friends") with other content.

Relational

> This type of content has a tightly defined structural relationship between multiple highly structured content types, much like a typical relational database. The Internet Movie Database, for example, has Movies, which have one or more Actors, zero or more Sequels, zero or more Trivia Items, etc. These relationships are enforced—for instance, you cannot add a Trivia Item for a Movie that doesn't exist. A Trivia Item is required to be linked to a Movie, and cannot be added until the Movie exists.

Different CMSs have different levels of ability to handle the different shapes of content. For example:

- WordPress is well suited to managing serial content (blog posts), but you couldn't easily run a highly hierarchical help topic database with it.

- MediaWiki is designed to handle networked content, but it would be extremely inefficient to try to run a blog from it.

- Webnodes is perfect for defining and managing tabular and relational content. Interestingly, this also gives it the ability to manage serial content well (a blog is essentially a database table ordered by a date field), but it wouldn't make sense to

---

2 "Tabular" meaning having the characteristics of tables, not tabs.

highly structure a networked wiki with it. Figure 7-2 shows an example of a complicated relational content model implemented in Webnodes.

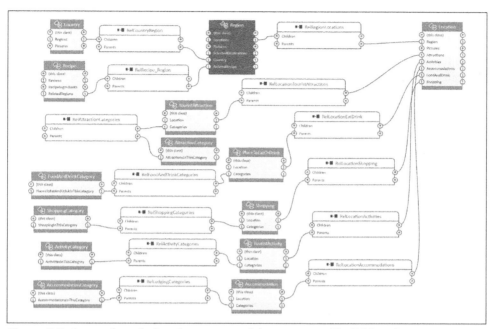

Figure 7-2. A complex relational content model as supported by Webnodes

In our examples, we simplified by pigeonholing websites to one shape, but the truth is that different sections of the same website will model content differently. The average corporate website might have many marketing pages organized into a tree (hierarchical), a dealer locator (tabular), and a news feed (serial). The content managed in each section has a different shape.

Additionally, when we say a particular system is not suited to a particular shape of content, what we're saying is that this system is not *best suited* to work with that shape of content. It's important to note that almost any system can be contorted to work with any type of content, though this either requires heroic development efforts or results in a very complex and confusing editor experience (often both).

Most mainstream CMSs are pursuing the middle of the road. They are usually particularly well suited to one or more of the listed shapes, but have some ability to handle any of them.

Content Geography

Most every system has some core method of organizing content. Very rarely do editors just throw content into a big bucket—normally, content is created *somewhere*, which means it exists in a location relative to other content.

Much like geography refers to the spatial relationships of countries, content geography refers to the spatial nature of content—where it exists "in space," or how it is organized relative to the content "around" it.

The quotes in that last paragraph underscore the idea that we're trying to place some physical characteristic on an abstract concept. Geographies attempt to treat content as a physical thing that exists in some location in a theoretical space representing the domain of all of your content.

The most common example of a geography is a "content tree" where content is organized as a parent/child structure (see Figure 7-3). All content objects can be the parent of one or more other content objects. Additionally, each object has its own parent and siblings (unless it's the root object, which means it's at the very top of the tree).

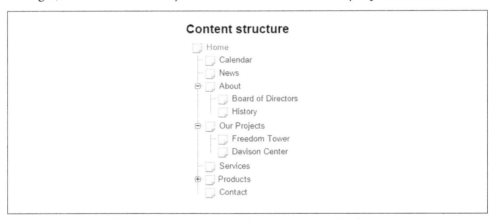

Figure 7-3. A typical content tree in an eZ Platform–powered website

In this sense, all content is created in some location. You add content as a child of some other content object, and because of this, it instantly has relationships with multiple other content objects. Depending on where it's placed, it might come into the world with siblings and (eventually) might have children, grandchildren, etc.

This content is hierarchical, and this geography allows us to traverse the tree and make decisions based on what we find. For instance, we may form our top navigation automatically from the children of the root object, or we may list the children of a certain page as navigation options when displaying that page to a user.

In a content tree geography, content is often discussed in terms of "levels." The most important pages in your site are top-level pages or first-level pages. Under that we have second-level pages, then third-level pages.

The Global Tree

A hierarchical tree is a natural way of organizing information for humans, as it tends to mirror how we think about and work with information—so much so that some systems use the tree globally, not just for content. These systems store *everything* in a tree, with the content of the website just being one node. Users, groups, templates, settings, even sometimes down to the button labels on rich text editors—it's all stored as objects in a tree, and all data is accessed via the same API. See Figure 7-4 for an example from Sitecore.

Figure 7-4. An example of a global tree from Sitecore—this system stores almost every bit of data in a tree structure, including templates and system settings

Less common is the folder structure of organizing content. Systems using this model have "folders" into which content can be placed, similar to files in an operating system.

This might seem very similar to the content tree in that it's hierarchical, but there's an important difference: *the folder is not itself a content object.* It's simply an administrative structure for editors to use to organize their content. Content objects are not children of other content objects, nor do they have children. Instead, we have folders and subfolders in which content objects are placed.

While this structure is generally clear for editors—we've been using files and folders for years in every operating system—it can be limiting in practice. The inability to directly relate content by parentage removes a valuable tool to aggregate content.

If we can't have children of a page, then we have to find another way to tie these pages together. The only spatial relationship content in these system exhibits is a sibling relationship with content in the same folder. (What makes this more complicated is that folders are often treated as simple buckets that don't allow arbitrary ordering of the content within them—more on that later in this chapter.)

Other systems might depend on a simple content type segregation model, where the content type of a particular piece of content is the major geography.[3] You can easily subdivide the entire domain of content by content type and perhaps some other parameters, but sometimes not much else. We can easily see all the News Releases, for example, but we don't create content in any specific location, and it doesn't exist with a spatial relationship to any other content. Figure 7-5 shows type segregation tools in Drupal.

Figure 7-5. Listing content by type in Drupal

Like the folder structure, this can limit our options considerably, but it can be appropriate in many cases. For instance, if your website is a high-volume blog, then your editors might not need to "place" their content anywhere. They might just need to create a Blog Post or a Movie Review and let the system itself sort out how to organize it. In these situations, editors are creating serial, isolated content that doesn't need any spatial relationships (or, rather, its spatial relationship to other content is automatically derived by date).

It's important to understand that a content geography is simply the main organization method a system exhibits. Systems usually offer multiple ways to aggregate content,

---

3 This could almost be viewed as the absence of *any* geography, since searching by type doesn't imply any spatial relationship to content. Nevertheless, it's quite common as a primary method of organization.

so when the core geography falls short there are typically multiple paths to accomplish the desired aggregation.

Geography Bias

As I've already mentioned, I was a huge James Bond fan in college. In the early days of the Internet, I spent hours on the *alt.fan.james-bond* Usenet group debating one of the most common topics for Bond fans: who was the best actor to play the role?[4] These debates often boiled down to this point: the first actor you ever saw play 007 is probably your favorite.

The same is true of geographies. The first geography style you worked with often imprints itself as the "right" way to organize content. This is important because the geography of a system is absolutely foundational to how developers and editors work with it. Geography plays an outsized role in forming a conceptual model of a system and the content that resides in it.

I've spent most of my career working with systems that have strong content trees. As such, my thought processes about CMSs have evolved around organizing content into a hierarchy. To this day, Drupal mystifies me, in this respect. I realize it's immensely popular and has thousands of adherents, but I struggle with anything that doesn't have a content tree at its core. I freely concede this is simply a bias that comes from the bulk of my professional experience.

Breaking biases like these can be difficult. Because of it, integrators can struggle when moving from one platform to another. They often try to force-fit the new platform into the old paradigm with which they're comfortable, and this rarely works well.

Editorial Limitations on Geography

Having editors intentionally "placing" content in a specific location in a geography might not be ideal. As we discussed in Chapter 4, there are different ways that editors' capabilities can be limited.

There are some editors who have limited responsibilities and might only be able to create certain types of content that can fit into the geography in one tightly controlled way. In these cases, you can limit them with permissions, but you might instead create a very simple interface for these editors to work with content.

The receptionist who manages the lunch menu on your intranet, for example, might only see a simple text box that allows him to enter some text for the next day's menu.

---

4 It was Timothy Dalton, for the record. This has been definitively and conclusively settled for all eternity and is now simply a nonnegotiable fact. If anyone disagrees, show them this footnote and back away slowly.

Behind the scenes, this interface places the content in the correct location relative to the larger geography without the editor being aware of it or being able to affect it in any way.

Secondary Geographies: Categories, Taxonomies, Tags, Lists, Collections, and Menus

When we talk about a geography of content, we're normally talking about the main way a CMS organizes its content. However, many systems have additional ways of grouping content, which might be pervasive enough to be considered secondary geographies.

Many systems are explicitly menued, which means there are menuing subsystems in which you create organizational structures and assign content to them. Menuing systems are generally very practical, in that they have to directly generate an HTML structure at some point. They're less about pure content, and more about providing an interface to generate a specific snippet of HTML. As such, you can assign content to a menu, but you also usually assign external URLs and sometimes even specify presentational information, like whether to open the link in a new window or whether to use an image in place of text. You sometimes even get all the way down to CSS classes and other details.

Menus are almost always hierarchical. This leads to the sometimes odd situation of having multiple trees. If your system uses a content tree as its core geography, you might have menus where relationships are reversed. Object B could be a child of Object A in the actual content tree, but Object A might be a child of Object B in one or more menu trees. This can either be handy or confusing, depending on the situation.

Some systems have flat structures they call *lists* or *collections*. These are just ordered lists of content which can be used in dozens of ways to aggregate content around a website. (Of course, a single-level menu, where the top-level items have no children, will basically accomplish the same thing.)

Categories, taxonomies, and tagging are other popular ways to organize content. Content objects can be assigned to a category or tag, which gives them some affinity relationship with other content in that category or tag, much like content in a folder or child content under a parent. The relationships in these secondary structures don't have to bear any resemblance to how content is organized in the primary structure.

Editors might find it easier to organize or relate to content in this way, and there are numerous ways to use these secondary geographies to display content to the end user.

Is There a Difference Between Categories and Tags?

If you implement both categories and tags in the same website, *be sure that you differentiate the usage clearly*. The logical architecture behind the two methods is the same—content is assigned to a larger structure (a category or tag) and retrieved by reference to that structure.

The biggest difference is that categories tend to be hierarchical and fixed, while tags are flatter and more dynamic. Editors can often make tags up on the fly, enter them as simple text strings, and generally treat them more casually than a rigid category tree.

However, in many cases, *editors will confuse categories and tags*. I have yet to see an implementation that used them both effectively, with a clear differentiation of when one was appropriate rather than the other. There's so much functional overlap that there just aren't many situations where a website needs both.

In one case, we completed an entire project with both categories and tags, only to discover that the editors had thought they were the same thing all along, and didn't understand why the finished website had both.

In general, content geographies are administrative concepts only. Visitors to a website will not usually be aware of the underlying geography. They may be vaguely aware that pages are ordered hierarchically, or that news items are ordered by date. However, at no time will the average website call attention to the content tree (with the possible exception of a sitemap) or explicitly name pages as "parent" or "child."

The Tyranny of the Tree

Content trees are very common in CMSs, but they can be problematic when large portions of functionality are bound to a single tree. In these cases, you can find that the tree exerts tyrannical control over your content, and simple problems become harder to resolve.

For instance, in various systems, the following functionality might be in some way related to where a piece of content resides in the tree:

- Permissions
- Allowed content types
- Workflow
- URL
- Template settings

If there's only *one* tree, then the tree can seem "tyrannical," forcing all this functionality onto content based solely on its position. For instance, you might group content into one location in the tree to make assigning permissions easier, but want more granular control over template selection than the tree position allows.

In these cases, a system needs to allow for settings and configuration to depart from the tree in some way. Applying this information based on tree position can certainly be efficient, but it might cross the line into restrictive, and a system needs to allow an intelligent and intuitive way to override this when necessary.

Additionally, binding navigation to a content object's position in the tree can become problematic when the same link needs to appear in two places on the site. If the website navigation is generated by traversing the tree, you are limited to what is present in the tree. If content needs to be in two places, how do you handle this?

Thankfully, most systems using a content tree have some mechanism for content to appear in more than one location. Usually, one of the appearances is designated as the "main" location, and the second is just a placeholder that references the first. Navigation can be handled one of two ways: the second location actually sends the user "across the tree" to the first location, or it renders the content "in place," essentially giving the same content two URLs. In practice, the former option is usually preferred.

When rendering external navigation links (to another website), these usually have to be represented by a content object. A type named External Url, or something similar, is modeled to contain the URL to which the editor wants to link. When rendered in navigation, this object displays a hyperlink off-site.

Aggregation Models: Implicit and Explicit

There are two major models for building aggregations:

- Implicit/internal
- Explicit/external

Content can implicitly be created as part of a larger structure. This is common in the content tree and type segregation models. When you create the page for Product X under the Products page, you have created a relationship. Those two pages are inextricably bound together as parent and child.

Put another way, their relationship is *internal* (or "implicit")—each content object knows where it lives in the structure. The fact that Product X is a child of Products, or that your Press Release is part of the larger aggregation of all Press Releases, is a characteristic that is inextricable from the content.

Conversely, an explicit aggregation means the relationship between these two content objects doesn't reside in the objects themselves. If we relate two objects in the Main

Menu, the fact that Product X is a child of Products is *only true in relationship to the Main Menu we created*. Taken in isolation, the two content objects don't know anything about each other or their relationship in this menu. The structure in these cases is *external* (or "explicit"). The structure doesn't exist within the content itself, but rather in a separate object—the menu. If that menu goes away, so does the relationship.

One of the benefits of explicitly creating aggregation structures is that content can take part in more than one structure. You might have a dozen different menus in use around your site, and the Products page could appear in all of them.

Should Your Aggregation Be a Content Object?

In some cases, your aggregation is really a managed content object with relationships to other content. However, most systems don't treat aggregations as core content objects, which means they're locked out of a lot of the functionality we consider inherent in the management of content. Sometimes, turning an aggregation into a content object is the right way to go.

Consider your team of technical writers. They would like to maintain several lists of help topics centered around certain subjects—topics about dealing with difficult customers, topics about the phone system, etc. These lists will always be manually curated and ordered, and each list should have a title, a few sentences of introductory text, and a date showing when the list was created and last reviewed.

Clearly, this is less of an aggregation and more of a full-fledged content object. Referring back to the concepts discussed in Chapter 6, this situation would call for a new content type: Topic List. It would have attributes of Title, Introduction, Date Created, Date Reviewed, and Topics. That last attribute would be a reference to multiple Help Topic objects from elsewhere in the geography.

By making this aggregation a content object, we gain several inherent features of content:

Permissions
    We could allow only certain editors to manage a particular Topic List.

Workflow
    Changes to a Topic List might have to be approved.

Versioning
    We might be able to capture and compare all changes to a particular Topic List.

URL addressability
    This aggregation now has a URL from which it can be retrieved (more on this in the next section).

When modeling content relationally, the line between content objects and content aggregations blurs because a referential attribute that allows multiple references *is a small aggregation in itself*. In these ways, aggregations can be "carried" on the backs of content objects.

Consider that the composition of an aggregation is really content in itself. A list of curated content objects, placed in a specific order, fulfills the two tests of content from Chapter 1: it's (1) created by editorial process, and (2) intended for human consumption. Not treating this aggregation as content can lead to problems.

Let's say your organization is legally required to list hazardous materials used in its manufacturing process on the company intranet. Someone might accidentally remove all the items from this list, putting the organization in violation of the law. How did the editor get permissions to do this? Did this change not trigger an approval? Could the organization not roll back to a previous version of the list?

Not every aggregation is as critical as this example, but in many cases, aggregations are not backed by the safeguards associated with other content objects. When planning and designing aggregations, your requirements might dictate that they be treated more like content.

The URL Addressability of Aggregations

In many systems, the only data structures that are assigned URLs are full-fledged content objects. This means that aggregations like menus, lists, and tags are not URL addressable—no visitor can type in a URL and view a menu, for instance.

In these cases, aggregations need to be "wrapped" in content objects in order for them to be displayed. For example, to create a list of content, an editor might have to create a Page object, then somehow embed this aggregation inside the page. Then, a visitor isn't viewing the aggregation so much as viewing the particular content object in which the aggregation is being displayed. Displaying the aggregation becomes indirect.

Not all systems work this way, though. Some systems have different mechanisms for assigning URLs to explicit aggregations and allowing them to be directly displayed as the target of a URL.

Aggregation Functionality

Content aggregations can have multiple features, the presence or absence of which will drastically affect an editor's ability to get the result she wants.

Static Versus Dynamic

A particular aggregation might be *static*, which means an editor has arbitrarily selected specific content objects to include in the aggregation, or *dynamic*, meaning the content of the aggregation is determined at any particular moment by specified criteria:

- A static aggregation might be an index of pages from your employee handbook that new employees should review. In this case, you have specifically found these pages and included them in this aggregation via editorial process. For a new page to be on this list, you need to manually include it (see Figure 7-6).

- A dynamic aggregation might simply be a list of all of the pages of the employee handbook. For a new page to be on this list, it just needs to be added to the employee handbook. Its appearance on this list is a byproduct of that action. A dynamic aggregation is essentially a "canned search"—a set of search criteria which are executed at any moment in time to return matching content.

Figure 7-6. A statically created list of content for an image carousel in Episerver

Dynamic aggregations are often a byproduct of the content geography. In the case of a content tree, the set of children of a parent page is a dynamic aggregation. With all such systems, it's possible to obtain an aggregation of child pages, and a new item will appear in this aggregation simply by virtue of being created under the parent. This is no different than a canned search with the criterion that the returned content must be the children of a particular parent.

Likewise, a dynamic aggregation might be "show me all the News Releases." In a system relying on type segregation as its core geography, simply adding a new News Release content object will cause a new item to appear in this aggregation.

Search criteria in dynamic aggregations

When creating a dynamic aggregation, editors will be dependent on the criteria that the CMS allows them to use to search for content, and the interface that the CMS gives them to configure it. They might be able to search by type, by date published, by author, and perhaps by property value.

When these methods fall short, it can be extremely frustrating. Either the CMS is deficient, or the editor simply wants to aggregate content using such an esoteric combination of criteria that no CMS can reasonably be expected to provide that level of specificity.

For example, suppose your editor wants to display an aggregation of all News Release objects from 2015 that are categorized under "Africa," but only when the text doesn't contain the phrase "AFRICON 2015" (since the preparations for a particular conference in Africa might confuse the results). Also included should be anything that contains the word "Africa" from any category, and any News Release written by an author assigned to a location in Africa during 2015.

There may be some CMSs that allow editors to configure this level of specificity from the interface, but they're few and far between. In these situations, it's usually necessary to have a developer assist by creating a custom aggregation from code.

Supplemental Indexing

I've read several books on organization and productivity that have boiled down to the same advice: externalize memory.[5] Write stuff down. This is unglamorous advice, certainly, but it's effective.

In data management, this is the process of "indexing" data. Databases store data in tables, but provide the ability to index data using other methods of organization to reduce query times. Just like the index of a book gives you an alternative method of finding information (as opposed to the table of contents, or just browsing the pages), an index provides a different and more efficient way of finding specific data in a larger repository.

In content management, it's sometimes helpful to create supplemental indexes to assist in esoteric searching. For instance, in the previous example, a developer could write some code that executed whenever a News Release was saved. If it matched the criteria specified, the unique ID of that content object could be added to a text file (or removed, if it didn't match). When the aggregation needed to be displayed, the IDs of the matching content objects would all be in one place.

Yes, this is unglamorous and low-tech, but like writing things down, it's highly effective. When you consider that this aggregation will likely be displayed more often than

---

5 The direct exhortation to "externalize memory" came from *The Organized Mind* by Daniel Levitan (Penguin). David Allen has talked about the same thing in the discussion of "collection systems" in his book *Getting Things Done* (Penguin).

any of the content will be created or updated, it becomes obvious that enduring computational complexity at those times is much more efficient.

Perhaps if the CMS allows searching by criteria, the developer could add a hidden true/false attribute to the content type: Africa Related. This attribute could be searched, but not set by an editor. When saving the content, the content could be evaluated by code and this attribute set to true or false. Then the editor could perform a simple search on that attribute and trust that it would only be set to true if the content matched the criteria.

This surfacing of deeper information into more consumable structures ("externalizing memory") is an acceptable strategy to circumvent aggregation criteria limitations and reduce real-time computational overhead.

Variable Versus Fixed

A subset of dynamic aggregations are those that can vary based on environmental variables. Even if the domain of content doesn't change and no content is added or altered, what appears in a dynamic aggregation might be different from day to day, or user to user.

Search is a classic example of a dynamic, variable aggregation. What is displayed in a search results page depends primarily on user input—what the user searches for. You may specify some other criteria, such as what content is searched and how the content is weighted or ordered, but a search is still created in real time based on user input.

Other aggregations might also be based on user behavior. For example, a sidebar widget displaying Recommended Articles might examine the content consumed by that visitor during the current session to determine similar content of interest.

Aggregations might be based on other variables, too—a "This Day in History" sidebar listing events, for example, clearly relies on the current date to aggregate its contents. Likewise, a list of "Events Near You" relies on a geolocation of the visitor's latitude and longitude.

Manual Ordering Versus Derived Ordering

Once we have content in our list, how is it ordered? What appears first, second, third, and so on? In some cases, we need to manually set this order. In other cases, we need or want the order to be derived from some other criteria possessed by the content itself:

- In the case of our employee handbook, if we were creating a curated guide of pages that new employees should read, then in addition to manually selecting those pages, we'd likely want to arbitrarily decide the order in which they appear.

We might want more foundational topics to appear first, with more specific topics appearing further down the list.

- If we had a list of Recently Updated Handbook Topics, then in addition to this list being dynamic (essentially a search based on the date the content was changed), we would want this content ordered reverse-chronologically, so the most recently updated topics appeared first. We would simply derive the search ordering by date.

It's obvious from our examples that the characteristics of static vs. dynamic and manual ordering vs. derived ordering often go hand in hand. It's relatively rare (though not impossible) to find an arbitrary aggregation that should have derived ordering. However, in most cases, if editors are manually aggregating content they also want the ability to manually order it (Figure 7-7).

Figure 7-7. Manually reordering a menu in Drupal

The opposite scenario—a dynamic aggregation that is manually ordered—is logically impossible. This gets a little abstract, but if an aggregation is dynamic, then its contents are not known at creation time (indeed, you're not building an aggregation as much as simply configuring search parameters), so there's no way this aggregation can be manually ordered. You can't manually order a group of things if the contents are unknown.

Manual ordering of dynamic aggregations can be approximated by "weighting" or "sort indexing," whereby content type has a property specifically designed to be used in sorting.

This works in most cases, but it can be quite loose. If one page has a sort index of 2 and another has an index of 4, then there's nothing stopping an editor from inserting something at index 3. Indeed, in many cases this is what the editor wants to do, but in other cases editors might do this in ignorance of the consequences (remember, they're editing the content itself, not the content's inclusion in the larger aggregation —they may not even be aware of the larger aggregation).

Furthermore, to allow this type of ordering, you need to have *a different sort index for every single dynamic aggregation in which the content might appear*. You would need some way to say, "Weight this result by X when Bob searches for *party*, but weight it at Y when Alice searches for *gathering*."

Obviously, this is nigh impossible. Dynamic aggregations, by definition, can be created to execute arbitrary searches, so there's no way to speculate on the sum total of all aggregations in which a content object might appear, nor is it possible to speculate on the *other* content in any particular aggregation, so as to manually tune a sort index.

Suffice it to say that in very few cases is it possible to manually order a dynamic aggregation of content.

 Lack of the ability to arbitrarily order content is one of the limitations of aggregation using categories or tags. It's normally not possible to assign content to a category or tag *in a specific order*. Content aggregated by these methods is essentially held in a big bucket, which can be dynamically ordered on retrieval.

Type Limitations

It's not uncommon to only allow certain content types in specific aggregations. If the aggregation is dynamic and we specify the type in our search criteria ("show me all the News Releases"), then this is natural. However, in other situations, we might want to limit types because the content has to conform to a specific format in order to be used in the output.

For instance, consider the image carousel frame depicted in Figure 7-8. This is one frame of a multiframe gallery, powered by an aggregation (a flat list or collection) of multiple content objects. This list is manually created and ordered.

Figure 7-8. An image carousel frame—the image carousel itself is an aggregation that depends on all its content being of a specific type.

To render correctly, every item in this aggregation must have:

- A title
- A short summary
- An image
- Some link text (the "Read the Article" text)
- A permanent URL (to route visitors to when they click on the link text)

Only content conforming to this pattern can be included in this aggregation. This means, for example, that an Employee Bio is out, because it doesn't have a summary.

Since this aggregation is most likely static (image carousels are always curated lists of content), then we need a way to limit editors to only select content that is of the type we need. If we can't limit by type, then we run the risk of our image carousel breaking if it encounters content not of the type it needs.

A smart template developer will account for this and simply ignore and skip over content that doesn't work. This prevents errors, but will likely confuse an editor who doesn't understand the type limitations and might result in a panicked phone call: "My new image isn't appearing in the front page carousel!"

These limitations are not uncommon in content tree geographies. It's quite common to be able to specify the type of content that can be created as a child of other content. For example, we might be able to specify that a Comment content type can only be created as a child of a Blog Post content type, and the inverse—Blog Posts can only accept children that are Comments.

Quantity Limitations

This is less common, but some aggregations can store more content than others, and some systems allow you to require a certain number of content objects, or prevent you from going over a maximum.

Consider our image carousel—it might need at least two items (or else it's not a carousel) and be limited to a maximum of five (or else the pager formatting will break). It will be helpful if the interface can limit editors to adding items only within those boundaries.

Permissions and Publication Status Filters

In one sense, an aggregation—be it static or dynamic—should be a "potential" list of content. Every aggregation on a site should be dynamically filtered for both the current visitor and the publication status of the content in it.

If you manually create an aggregation with ten items, but the current visitor only has permission to view three of them, what happens? Ideally that list should be dynamically filtered to remove the seven items that shouldn't be viewed. The same is true with publication status, and specifically start and end publish dates. If the current date is prior to the start date of the current (or after the end date), then it shouldn't be included.

What this means is that an aggregation—even a static one—might show different content for different visitors, and under certain conditions *some visitors might not see any content at all*. This is an edge case that your template developer should be aware of and will need to account for.

Flat Versus Hierarchical

Many aggregations are simply flat—our list of employee handbook pages, for example, or our image carousel. But other aggregations are often hierarchical structures of content.

In these cases, we have multiple flat aggregations with relationships to each other. A hierarchical list is basically multiple flat lists nested in one another. The top level is one flat list, and each subsequent level can either be a single content object or another flat list, and so on all the way down. The only difference (and it's an important one) is that these flat aggregations are aware of each other—any one of them knows that it has children, or a parent.

The main menu for a website is a clear example. Websites often have an overhead menu bar that either contains drop-down submenus for second-level pages, or secondary navigation that appears in the sidebar menu. [6]

Interstitial Aggregations

In some situations, the inclusion of content in an aggregation requires additional information to make sense. In these cases, the inclusion of content becomes a content object in itself.

For example, let's say we're aggregating a group of Employee Bio content objects to represent the team planning the company Christmas party. To do this, we will create a static aggregation of content.

However, in addition to the simple inclusion in this aggregation, we want to indicate the role each employee plays in the group represented by the aggregation. So, in the case of Mary Jones, we want to indicate that she is the Committee Chair. Mary is

---

6 And I hope it's obvious by this point that a content tree geography is one big, hierarchical content aggregation. It just happens to be the core aggregation for many CMSs.

actually the receptionist at the company, and this is the title modeled into her Employee Bio object.

The title of Committee Chair only makes sense *relative to her inclusion in this aggregation*, and nowhere else. Therefore, this attribute is neither on the aggregation nor on the Employee Bio. As Figure 7-9 demonstrates, this attribute rightfully belongs on the attachment point between the two; it describes Mary's assignment to this committee.

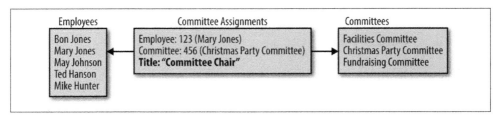

Figure 7-9. The title "Committee Chair" belongs to neither Mary nor the committee; rather, it correctly belongs to the intersection between the two

In this sense, her inclusion in this aggregation *is a content object in itself*, and our committee is really an aggregation of Committee Assignment content objects, which are modeled to have a Title and a reference to an Employee Bio. The Employee Bio object is included in the aggregation "through" a Committee Assignment object, for which we need a new content type.

Now, clearly, this gets complicated quickly, and this isn't something you would do for a one-off situation. But if situations like this are part of your requirements, then modeling an aggregation assignment as a content type by itself can allow you to model the relationships.

By Configuration or by Code

As we briefly discussed in Chapter 2, certain things in a CMS environment can be accomplished by non-technical editors working from the interface, and other tasks need to be handled by developers working with the templating or the core code of the system.

Aggregations are no different. As a general rule, developers can aggregate content any which way the API allows—they have complete freedom. A subset of these capabilities are provided to editors to create and display aggregations as part of content creation. How big this overlap is depends highly on the system, and partially on the sophistication of your editors.

Aggregations can get complicated. A list of blog posts seems quite simple, but the number of variables it involves can spiral out of control more quickly than you might think:

- What content should be included?
- Where should this content be retrieved from?
- How many posts should be included?
- Will the aggregation be subdivided into pages?
- How should the posts be ordered? Should there be controls for visitors to order by a different criterion?
- Should the posts come from one category? From one tag? From more than one tag?
- Should they be filtered for permissions?
- Should they be filtered by date?
- Are there any other criteria that they should be filtered for?

These variables are usually quite simple for a developer to code, but they get very complicated for an editor to configure via an interface.

The Drupal Views module provides a wonderful example of this basic complexity. Views is a module that allows editors to create dynamic aggregations of content by configuring search parameters and formatting information. It provides an enormous number of options in order to provide editors with extreme flexibility.

Views has been developed over many years, and the interface has been through several rewrites with the goal of making it as simple and usable as possible. However, complexity remains. There's simply a basic, unresolvable level of complexity that goes with the flexibility that Views offers. Fisher-Price doesn't make a "Nuclear Fission Playset" for the same reason—all the bright primary colors in the world aren't going to make splitting the atom any less complicated.

Consider the interface presented in Figure 7-10. You could very easily spend an entire day training editors on just the functionality that Views offers.

Figure 7-10. Drupal Views module configuration—note that many of the buttons and hyperlinks hide entirely different subinterfaces for those particular aspects of the aggregation

Developers have it easier, since code is more succinct and exact, and they're more accustomed to thinking abstractly about information concepts and codifying those abstractions. That said, the quality of the APIs provided varies greatly. Some are elegant, succinct, and comprehensive, while others are awkward, verbose, and have frustrating gaps that prevent even a developer from aggregating the desired content in the desired format.

Training and Repetition

They say that practice makes perfect, and the same is true of content editing. Editors will remember things they do often, and forget things they do seldom. Editing content is something they do often. Creating content aggregations is generally done much less frequently.

This means that no matter how well they were trained originally, editors will tend to forget those seldom-used features that require intricate functional knowledge, and content aggregation configuration clearly fits this description.

Consequently, a system designed to give editors control over aggregated content is often more effective at generating a support call every time an editor tries to use it. It's not uncommon for developers to have to configure aggregations for editors, using the interface, that ironically, was created to allow them to do it *without* developers.

A Summary of Content Aggregation Features

Here are some questions to ask about the content aggregation features of any CMS:

- What is the core content geography in use by the system? Does it have a master aggregation model, into which all content is structured?
- Can parent/child relationships be easily represented?
- What abilities do developers have to aggregate content by code?
- What abilities do editors have to aggregate content by configuration in the interface?
- What secondary aggregations, such as categories, tags, menus, and lists, are available?
- Can editors create static aggregations?
- Are these aggregations flat or hierarchical?
- Can static aggregations be manually ordered?
- Can static aggregations be limited by type?
- Can editors configure dynamic aggregations? Based on what available criteria?

CHAPTER 8

Editorial Tools and Workflow

The hosts of the TV show *MythBusters* did an experiment once where they interleaved the pages of two phone books. In effect, they set two phone books together, then pushed them into each other so that their pages alternated, and every page of one phone book was lying between two pages of the other.[1] The only thing holding the two phone books together was the friction of the pages on one another.

Then they tried to pull the two phone books apart.

They tried pulling with a dozen people, then they dangled a person from one of them, then they lifted a car off the ground, then they tried to use power equipment in the shop, then they tried two cars moving in opposite directions. Nothing could pull the two books apart until they got *two World War II–era armored vehicles*. The phone books finally came apart under 8,000 lbs of force.

Do not underestimate friction. It can sneak up on you and bring everything to a grinding halt.

Your CMS necessarily introduces some degree of editorial friction. To do their jobs, your editors will have to interact with the CMS, use the tools it offers, and suffer without the tools it doesn't. The CMS can either enable them to efficiently breeze through their work, or introduce friction through poor usability, needless repetition, error-prone interfaces, and poor conceptual models.

The capabilities of the CMS that editors use to perform the editorial process are collectively known as *editorial tools* or *editorial workflow* (literally meaning "flow of

---

1 It actually wasn't that simple. They had to individually turn thousands of phone book pages over each other. That part is boring, but the rest of the video (*https://www.youtube.com/watch?v=QMW_uYWwHWQ*) is incredibly entertaining.

work," rather than workflow as a specific CMS concept, which we'll discuss further later in this chapter).

This is really the "management" of content management systems. These are the tools that increase editors' ability to create better content and gain more control over the content under their care. This is the side of the CMS that editors are going to use, day in and day out.

This is a critical area of functionality, because poor tools and workflow can cripple editors and destroy morale. Sadly, editorial usability is one area of CMS development that gets skipped over too often. As we've discussed, CMSs are created by developers, but they're often also created *for* developers, first and only. A developer understands things differently than the average content editor, and when designing editorial interfaces and tools, developers will often take leaps and liberties that make sense *to them*, but not necessarily to people with other perspectives.

With commercial systems and larger open source systems, these usability shortcomings are corrected due to market pressures and large editorial usage. However, in smaller open source systems that don't have to collect a license fee and might not have a large editor community, editorial usability problems can persist for *years* without correction.

While editorial friction directly impedes editor productivity in the short term, the more damaging aspect is the chronic drag it has on morale in the long term. Many an editorial team has grown increasingly frustrated and resentful over time with a poorly architected or implemented CMS. More than once, I've encountered teams that were fraying at the edges and losing staff because they were tired of the extra workload imposed on them by the system they were forced to use.

Solid, well-implemented editorial tools enhance the editorial process. Poor or nonexistent tools will destroy it over time. At an absolute minimum, a CMS needs to stay out of the way and not impose any friction beyond what's absolutely necessary.

The Content Lifecycle

From the moment it's conceived to the moment it's irrevocably deleted, content goes through multiple stages of "life." The stage where it's actually published on a website and can be consumed by a visitor is just one among many (and might sometimes be quite short—a news release announcing an event might be created then deleted a week later).

These stages are collectively called the "lifecycle" of content. There is no universally accepted definition of the exact stages and their order, but I'll try to present a definition here that encompasses many of the commonly accepted stages.

Not represented here is the informal "Conception" phase of the content lifecycle, where someone thinks up an idea for new content, tosses the idea around with colleagues, and maybe starts writing something in Microsoft Word or Google Docs. We're skipping this and only accounting for what happens inside the CMS itself.

The content lifecycle can be described as having the following stages:

Create
Content is initiated in the CMS. It is not complete, but exists as a managed content object. It is not visible to the content consumer.

Edit and Collaborate
Content is actively edited and/or collaborated on by one or more editors. Content is still not visible.

Submit and Approve
Content is created and edited, and has been submitted for one or more approvals. Content is still not visible.

Publish
Content has been approved and is published on the website. *Content in this state is visible to the content consumer.*

Archive
Content is removed from public access, but not deleted. It is usually no longer visible.

Delete
Content is irreversibly deleted from the CMS.

Some of these stages are iterative and may apply simultaneously to different versions of the same content.

For example, a piece of content may be published for some time, then need to be changed. At this time (and depending on the CMS), a new version is created as a draft (Edit and Collaborate), is submitted for approval (Submit and Approve), and then is finally Published, which causes the previous version to Archive. There are now two versions of this content, in different stages of their lifecycles—one is archived, the other is published.

This is not the only way the content lifecycle can be described, and the language used depends highly on the perspective and professional role of the observer. Marketers, for instance, would tend to describe content in terms of "creating, distributing, and analyzing," without getting into the nitty-gritty of editing, approval, and archiving that a content manager is concerned with.

The Archive stage is particularly nebulous, with very few practitioners completely agreeing on its definition. For some, to archive content just means to make it not visible to the end consumer, without deleting it. For others, it means moving it "somewhere else" in the CMS, out of the way of the non-archived content, but perhaps still leaving it accessible to visitors via a different method. For others, it may mean moving it to different storage—even into offline archival storage media.[2]

Regardless of the particular stages of the lifecycle, a good CMS provides functionality across the entire scope of a content object's existence in your website.

 One inevitable constant of the content lifecycle is that it's circular. Search Google Images for "content lifecycle," and you're invariably presented with a browser full of circles. While somewhat amusing, this also demonstrates the circular nature of content. It tends to be created, evaluated, edited, and republished in a cycle, over and over.

The Editing Interface

The first job of an editing environment is to be usable and to provide content editors with a competent and functional interface in which to create and edit content. If a CMS fails at this, it's tough to recover. Editors who hate working with content in their CMS will be hard pressed to create anything of value over the long term.

Content Findability and Traversal

To edit content, an editor first has to find it. In some websites, this is simple—if a website has 20 pages, it's not hard to locate the right one. However, when a website has thousands and thousands of pages, it becomes more difficult. How do you keep track of them all?

Traditionally, websites offered dedicated management interfaces designed to be used by editors solely to browse the content in the repository. Content would be listed in a simple table, with search tools to assist in finding it.

As more and more CMSs embraced the content tree geography, management interfaces moved into a collapsible tree structure, where editors would traverse down through parent and child relationships to identify content.

---

2 On LinkedIn, a group of content managers attempted to define "archiving." The range of responses was considerable, and they were collected in "Perspectives On What 'Archiving' Means in Content Management" (*http://gadgetopia.com/post/9070*).

Today, these interfaces are increasingly giving way to in-context management, where editors simply browse their websites like content consumers do. When the editors are authenticated to the CMS, however, they have editing tools available, ranging from a simple "Edit This Page" link to more complex pop-up/overlay interfaces that allow them to enter an editing mode.

 I can still remember visiting the vendor floor of Intranets 2001 in Santa Clara, California, and seeing a demo of RedDot where the salesman exclaimed, "When you're logged in as an editor, anything you can edit will have a little red dot next to it!" (Hence the product name, obviously.) We were all suitably impressed. It was like magic at the time.

This style of finding content can be difficult for decoupled systems. When the publishing/delivery server is separate from the management/repository server, it often has no capability to authenticate someone as an editor, and therefore has no way to show these users editing tools on the page. Many systems get around this by generating a proxied version of the site—editors browse in a management interface that shows the website in an `IFRAME` or proxies the entire website to another server, to which the editor is authenticated.

This method of content traversal has become common because as website usability has increased, the tools available for content consumers to find content have become more similar to the tools editors use. Why build a set of editor tools when the CMS has already provided the end user with an array of sorting and search functionality? As we come up with better and better search technologies and interfaces for our visitors, we're becoming hard pressed to improve on these for editors. And it would be tough to explain if your editors had to use tools that were actually *worse* than what site visitors used.

However, there are still content filtering tools that can be considered editor-specific. These are tools that allow you to filter.

- By workflow or publication status
- By administrative task status
- By content owner
- By archival or deletion status
- By custom editorial metadata (for example, locating content tagged with "needs review")

In all these situations, the criterion for locating content is not something that would be visible to the content consumer, and therefore a CMS might have special editorial tools with which to handle these situations.

Given that editors will always have some special needs beyond those of content consumers, most CMSs pursue a hybrid approach. There is a dedicated administrative interface, supplemented by in-context editing tools of varying depth.

Scaling the Admin Interface

If there's a dedicated admin or edit interface for a CMS, make sure it will scale to a large amount of content if needed. Many interfaces work fine with a few hundred content objects, but fall apart when the number of objects reaches, say, 100,000.

Content trees with large amounts of objects under a single parent can be especially problematic. If you have 10,000 news articles under a single parent, how will the tree interface handle this? Scrolling through 10,000 articles is basically pointless, and expanding that node in the tree will likely slow the interface down or break it entirely. Can the tree paginate that list? Can it present you with a searchable interface for just that node in the tree?

Developers writing these interfaces often don't test with large amounts of content. If managing high-volume content is one of your requirements, be sure the interface can handle it.

Type Selection

When creating a new content object, the first task of an editor is usually to select the content type on which to base it (see Chapter 6). The CMS needs to ensure the editor can select the appropriate content type for the situation, and not a content type that doesn't work quite right, or will break the website should it be published.

In many cases, the integrity of a content tree is enforced through restrictions on type parentage. We may have an Issue type, which contains one or more Article Category types, which each contain one or more Article objects. The hierarchy is logical and necessary to the proper modeling and rendering of content.

If an editor was allowed to create content based on the Issue type as a child of an Article, what would happen? The code in the template wouldn't be expecting content of that particular type in that location. In the best case, if the developer were checking the type of everything, the template would simply ignore it. However, in many situations, the templating would break—the developer would probably assume that the CMS would enforce the type hierarchy, and would thus trust that an Issue would never be found as a child of an Article.[3]

---

3 Yes, clearly, this would be a failure in error checking. But when working with a CMS, developers will often trust it to enforce certain standards and forgo exhaustive error checking for the sake of practicality.

In these situations, the CMS needs to be able to dictate the correct relationship between types. Editors create content in specific locations in the content geography, and the CMS should be able to dictate what content they can create at any particular location. Content types therefore need to indicate what types can be created as children of a specific type.

Additionally, some content types might be restricted from certain editors. It's common that certain types are more volatile and advanced than others. As we discussed in Chapter 4, not all editors are created equal. A power editor might be allowed greater liberties than others, and the content types to which these editors have access should reflect this.

In some installations, for example, a power editor might have access to a content type that allows raw HTML inclusion—the editor might be able to type raw HTML/JavaScript code that is included into the page, unchanged. Clearly, this can be dangerous —HTML could be introduced that prematurely closed tags, or JavaScript could be added that opened the site to cross-site scripting attacks.

Other items, like image carousels, might require more care and experience than the training of the mainstream editor allows. Editors might need to understand how to select and edit images, address accessibility concerns of image inclusion, and deal with other usability issues.

In these cases, these content types should be restricted to editors trained to use them correctly.

Finally, in some installations, the list of available content types can become quite large, occasionally numbering in the dozens. Several different features can make type selection easier for editors:

- Intelligent naming can help with content type selection. Types often have a "system name" for reference from code and a "display name," which can be expanded to make more sense for editors.

- Some CMSs will allow a sentence or two of description about what the type does to further explain its usage.

- Others will allow a thumbnail image of an example of a fully rendered type that can jog an editor's memory as to its correct usage.

- Some CMSs will even learn over time, and present editors with their most commonly used types, or types most commonly used in similar situations—as children of the parent type, or example (see Figure 8-1).

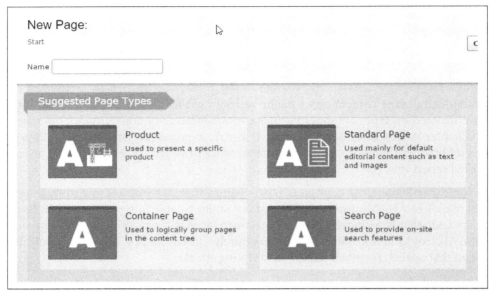

Figure 8-1. The type selection interface in Episerver

In all cases, the goal is to provide editors with a list of content types that are allowed and appropriate to the current content problem. A CMS should be able to alter this list based on the location of the desired content object and the role of the particular editor.

Content Preview

While we'll discuss the actual editing interface shortly, it's important to consider the relationship between editing content and previewing it. When editors make changes to content, they usually want to see those changes before they publish their content to the world. Hence, editors need preview functionality to enable them to see these changes "in context," which means in the visual environment to which they're about to be published.

There are two schools of thought about how content preview should relate to the editing interface:

- *Presentation-free editing* was the default standard for many years. In this case, the editor works in a standard web form, with text boxes, text areas, drop-down lists, etc. To preview content, the editor navigates to a separate interface, then back again to continue editing.

- *In-context editing*, by contrast, seeks to make the editing interface look as close to the final content production as possible. An editor might find himself editing in something that looks very much like the finished page, complete with styling. When he types the title, for instance, the letters come out in 24 pt Arial Bold, just like when the page will be published. The goal is to try to disguise that this is an editing interface at all, and make it seem like the editor is simply working in the finished page. Preview becomes effectively real-time.

While in-context editing seems advantageous on its face—who wouldn't want to see live, real-time previews?—there are a couple of extenuating issues:

- In-context editing doesn't handle nonvisual properties, like META tag content, or configuration content, such as a checkbox for "Show Sidebar," for instance. If the content is meant to alter page behavior rather than be consumed as content itself, it's harder to work into an in-context interface.

- In-context editing will often only represent a single view of the content—that of a single web page. In today's multichannel world, content might be published in many places around the Internet and consumed by many different devices, so the question becomes, what preview are you viewing?

Mark Boulton considered this very issue in a blog post:

> The problem is this: The question content people ask when finishing adding content to a CMS is "how does this look?". And this is not a question a CMS can answer any more--even with a preview. How we use the web today has meant that the answer to that questions is, "in what?"[4]

More modern CMSs have multipreview features where an editor can pick a view to preview the content—as a web page, a tweet, or an RSS item, for example. However, this preview functionality is not common, and it generally requires additional setup, development, and templating to provide accurate views for all possible content channels.

Understand that multichannel preview is not just a technical issue. Left to their own devices, editors will be biased toward the main, intended output format, which will likely be HTML. Don't underestimate the workflow, training, and governance challenges involved with mandating multichannel preview before publication.[5]

---

4 "WYSIWTFFTWOMG!" (*http://www.markboulton.co.uk/journal/wysiwtfftwomg*), September 3, 2013.

5 I wrote this book in O'Reilly's Atlas editing platform. I wrote in a text format called AsciiDoc, and could "build" into multiple formats at any given time. I *obsessed* over the formatting of the print (PDF) version of the book, showing a clear bias toward what it would look like when printed. Only later in the writing process did I start looking at the EPUB, MOBI, and HTML output options. Often, formatting that worked in one was problematic in another.

The problem of personalization and preview

One of the new frontiers in content management over the last half-decade has been *personalization* (discussed more in Chapter 10), or the use of behaviors and contextual information to personalize the web experience for each visitor.

Unfortunately, this complicates preview even further. When previewing content, how can you account for all the possible permutations and combinations of factors that might affect that content?

For example, if a visitor has viewed three pages in the section of a university's website about the nursing program, then a stock image of a nursing student should be displayed on the Admissions page, rather than a more generic image.

How can you preview this? Will you have to manually view three pages yourself in order to mock up the behavior your CMS requires? Or does your CMS have tools to allow you to "spoof" your membership in a personalization group?

Combine this with device and distribution channels, and the possible outcomes can be endless. For one web page, an editor could conceivably create hundreds of different combinations of visitor behavior, consuming device, and distribution channel, all with their own specific previews.

Editing Interface Elements

The editorial rubber meets the road in the interface. There comes a point where an editor actually types or clicks something and creates some content. Generally speaking, a CMS should present editors with the correct editing element for the information they're trying to edit. A good editing interface guides editors into the right decisions and protects them from doing damage.

Imagine if the editing interface was simply a list of empty text boxes for all attributes. For text, this might be appropriate, but what about for a yes/no value? Should the editor just type "yes" or "no"? How about "true" or "false"? Does capitalization matter? Clearly in this instance the appropriate interface element is a checkbox, which is checked for "yes" and unchecked for "no."

A CMS should render the editing interface to conform to the content model, making intelligent assumptions when selecting the correct element to present to editors (and allowing administrative overrides where needed). The goal is to present a highly productive working environment avoiding unnecessary error or guesswork.

In addition to the aforementioned checkbox, here are some other element choices:

- A simple text box or text area for long or short text entry
- A checkbox list for an attribute that can support multiple values from a predefined list

---

- A radio button list or drop-down selector for an attribute that allows only one value from a predefined list
- A rich text (WYSIWYG) editor for editing HTML
- A calendar drop-down for selecting a date
- A Google Maps interface for selecting a geographic point on a map
- A custom interface providing a search tool to locate an SKU from your product catalog

Validation

In addition to accepting input, a content editing interface must ensure the input is valid to prevent errors from compromising the content. Validation can be guided by the use of editing interface elements, as discussed in the previous section; however, the CMS should always validate data independently of the interface in the case of data being entered through an API or service (and therefore not being subject to the restrictions of the editing interface).

Understand that the validation of content is related to its *logical value*, not necessarily its pure datatype. Datatypes do not understand context; they only understand pure data, completely separate from how the data will be used.

As we discussed in Chapter 6, if an attribute represents a year, then the underlying datatype might be number (or integer). However, the logical idea of a year presupposes several other restrictions:

- It must have four digits.
- It might have to be in the past.
- It might have to fit into a logical range (while AD 4538 might make for a good science fiction novel, it does not work in the context of when a movie was released).

In this case, the datatype of *number* is wholly insufficient to enforce the necessary restrictions around the logical value type of *year*. Additional validation will have to take place.

Some systems offer expanded validation types for these instances. For instance, in the case of a number, a range might be allowed to ensure the number is valid. The same could be true of dates, to ensure an entered date in the future, in the past, or between two landmark dates.

Regular expressions ("regexes") can be used in many cases to validate text patterns. While a discussion of regex is far beyond the scope of this book,[6] at a high level a regex is a definition of a text pattern, which can be tested for validity.

For example, in the case of our movie release date, we can define a regular expression to enforce:

```
(19|20)\d{2}
```

This pattern, when applied to entered text, will ensure that the first two digits are "19" or "20" and that they are followed by two additional digits. This would limit data to years between 1900 and 2099.

If we know that our product numbers begin with "A," followed by two other alphabetic characters, then a dash and four digits, we can write a pattern like this:

```
A[A-Z]{2}-\d{4}
```

Invariably, some validation needs simply can't be predefined by a CMS and must be implemented by custom code. In this example, we can certainly enforce the format of a product number, but we can't ensure that this product exists in our catalog.

To validate that fact, we will need to write custom code to connect to our product database, check for the entered product number, then tell the interface whether to accept the entered data or display an error to the editor. Different CMSs will offer different levels of functionality in this regard.

Rich text editing

Most CMSs include a rich text interface to allow editors to create HTML content as an attribute of a content object.

For example, almost all implementations will have a content type for Text Page or Standard Page. This content type can be as simple as a Title and a Body, which will often be rich text. Inside the editing interface for the Body, the editor will have buttons for formatting items like bold text, italics, bulleted and numbered lists, image insertion, hyperlink creation, etc. "Just like Microsoft Word," is a common phrase used to describe these editors.

Usage of rich text can be divisive. Editors enjoy the control, but developers and designers can get nervous about the freedom it allows. Editors have been known to use formatting liberally, and often in defiance of style guides and conventions. Additionally, if they have access to the HTML source, they can manually edit the HTML, which might cause rendering problems with the template in which the content is dis-

---

6 *Mastering Regular Expressions* by Jeffrey E. F. Friedl (O'Reilly), currently in its third edition, is the seminal and authoritative text on regexes.

played (worse, a nefarious editor can write HTML that compromises the security of the site itself).

Ideally, a CMS should be very careful about the formatting and access to source it allows. Some common protective features include:

- The buttons displayed in the formatting toolbar should be centrally controlled and contextual to both editor (certain editors get more options than others) and attribute (more options are available when editing the Body than when editing an Author Note, for instance).
- Regardless of editor or context, formatting tools should be heavily scrubbed of anything that might compromise the style of the site, including font selectors, text color palettes, font size controls, etc.
- Access to HTML source should be carefully controlled. Invalid HTML can be introduced through direct HTML editing, in addition to malicious JavaScript opening the site up to cross-site scripting attacks.
- HTML validation should be enabled and strict. When rich text content is saved, it should be checked and corrected for invalid HTML.

There is a recent trend to avoid rich text altogether, and instead attempt to "structure away" the problem by breaking content down into attributes small enough to not need rich text at all. While this might make developers happy, it's probably not entirely realistic. Most editors will always want formatting tools.

Alternatively, some implementations are moving toward very lightweight markup languages rather than HTML. These languages can be edited inside simple text area elements and use character combinations that convert to HTML later, in the page rendering stage. The most common example is Markdown, which looks like this:

```
This text is in _italics_ and this text is *bold.*
This is [a link](http://oreilly.com/).
```

Other examples of alternative markup languages are Textile, PanDoc, and WikiText.[7] Some CMSs, like Ghost, offer real-time preview of these languages in a side-by-side style interface, with changes in one pane reflected in the other (see Figure 8-2 for an example).

---

7 As mentioned earlier, I wrote this entire book in a variant of Markdown called AsciiDoc.

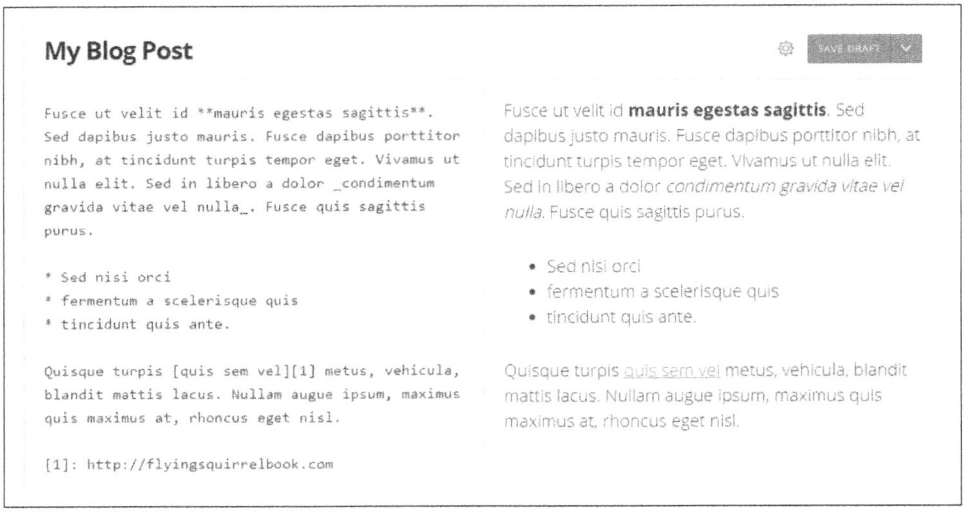

My Blog Post

SAVE DRAFT

```
Fusce ut velit id **mauris egestas sagittis**.
Sed dapibus justo mauris. Fusce dapibus porttitor
nibh, at tincidunt turpis tempor eget. Vivamus ut
nulla elit. Sed in libero a dolor _condimentum
gravida vitae vel nulla_. Fusce quis sagittis
purus.

* Sed nisi orci
* fermentum a scelerisque quis
* tincidunt quis ante.

Quisque turpis [quis sem vel][1] metus, vehicula,
blandit mattis lacus. Nullam augue ipsum, maximus
quis maximus at, rhoncus eget nisl.

[1]: http://flyingsquirrelbook.com
```

Fusce ut velit id **mauris egestas sagittis**. Sed dapibus justo mauris. Fusce dapibus porttitor nibh, at tincidunt turpis tempor eget. Vivamus ut nulla elit. Sed in libero a dolor *condimentum gravida vitae vel nulla*. Fusce quis sagittis purus.

- Sed nisi orci
- fermentum a scelerisque quis
- tincidunt quis ante.

Quisque turpis quis sem vel metus, vehicula, blandit mattis lacus. Nullam augue ipsum, maximus quis maximus at, rhoncus eget nisl.

Figure 8-2. Editing in Ghost using the Markdown syntax in the lefthand pane with real-time preview in the righthand pane

Reference content selection

In most implementations, content will need to be linked together, in one or more ways:

- The rich text in one content object might contain a hyperlink to another content object.
- A content object might use an image stored elsewhere in the repository.
- A content object might have an attribute that references another content object.

In all these cases, an editor will need to find the remote content object from the editing interface. Methods of doing this vary, but commonly the editor will be presented with a pop-up window that offers multiple methods to find the content—editors will usually be able to browse for it, and might be able to search for it. This becomes more and more important as the number of content objects scales up. Trying to browse for a specific article among thousands can be frustratingly difficult.

What becomes critical is the ways in which this interface can be restricted. For example:

- An attribute reference might only be allowed to a specific content type. The Manager attribute of an Employee content object should only be linked to another Employee content object.

- An attribute reference might be restricted to a specific location in the geography. Perhaps the editor can only select children of the current issue for the Featured Article.

Additionally, a subtle but critical point is whether the reference to an object is attached to the object itself, or to the current URL of the object. The latter is always going to be problematic. If a CMS requires an editor to simply find the URL of another page and paste it into the hyperlink box, what happens if the URL of that second content object changes?

URLs can change, so links between content should be resolved as late as possible in the content delivery cycle. Any inserted link should just be a *reference* to the content, not its actual, current URL. The reference should then be replaced with the correct and current URL to that content when the content is rendered.

In-context help and documentation

You can't merely assume that editors will always understand all the nuances of the content model. Content changes can have subtle implications that it may be hard for them to keep track of after the training session. This is especially true of seldom-used properties and features.

Systems vary in their ability to provide editors with help in the editing interface itself. At the very least, properties should be labeled clearly. The ability to provide a few sentences of documentation sometimes makes all the difference.

For example, when presented with a summary field, these few sentences might be invaluable:

> Content entered in the summary will be used along with the title when this content is referenced from other locations in the website. If left blank (not recommended), the first paragraph from the body will be used for the summary.

If there's one thing an editor hates, it's not knowing what to do and getting stuck. Worse still is doing something and having it cause unintended side effects, or even an error. In-context documentation vastly reduces uncertainty along with the ensuing questions and frustration.

Perspective: Editors Will Circumvent Poor Tools

by Rahel Anne Bailie

The great irony of content management systems is that they don't actually manage content. What they manage, as Deane points out, is the editorial flow of work. Therein lies the problem.

Because the engineers who develop editing interfaces don't really understand the tensions that content editors face when creating content for multiple products, audiences, channels, markets, and locales, the editing interfaces tend to be underdeveloped. The interfaces rely on workflow to compensate for the shortcomings of actual management of content.

I've watched a writer "break" the schema because she knew the amount of machination it would take to finish her task would mean she would miss her train home. Writers will work offline and copy-paste from Word into the editing interface. They will avoid entering metadata that they don't understand, or they will delegate "entering stuff into the CMS" to the lowest-paid person on the team. That person will have little understanding of what the ultimate intent is, and will merrily do the rote work of copying and pasting. Even when there is a willingness to work within the system, there tends to be a lot of experimentation to figure out which fields are displayed where, in which templates, because the documentation provided tends to be less than useful.

The fact of the matter is that unless the content editing environments make the jobs of writers easier, they will do everything in their power to circumvent the system. And why shouldn't they? Developers regularly tell me that they code with the easiest solution in mind—for them, not necessarily for the content or the writers who use the system. That leaves content editors to "work harder, not smarter" for years afterward.

The one caveat about how content is created within a CMS is that this book deals with the class of software generally known as a web CMS. The class of software called a component (CCMS) actually does manage content as well as workflow, and is more suited to use by content developers—the gap between writers or editors and content developers is as large as the difference between visual designers and software designers. In a CCMS, changeset publication is simply a nonissue; content developers don't need formatting to do their work effectively, and the editing environment allows them to structure, chunk, and tag content in quite sophisticated ways.

Rahel Anne Bailie integrates the best from several disciplines to do content strategy her way. She coauthored Content Strategy: Connecting the Dots Between Business, Brand, and Benefits *(XML Press).*

Versioning, Version Control, and Version Labels

Versioning is the act of not overwriting content with changes, but instead saving content in a new version of an existing content object. This means that content objects that have been edited have multiple versions—indeed, they might have hundreds of versions—each representing how that content object looked at a certain moment in time.

Editors can use versioning in several ways:

- As a safeguard against improper or malicious changes. Versioning is like real-time backup for that single content object.
- As an audit trail to ensure they always have a record of what content was presented to the public at any given time, perhaps for legal and compliance reasons.
- To separate changes to content from the currently published content, so that changes can be approved and scheduled independently of the content currently shown to the public.
- To enable one version to be compared to another to determine what has changed, which is helpful for approvals (discussed later in this chapter).

Some systems make versioning automatic, while others require it to be specified by content type. Some systems just version content, while others version everything—content, users, media, and settings.

At any given time, an editor should be able to review a timeline of content changes for an object and see who changed the content and when. Some systems take this a step further by allowing editors to compare versions, either in side-by-side windows or sometimes in a "Track Changes" style where additions, deletions, and edits are shown inline.

Conceptually, versions become a "stack," stretching back in time. The initial version of content is on the bottom of the stack, with new versions stacked on top of it. Versions are usually labeled with a status, with one of the versions being considered the "published" version.

You might envision an arrow pointing to one version on the stack, which is the published version. This is hypothetical, and the actual implementation of the concept might vary, but it's a handy metaphor to envision the relationship between the version stack and the various states of content within it.

To change which version is published is to "roll back" to a previous version. Different systems handle this different ways—some will simply move the "published" arrow to a different version, while others will copy the desired older version and make it a new draft version at the top of the stack (thus ensuring that the published version of the content is always the latest version).

Changes to content are considered a new unpublished version—with a label of Draft or Awaiting Publication—sitting on top of the stack. When a new version is published, the publication arrow is simply moved. In some systems you can edit a prior version, while in others you cannot; any change to any version becomes a new version at the top of the stack.

Logically, only one version of content can be published at any one time. Figure 8-3 shows a visual representation of this concept.

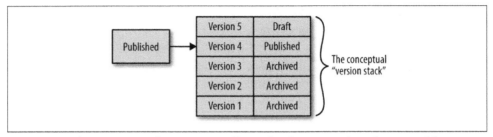

Figure 8-3. The version stack is conceptually a pile of versions, from latest to oldest, sometimes with a designator showing which one is published (other implementations might just consider the top version published)

Some systems will also allow mass rollback, which will allow an editor to essentially step back in time and view the entire site as if all content was rolled back to its version at that moment.

Almost all versioning in web content management is "serial," meaning versions to a content object are simply stacked in order of date. Some more advanced document management systems, however, offer *branching*, where content can be split into multiple branches—version 1 can have version 1.1 and 1.2, which is further split into 1.2.1, etc. This gets *very* confusing for most editors, and is only required in highly controlled document scenarios (this is common in the management of technical documentation, for example).

Even if never used, versioning is a handy feature to have lurking in the background. The only reasons *against* using versioning might be storage, since multiple versions will obviously consume more disk space.

Versioning is designed to keep content safe, so the ability to delete or purge versions is usually not available by default. A limit can often be set and a scheduled job will delete excess versions beyond that limit (in the event that there are storage limitations), or the permission to delete individual versions can be granted on an exception basis to specific editors.

When considering versioning, remember that without it, the power to edit is essentially the power to delete. An innocent mistake by an editor who is too quick with the save button can be disastrous.

 Even if you're versioning content, delete is still delete. If you delete a content object, it's usually gone, *with all of its versions*. There's often no version trail left when something is deleted. Many systems will "soft delete" to a Recycle Bin or Trash, but once it's gone from there, understand that the object and all of its version history are *gone*.

Version control

Version control is about the management of versions of content between multiple editors working simultaneously. If two editors want to work on the same piece of content, how does this get managed? There are a few options:

- Does the system create a version for each, calling them both "Draft"? This can be a bit frustrating, since the two editors might not realize someone else is working on the same content. When they go to publish, they will realize that they have to reconcile changes between two versions for the content to be correct.

- Does the system allow an editor to "lock" a content object to prevent anyone else from working on it? This is certainly effective, but it essentially blocks the workflow of other editors, and if used haphazardly can cause a piece of content to be locked for longer than necessary, perhaps even while a careless editor goes on vacation.

- Does the system allow two editors to work simultaneously on the same version, *à la* Google Docs?

At the very least, a CMS should have some indication that a content object is being edited, or that there's a draft version of this content object above the published version on the version stack. The editor should be notified of this, and given the option of working with the existing draft version (which might be locked), or creating a new draft (which might require change reconciliation with the existing draft at some point in the future).

Dependency Management

Two content objects can be related in a number of ways:

- The HTML of an attribute might contain a hyperlink to another content object.
- An attribute reference might link to another content object.

- A content object might be embedded in the rich text of another content object.

- The HTML of an attribute might contain embedded media that is a separate content object.

Many CMSs will keep track of these links and their purpose (HTML link, attribute reference, media embed, etc.) so it's possible to know which content depends on which other content. This enables some helpful functionality:

- A predeletion check can inform the editor that the content he's about to delete is referenced from other content (see Figure 8-4).

- Broken link reports can identify content that links to a target that is no longer available, either due to forced deletion, content expiration, or permission changes.

- An orphaned content report could identify content not in use by any other content.

- Dependencies can be used to determine the cascading scope of changes. When content is published, for example, the system can know what other content needs to be republished, in the case of a decoupled CMS, or reindexed for search.

- Search optimization can use dependencies when weighting result pages, assuming that popular content is referenced more often and should be more heavily weighted. Other information architecture functionality might use the link graph to extract information from content relationships.

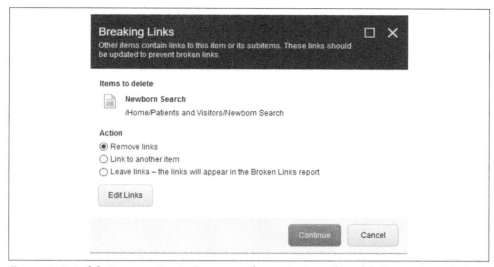

Figure 8-4. A deletion warning in Sitecore—the content pending deletion is depended on by other content, and the system needs to know how the editor wants to handle the broken dependencies

Content Scheduling and Expiration

Often, an editor doesn't want content to be published immediately. Rather, content should be scheduled for publication in the future.

This is intertwined with versioning, because what an editor is essentially doing is scheduling the change in version labels. The content she's scheduling is considered to be Draft, with the version label to be changed to Published in the future. (Remember our conceptual "publication arrow"? All the editor is doing is scheduling a time where it moves to a different version in the stack.)

Publication scheduling has two basic forms:

Scheduling of new content
> The ontent object isn't displayed anywhere on the site until a point in time at which it appears.

Scheduling of a new version
> The content object is displayed in its current form until a point in time, when a new version takes its place.

This can be slightly complex in some cases when editors begin working on a new version of content before the latest version of content has been published. In these cases, you have the published version several levels back, then one or more versions awaiting publication, then one or more versions ahead of those in draft, which might then get scheduled.

And what happens if an editor elects to publish a new version directly? Or schedules it to publish before one of the versions behind it in the version stack? Some systems might not allow this, others might negate the scheduled publication of anything behind it in the stack, and others might simply blindly follow instructions, which means the scheduled publication would actually move the publication arrow backward in the stack, rather than forward.

Thankfully, it almost never gets this complicated, but poor communication between editors can sometimes bring about complicated scheduling logic problems that can be tricky to sort out.

Changeset Publication

Oftentimes, editors are working on a content project that requires changes to multiple content objects separately. Editors would like these changes tracked as a group and scheduled, approved, and published together.

This is known by several names, but most commonly as a *changeset* (other common names are "project," "edition," and "package"). A changeset is created with all related content bound to it. The changeset itself is scheduled, rather than the individual content versions. When the changeset reaches publication, all of the content objects are published simultaneously.

Content Expiration

Mercifully, content expiration is quite a bit simpler. At a given point in time, content is simply removed from publication. This means our imaginary arrow disappears from the stack completely, and no version of the content is considered to be published. This is *not* a deletion. The content still exists, it's just not viewable.

The only caveat here is that the unattended removal of content from a site can cause some issues when an editor is not available to be notified. When attempting to delete content directly, for example, an editor might be notified that the content is linked to and from several other content objects and that deleting it will break these links. If content is expired unattended, links might break silently without warning.[8]

---

8 I once had a client who was concerned about this exact scenario. While the logical problem could not be solved short of simply not allowing expiration on objects that were the target of links, we did create a scheduled job that emailed the webmaster every night if it found content that (1) was the target of one or more links, and (2) was expiring in the next 72 hours. This at least gave the client some notice so they could resolve the situation gracefully rather than have links break.

Workflow and Approvals

Workflow is the logical movement of a content object through various steps or stages (though we'll avoid using the word for "stage" from here on out so as not to confuse this with the content lifecycle discussed previously). Workflow is often conflated with approvals, and they overlap heavily, so we'll discuss both.

Approvals

After an editor makes a change to content, he might be able to publish it directly, or he might have to submit the change for approval. Many systems separate Edit and Publish permissions. If an editor can edit but not publish, then he can make a change, but it can only be published by someone with that permission.

Conceptually, the editor needs a way to signify, "I am done working on this content, but cannot publish it directly. Someone who can publish it directly needs to review the content and publish it for me."

Two questions need to be resolved:

- Who gets notified?
- How are they notified?

For the former, the "owning user" (or group of users) can be specified to receive notices of changes or submissions. In other cases, any editor with permission to publish might be notified. In still other cases, specific workflows are created (see the next section) that identify the responsible party.

Notification is usually handled via simple email or through the CMS's task management system (discussed in "Collaboration" on page 160), which might also generate an email.

Workflow

Generally, workflow is a larger, more abstract concept than simple approval. The approval of content can be a type of workflow, but many workflows have nothing to do with content approval. Workflow is more broad than simple approval.

Workflow is the movement of content through a map or network of discrete steps. A workflow step can be almost any process that takes some action before moving the content to another step. As a rule, content can only be in a single step at any time in a given workflow. A workflow step (sometimes called an "activity" or a "task") is a clear boundary that defines a state the content is in at a moment in time.

Some examples:

- Content is waiting in a step for an editor to approve its movement to the next step, which publishes it. It might wait in this step for three minutes or three days, depending on how long it takes for the editor to take the action necessary for it to continue.

- Content is moved to a step that triggers the execution of code to post a summary of the content to Twitter. When this is complete, the content is automatically moved to the next step.

- Content is waiting in a step for a translator to complete a Spanish translation of the content. When this is done, the translator will signify this completion and move the content to the next step, which creates a task for a reviewer.

In all cases, one or more steps will have no subsequent step, which ends the workflow. Any content currently in a step is in an active workflow, and when the content progresses past the last step, the workflow ends.

It's important to differentiate between a workflow *template* and an actual running workflow. Nomenclature varies, but like content, workflows have types (templates) and actual instantiations of those templates currently operating on content.[9]

For example, a news publishing organization might have a News Approval workflow that moves content from Submitted to Published. This is a template that defines how the workflow should operate. In a busy newsroom, articles might be submitted for publication every 5 minutes, so while there is one News Approval workflow template, there may be 20–30 *instances* of this workflow active at any given time, all moving individual content items through steps toward publication.

Many systems have reporting interfaces to view all the running instances of a particular workflow, including which step the content is currently in. In some cases, content can get "stuck" in a workflow step, which means it is waiting for an action that will never take place, for whatever reason. Content stuck in a workflow can usually be manually progressed, or have its workflow forcibly ended.

While not common for most organizations, content can even be in more than one workflow at a time. For example, a news article might be in the News Approval workflow, while at the same time it is in the Media Request workflow, awaiting photography.

What constitutes a workflow step can be vague, and it depends highly on what a particular system allows. In some cases, workflow steps are only human-based approvals

---

9 While it would be convenient to call them "workflow types" to parallel "content types," it seems to be an industry convention to call them "workflow templates."

(one system even calls workflows "approval chains"), while in other cases there are numerous prepackaged activities and actions that can happen, and many allow arbitrary code execution.

External Event Engines

There are some interesting things happening in the world of external event engines, which are commercial services that can be notified of events and then perform actions on other systems. These systems, such as Zapier (*http://zapier.com*) and If This Then That (*http://ifttt.com*), can be triggered by things like webhooks (a formatted HTTP request) or the appearance of a new item in an RSS feed, and can perform hundreds of possible actions on other systems in response.

In some ways, these systems are defining a generic event API for the Internet itself, and serving as the "glue" between standalone software platforms. Traditionally complex and expensive system integration can be simplified enormously.

While editors tend to envision workflows as human-centered processes, some workflows have no human-powered steps at all, and are more accurately considered arbitrary processes that can be initiated and performed on content. For example:

- A Post to Twitter workflow might have one step that takes mere seconds to execute, then the workflow ends.
- An Export Content workflow could serialize content to a file, write it to the filesystem, and notify an external process that the file is available to be moved to offline storage.

In these cases, workflow is perhaps more accurately described as "work actions." The initiator is, in effect, saying "execute this action on this content," and there might not be multiple steps through which it progresses. Rather, there might be a single conceptual action that happens at a moment in time and then ends.

Clearly, workflow is a broad and vague concept that defies attempts at clear definition.[10] What one system calls "workflow" might be simple approvals in another, or code-level events in a third. Additionally, the scope and functionality of a workflow event vary widely. Some systems allow workflow to be used for approvals only, others

---

10 If you have an interest in workflow as a general process, the Workflow Patterns website (*http://www.workflow patterns.com*) is a project by two universities "to provide a conceptual basis for process technology." If nothing else, the site demonstrates that workflow is a discipline that originated and is practiced far beyond the bounds of content management.

allow a broad definition of processes to be performed on content, and still others use their own internal workflow framework to manage content publication.

The Dirty Little Secret of Content Approval and Workflow

Complicated content approvals are the white whale of content management. During the planning and sales phases of a project, editors often discuss their great need for long, complicated workflows full of critical approvals and processes, with complex branching logic and automated collaboration and auditing.

In reality, these scenarios almost never happen. I fully believe that 95% of content approvals are simple, serial workflows, and 95% of those have a single step. An editor submits content to be published, and an approver publishes it.

In fact, in most cases, workflow never even enters into the process and approval is managed entirely with permissions. Removing the Publish permission from one editor and granting it to another effectively institutes a single-step serial workflow approval.

In other cases, informal workflow happens outside the CMS, consisting of an editor yelling to her manager, "Hey, can you come look at this and tell me if I can publish it?" No, it's not sophisticated, but that's often how it happens.

I even know of a CMS that changed its architecture to ensure that unpublished content was assigned a private URL specifically to account for the ubiquitous scenario of an editor emailing a link to someone with the note, "Can you look at this and make sure it's okay?" This is effectively approval via email.

While I concede there are situations where workflow and approval can and do get complicated (lawyers can do this to an organization), I maintain that workflow is the single most overpurchased aspect of any CMS. An astonishing amount of money has been wasted in pursuit of hypothetical workflow fantasies that will simply never see the light of day. And, in the event that they were ever actually realized, the volume of content pushed through them would have to be very high and prolonged to justify the expense of making them happen.

Unless you're the *New York Times*, it's best to keep your workflow goals modest.

Collaboration

In multieditor scenarios, there's often a need to specify a unit of work, or have a discussion or collaboration session, specifically related to a piece of content.

To address this, some systems have task management or lightweight groupware built in. The utility varies widely, but some common features include:

- The ability to create and assign a task, specifically bound to a content object or changeset. An editor might create a task entitled "Update the Privacy Policy," then attach that content object to the task, and assign it to another editor. This often dovetails into workflow, as the act of creating the task might have created a workflow. Alternatively, a workflow might use the task subsystem heavily when notifying editors of pending approvals. In some cases, the tasks attached to a content object can be viewable in the administrative interface from that object.
- The ability to leave notes for other editors regarding specific content; provide notes on specific versions explaining what was changed; or have threaded, multi-user discussions about content.
- The ability to store editorial metadata (in the event that you want this data separate from the actual content model).
- The ability to have real-time group chats within the CMS interface.

Clearly, this functionality overlaps heavily with non-CMS tools that editors might be using, such as Slack, Skype, Exchange, and even email. The specific difference is the ability for these discussions and tasks to be bound to and make changes to specific content, and for this information to be displayed in the CMS interface. Within the context of the CMS, these features are aware of the content and can be directed in relation to it.

Like with workflow, though, it's worth mentioning that these features are not often used. Collaboration tools inside a CMS are not the primary focus of the software, and their functionality won't be able to compete with the dedicated collaboration tools your organization likely uses every day. Left to their own devices, editors will usually revert to things like email and group chat to work with other editors on content.

The key in evaluating the usefulness of a CMS collaboration system is determining what advantages it offers by being embedded in the CMS. Sometimes, that intimacy with content brings nice advantages. But in many cases, the advantages aren't worth the disruption of yet one more collaboration environment.

Content File Management

Content files are the files (usually binary[11]) that support the editorial process. These are images, PDF files, Word documents, or other downloads that are not structured, modeled content, but are delivered as fully intact files by the CMS.

In many systems, files are "second-class" content. You can manage them, but in a more rudimentary fashion than "first-class" content (modeled content types). In these instances, binary files are often *missing* the following features:

- Granular permissions
- Workflow
- Language translation
- Metadata, or additional modeled data
- Personalization

In a more pure and functional implementation, binary files are simply managed content types like any other, with one additional property—the content of the binary file itself. So, the file is "wrapped" in a full-fledged content object that allows modeling of additional information (copyright notice, image caption, etc.), workflow, permissions, and so on.

Adding Content Files

Until the last few years, browsers were never stellar at file uploads, and web CMSs were bound by these limitations. Uploading dozens of files was a tedious exercise, with editors having to manually transfer one file after another.

Simple file upload still works and is available, but better methods now exist for getting files into your CMS. These include:

Drag and drop
>   Many systems will allow editors to simply drag one or more files into the browser window and onto a designated location in the interface. All files will then upload simultaneously.

Pseudo filesystem access
>   Some systems support protocols allowing for the repository to be accessed like a filesystem. Users might be able to "map a drive" to the CMS, or access the system

---

11 Many systems refer to content files as "binary files," even though they're not technically required to be binary. There's nothing stopping an editor from uploading a text file to the CMS, for example (and even a text file could be considered a "binary file" at some level).

via FTP or WebDAV clients. Additionally, when the repository is available natively to the filesystem, it's much easier for automated processes to upload content files—a scheduled script might copy files into the system every night, for instance.

External repository integrations

Many systems have "connectors" that expose other repositories to the CMS, such as DAM systems, ECM systems, or even remote services like Amazon S3 or Dropbox. Editors working with content might be able to insert images directly from a SharePoint library, for instance, without having to upload it first.

Content Association

Files are different from other content in that they rarely exist in isolation. To get to a file, a user has to navigate to other content, and a file download is almost always represented by a link on an HTML page (which is likely represented by a content object).

Consider how you typically download files. Unless someone has emailed you a direct link, how often do you navigate directly to a file download without touching any other page on a website? Usually you access a download page, then click a download link.

Additionally, many content files serve solely in support of specific content. A photo gallery will have multiple images that it renders. These images might not be used anywhere else on the site, and serve no purpose other than in support of that single photo gallery.

This means that files are often associated with specific content—they are "attached" to that content and operate under the same management umbrella. In these cases, the content objects and the files that support them should be managed as a package.

For example:

- A file associated with a page of content might need to mirror the permissions of that page. If the page is only available to logged-in users, the file should have that same limitation. If the permissions of the page change, the file permissions should change as well.

- When selecting files to link or insert, editors should have the option to isolate that selection to files associated with that page, rather than wading through all the files in the system.

- When a page of content is deleted or archived, any associated files should suffer the same fate. The lack of this feature inevitably results in a massive archive of old content files, the vast majority of which are not in use by the CMS any longer.

Many systems will provide for this by having files that are specifically associated with another content object and only available for use by that object, while also allowing for global files that are available to all the content in the system.

Image Processing

There's a difference between an image itself (the original) and a specific file representation of that image. An image of a sailboat might need to be converted into multiple files at different resolutions and file sizes for insertion in content at different locations.

Many systems will preserve the original uploaded image, but create additional renditions of it based on a set of configurable rules that allow for multiple styles of the image to be available to editors and template developers. For example, upon uploading an image, the CMS might resize it to three different sizes.

This manifests itself in two main ways:

- When an image is delivered, the templating system might have constructs for the selection of different renditions, or even the detection of the container and automatic insertion of the correct size.
- Editors might be able to select from different sizes and renditions when inserting images into rich text content.

In addition to automatic image manipulation, many systems provide some manual image editing capability—the unspoken goal being "Photoshop in the browser"—with varying degrees of effectiveness. Simple image editing, such as resizing and cropping, is common, but more in-depth transforms usually require images to be edited offline, and might require additional training for editors.

 Image management is one area where external vendors do quite well, by selling digital asset management (DAM) add-on tools. Many CMSs have high-end image management, editing, and processing suites available through third parties, which are either pure add-ons for that CMS only or standalone tools with integration hooks into the CMS. These tools allow the DAM to act as an integrated part of the CMS, and greatly expand its image management and processing capabilities.

Permissions

Content permissions are meant to prevent malicious manipulation of content, or (more likely) to protect editors from doing things they don't intend to do. Preventing an editor from changing the home page is both good editorial policy and helpful for the editor, who might accidentally be making global changes without realizing it.

The concept of permissions in a CMS ties heavily into (and borrows liberally from) the permissions systems that have been in use on filesystems for years. Windows and Linux filesystems have had global permissions models since they were invented, and many of the concepts in the modern CMS are based around them.

For example, an "access control list" or ACL is a generic computing concept. The definition from Wikipedia:

> An access control list (ACL), with respect to a computer filesystem, is a list of permissions attached to an object. An ACL specifies which users or system processes are granted access to objects, as well as what operations are allowed on given objects.

In the case of a CMS, an "object" is usually a content object, as opposed to a file on a hard disk. Many CMSs use both the concept and nomenclature of an ACL to control their own permissions.

A permission—or, technically, an access control entry (ACE), an ACL is a bundle of ACEs—is an intersection between three things:

- User
- Action
- Object

In any situation involving permissions, we must ask ourselves: (1) who is trying to, (2) do what action, (3) on what object? An ACE, bundled into an ACL, governs what is allowable.

Authorization vs. Authentication

Permissions are technically *authorization*, which is the granting of abilities to users. This is not the same as *authentication*, which is the process of making sure someone is who he says he is.

We could talk all day about authorizing Michelle to take some action, but that's not really what we're doing. We're actually authorizing *Michelle's user account* to take some action. We're simply hoping that the user account we know as Michelle is being controlled by the *human* we know as Michelle at any given time.

The process of authenticating this user and ensuring her identity by logging her into the CMS is a completely separate system and discipline from the one authorizing her to do things once she's inside.

Users

First, we must identify the user context in which an action will take place. For this, we must take into account roles and permissions. For example:

- Fred the Editor has been given Edit permission for the privacy policy, but not Publish permission.
- Mary the Corporate Counsel has been given Publish permission for the privacy policy.

Users can be identified directly (Mary and Fred in the preceding examples), or by group. A group or role is an aggregation of users. Users are assigned to a group, or are considered "in" that group. If a permission is granted to a group, then any user who is a member of that group gets that permission.

Thus, we can adjust our previous examples as follows:

- *Anyone in the Editors group* has been given Edit permission for the privacy policy, but not Publish permission.
- *Anyone in the Corporate Counsel group* has been given Publish permission for the privacy policy.

In most cases, this will make more sense.

In general, permissions should always be assigned by group, even when just a single user is in that group. Permissions are usually related to the role someone is performing, rather than to that user as a specific person.

For example, if posts to the CEO's blog have to be approved by Jessica the CEO, is this because she's…well, *Jessica*? No, clearly it's because she's the CEO, and if she's ever *not* the CEO, then she should lose this permission. The permission belongs to the *role of CEO*, not the person fulfilling that role.

In this situation, it would be entirely appropriate to create a group called "CEO," put Jessica in it as the only member, and assign the permission to the group. When Tilly deposes Jessica in a coup and assumes control of the company, we simply remove Jessica from the CEO group and add Tilly to the group, and Tilly assumes all of Jessica's powers. [Insert maniacal laugh here.]

 There is typically an "Anonymous" or "Everyone" group that represents all visitors not authenticated to the system. Protecting content is usually a matter of adjusting permissions for this group—removing Read access from the "Anonymous" group and granting it only to an "Authenticated Users" group, for instance.

Group management can get complex. In some cases, groups can contain other groups. So, the Corporate Counsel group could contain a subgroup called Really Important Lawyers. Being in the Really Important Lawyers group would allow all the rights and roles of the larger Corporate Counsel group, plus perhaps some additional rights.

Additionally, some systems have a differentiation between groups and *roles*. Groups identify users as a members, while roles indicate what they do.

For example, you may have an Editor group, in which you place all your editors, and then have multiple roles for News Article Editor, Media Editor, etc. Permissions are assigned to the roles, which are *then* assigned to the groups. Users are aggregated into groups, permissions are aggregated into roles, and then roles and groups meet to allow actions to take place.

Yes, this can get confusing. There's actually an entire discipline and body of theory called *identity management*. Again, from Wikipedia:

> In computing, identity management (IdM) describes the management of individual principals, their authentication, authorization, and privileges within or across system and enterprise boundaries.

In most situations, however, groups and roles are simply conflated. Even in situations where they're separated, the benefit in most cases is merely hypothetical and semantic. There are no doubt scenarios where the differentiation is important, but it's not common. Most systems will have a method of aggregating users and assigning permissions to those aggregations, whether they are called "groups" or "roles" or something else.

Objects

In an abstract sense, an "object" is anything in a system that may need to be acted upon. This includes:

- Content objects
- Users
- Content types
- Settings
- Templates

Different systems have different granularity in assigning and managing the permissions to act upon different objects. It's quite possible that a CMS will have a complex group/role ACL structure in place for everything. In many other cases, ACL-style permissions are reserved for content, and permissions for managing other items in the system—like templates or users—are simply binary: designated people can do it, and other people cannot.

In most cases, permissions apply to content. These permissions are granted or denied on specific objects, but rarely are they *directly assigned* to those objects. Permissions are usually inferred from either the type of content or its location in the larger content geography. For example:

- A user has full rights to any News Release anywhere in the system.
- A user can create any allowable object under the News section of the content tree.

Occasions exist when a specific content object has different permissions from other content of the same type or in the same location, but this is rare. Specifying those objects as such would become unmanageable over the long term. Therefore, managing permissions in aggregate becomes the only reasonable method.

In many cases, permissions are inherited from some other object—often the parent object or folder. Changing the permission of an object will also change the permissions of all its descendent objects, unless that descendant has been specifically declared to "break" this inheritance and manage its own permissions (at which point it might be the target for the inheritance of its child objects). This is appropriate as permissions are often based on location, and this effectively cascades permissions down branches of a tree.

This is an example of CMS permission models often mimicking filesystems. In Windows, for example, a new file inherits the permissions of its containing folder, unless this connection is specifically broken. Many CMSs use this same logical model.

Actions

Once we know the user and the object to be acted on, we need to allow or deny specific actions. While a user could have so-called "full control" of an object (a phrase borrowed from the Windows permissions model), there's a greater chance that what the editor can do is limited.

Some of the more common permissions in relation to a content object are:

- Creating content of a specific type
- Editing a content object
- Publishing a content object
- Viewing an unpublished content object
- Rolling back to a previous version of a content object
- Initiating a specific workflow on a type of content object

- Editing a single spec of an object of a specific type
- So-called "soft deleting" an object by moving it to the Trash or the Recycle Bin
- Irretrievably "hard deleting" a content object

Different systems have different granularity around what permissions can be assigned to an object. Some just have binary access—either you can create/edit/publish content, or you can't. Others have extremely fine-grained control over specific actions.

Some actions might presuppose other actions. It could be that the right to publish content also confers the right to create and edit it, though situations could be conceived where this doesn't apply. Likewise, an editor might be given the right to delete content but do nothing else to it, though envisioning a realistic usage scenario for this is harder.

Some systems are also extensible, allowing developers to create their own permissions to govern customizations and extensions they write to a CMS. Figure 8-5 shows one of the permissions interfaces in the Sitecore CMS, which offers fine-grained control.

Figure 8-5. One of several permissions interfaces in Sitecore—permissions can be allowed or denied to both content and administrative objects, and permissions "cascade" down the tree to child objects, unless overridden

Permission conflict resolution

Permissions can get complex, especially when different rules come into conflict. In these cases, each system will have some defined method of resolution.

For example, some systems simplify by only offering Allow permissions, but others have explicit Deny permissions as well, which often take precedence over Allow. Additionally, inheritance rules can come into play. Does an inherited permission take precedence over an explicit permission? Usually not; however, as Deny often takes precedence over Allow, an inherited Deny *might* overrule an explicit Allow.

It all depends on the system, and how that system implements its security model. The simpler you can keep your permissions model, the better. A more distributed editorial base requires more complicated permissions, which can lead to some complex models, and occasionally extended debugging when an editor can't do what he should be able to do.

 Consequences of permissions errors can be swift and painful. Revoking read access to the Anonymous group on the root content node of the tree might result in instantly locking everyone out of the website. This is one of the few situations where all that stands between your website and a giant swan dive into the abyss is a couple of mouse clicks.

A Summary of Editorial Tools

We've covered a lot of ground here. Here are some questions you might want to keep in mind. More than in any other chapter, the warning applies here that these checklists are simplistic and crude tools for analysis. Editorial tools run the gamut of functionality and polish. The room for interpretation is wide, and wide-eyed editors sick of their current CMSs can be easily seduced by glamorous features they might never use.

Content Traversal and Navigation

- Is there a dedicated administrative interface?
- Are there in-context editorial tools for authenticated editors?
- How is content presented and organized for review and selection?
- How can content be organized and grouped for editors?

Type Selection

- How are editors presented with types for creation? Is the interface usable and helpful? How will it scale for potentially dozens of different content types?
- Can available types be restricted by editor role?
- Can available types be restricted by parentage or location in the geography?

Content Preview

- Can the content be previewed prior to publication?

- Can the content be edited in preview mode?
- Can the editor select multiple preview modes to see how the content will appear in different channels?
- Can the editor spoof demographic or session information to invoke various personalization states?

The Editing Interface

- How usable are the editorial interface elements?
- What interface elements can be selected and configured for each property type?
- How can content be validated during entry? How much control is available for error messages?
- Is in-context help available to assist editors during content creation?
- How can the editorial interface be customized? Is it possible to remove functionality based on role? Is it possible to add links, buttons, and other functionality?

Versioning, Version Control, Scheduling, and Expiration

- Does the system version content at all? Is it optional or required?
- Is the versioning serial or branching?
- Can content be rolled back to a prior version?
- How can versions be compared?
- Can new content be scheduled for publication?
- Can a new *version* of existing content be scheduled for publication?
- Can content be scheduled for expiration?
- Is there a concept of archiving, and what does it mean? Is content actually moved to another location in the geography? Is it deleted? Can it be retrieved?

Workflow and Approvals

- What is the process for content approvals?
- Can approvals be achieved through simple manipulation of permissions?
- How are approvers for specific content identified?
- How are approvers notified that there is content awaiting their review?
- Is there a workflow engine?

- How are workflows created? From the interface? From code? By configuration?
- What constitutes a workflow step? Are there predefined actions that can be taken in a step? Can these steps be customized?
- Is there a task management system? How does this differ from the non-CMS collaboration tools your organization uses today?

Content File Management

- Can content files be managed from the CMS?
- Can these files be associated with specific content?
- Can their permissions and archiving/deletion be synced with content?
- How are files uploaded? Is there a mass-upload feature?
- Can external file repositories be connected to the CMS?
- What automatic image processing features are available?
- What in-browser image editing is available?

Permissions

- What level of permissions does the system offer beyond binary "full control" access?
- How can users be aggregated? Does the system offer both groups and roles?
- How can content be identified for the application of permissions? By location in the geography? By content type?
- Can content inherit or reference its permissions from another location or object, or are all permissions directly applied?
- What types of permissions are available?

CHAPTER 9

Output and Publication Management

There's a funny *Far Side* cartoon showing a group of people in a karate studio. Through the window, you can see a flying saucer has landed on the street outside and "aliens" made of bricks and boards are walking down the ramp, preparing to terrorize the town.

The caption reads:

> The class abruptly stopped practicing. Here was an opportunity to not only employ their skills, but also to save the entire town.

The implication is that the karate students were very skilled at breaking boards and bricks, and never expected they'd have a chance to use these skills to actually do something productive in the real world.

The same goes for our CMS. Now we're to a point where we have to output some content for a visitor to consume. Up to this point, we've basically been practicing. We've modeled our content, determined how to aggregate it into groups, and identified the editorial tools necessary to enable our editors to work with it.

The one thing we haven't done is actually publish it. To provide value, a *web* content management system has to generate *web* content at some point. We have to get the abstract notion of content out of our CMS and into a form and location where it does some good.

In other words, it's time to get out of the studio, break some boards, and save the town.

The Difference Between Content and Presentation

As I've said before, there's a tendency to look at a news article that you've modeled using your CMS and delivered into a browser window and say, "That's my content."

But it's not. *That's a web page.* It just happens to be displaying your news article. Your news article and the web page it rode in on are not the same thing.

What if you published the same article (in a shortened form) to Twitter? Would that be your news article? No, that would be a tweet, just displaying some different information from your article.

The fact is, that same article might be published into 20 different distribution channels, your website just being one among many. In each one, a new presentation artifact is created using information from your news article. These artifacts are not your news article; they're just things created from it.

The article might even be presented in different ways on the same website. For example, while the article has a "main" view where a reader can consume the entire thing, it likely appears in some other form on several news listing pages, which just use the title, the summary, and perhaps an image. And what about when the article appears in search listings? That's yet another presentation of the same article.

The key here is to separate your content in its pure form—its raw, naked data—from the ways in which it's used. Your article might consist of the following information (attributes, in the content model):

- Title
- Summary
- Image
- Byline
- Body

This is the pure content that makes up the article. It might also need to have multiple attributes to help when it's presented in various channels, such as:

- Tweet Body
- Sidebar Position
- Facebook Link Text

This information isn't your content. It's not critical to the "spirit" or core of the news article. It exists merely to aid in the translation of your news article into a format necessary for one or more channels.

In the end, does this matter? In many cases, no, this is merely an academic argument. But as we continue, it's important to note the difference between the content and the presentation in which it's displayed. Some practices are universal to both, while others only make sense in the context of one or the other.

Templating

Templating is the process of generating output based on managed content. In a very general sense, the output will be a string of text characters, usually HTML. Less commonly, a CMS will generate binary content such as PDFs.

Nomenclature: Template vs. Type

Be warned that some systems use "template" to refer to what we've called content types. For example, in Sitecore, your model of a news article is called a *template*, and templates (as we discuss them here) are called *renderings*.

This usage is not consistent with the nomenclature of this book. I'm not saying it's wrong; it's just different and less common and might have caused considerable confusion over the next couple of dozen pages if you weren't aware of it.

For the purposes of this book, a template is the set of code applied to a content object to generate output.

A CMS blends two things together to generate output:

- Templating code, or text entered by a developer, usually created and stored in a file. Different templates create different output. One template might generate a web page, while another might generate a tweet (see Figure 9-1).
- Managed content, or text managed by an editor, created and stored in the CMS.

The combination of both is the final, rendered output.

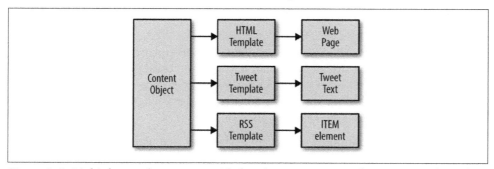

Figure 9-1. Multiple templates are provided to the same content object to provide multiple outputs

One of the constant balancing acts in a CMS implementation is where this dichotomy lies. How much of the rendered output should be created and managed by a developer in the template, and how much should be created and managed by the editor in the CMS as content? The answer to this question has a huge impact on the usability and manageability of the final system.

Load-Bearing Walls

A house can be modified by its owners. They can paint it, move furniture around, and maybe even knock down a wall or two.

However, eventually the homeowners will run into *load-bearing walls*. These walls hold up the roof, so they can't be moved or taken down. The owners simply have to work around them, or call a contractor to perform major structural modifications. The architects who designed the house can affect its future value by where they place the load-bearing walls, since those are set in stone (sometimes literally).

The same goes for a CMS implementation. While an editor might be able to change the layout, colors, and other superficial aspects of a page, eventually she's going to run into load-bearing walls. These walls are things that editors cannot change. They either have to work around them, or call a developer to perform major modifications.

Many of these aspects exist at the template level. The developer bakes items into the template that cannot be controlled by content or the CMS interface. These are the load-bearing walls. How many of these exist and where they're figuratively placed will have a *huge* impact on the value of the CMS implementation over time.

Some might argue that editors should have as much control over the page design and layout as possible, which can be accomplished either by providing configuration options for every possible bit of output, or by allowing editors free access to the templates (often from the CMS interface). This rarely works well. HTML/CSS technologies have advanced to the point where someone without training can do real damage if they're careless.

Additionally, in most cases, templated content is an advantage, not a limitation. As I mentioned earlier when discussing dynamic page composition, allowing an editor to change a page for no other reason than aesthetic preference might violate the site's style guidelines, and dealing with exceptions (e.g., where all content is a certain way *except* News Release X), is very rarely a good thing.

In general, clean separation of responsibility between templating code and editorial content is a desirable thing to have.

Warning: Code Ahead

If you're a developer, a lot of the information in this section will be redundant. While it differs in some ways, templating is closely aligned with mainstream web programming. Much of the information in this section is simply a lightweight introduction to those concepts.

If you're not a developer, you're going to see fictitious code. It's fictitious in the sense that it's not any actual language, but it's representative of the basic concepts of programming/templating languages.

The idea here is *not* to try to turn you into a developer. The aim is simply to provide an introduction to some of the issues that developers deal with when putting together a content-managed website.

Don't look at this as a practical tutorial. Rather, just skim the concepts and try to understand the larger logical issues at stake.

Templating Philosophy

There are varying schools of thought on the scope of templating that revolve around how much power the templates should have. The two sides of the argument look like this:

- Templates should not have any data that they are not directly given. Templates should be given a defined bundle of data, and they can format this data only.

- Templates should be able to retrieve and generate data as necessary. They should be small, encapsulated units of code that can reach "outside" themselves if they need to.

The first option is clearly more limiting. The CMS will "give" the template some data, and that's all the template has to work with. The argument in favor of this is one of maintainability. Template developers shouldn't be allowed unrestricted logic, or confusion will result because there's now one more location for something to go wrong.

Terence Parr, the creator of the StringTemplate templating engine, has written an entire white paper on this subject. In it, he says:

> The mantra of every experienced web application developer is the same: *thou shalt separate business logic from display*. Ironically, almost all template engines allow violation of this separation principle, which is the very impetus for HTML template engine development.[1]

---

1 "Enforcing Strict Model-View Separation in Template Engines," (*http://www.cs.usfca.edu/~parrt/papers/mvc.templates.pdf*) May 2004.

It's a valid point. If a template can do anything, then in what sense is it a "template" at all, and how is it different from any other code?

The other side of the debate might argue that this is limiting and that logic as it relates to presentation is perfectly acceptable. If a template needs to present a certain set of data, it's simpler for the template to be able to retrieve that data instead of having to depend on the invoking code or system to provide it. Templates only exist to make it easier to intersperse code amongst presentational markup, not to set the code apart for any other reason.

Regardless of your position, the fact is that different systems enforce different models, and many are settling into a hybrid approach: the template is given a bundle of data but can perform other operations as necessary, unless explicitly disallowed by configuration.

In practical terms, this means that most templates will execute *in the context of a known set of data*. Data will be provided, and most operations in the template will be specifically to format this data.

For instance, in ASP.NET MVC's Razor templating language, the data structure is conventionally known as the "model."[2] This model is given to the template, and is referred to as such. For instance, to display the TITLE tag of a page, that piece of data is retrieved from the model:

```
<title>@Model.PageTitle</title>
```

In Symfony, multiple variables are defined and given to the template, where they're retrieved by name:

```
<title>{{title}}</title>
```

The point here is not to survey templating languages but merely to demonstrate that in most situations, templates are "dumb" and *intended to act on provided data*.

URL mapping and the operative content object

Closely related to the architectural concept of how the template engine operates is how the CMS determines what information to give the template to work with. In a coupled system, this is usually accomplished by mapping a URL to a content object to be operated on—what we'll call the *operative* content object.

Consider the inbound URL:

```
/politics/2015/debate-report
```

---

2 This is both philosophical and practical. Philosophically, "Model" is the "M" in "MVC." Practically, this data is referred to in the template as the variable named Model.

In a coupled system, there is no "politics" or "2015" directory, and no file named "debate-report." Rather, this URL is mapped to the operative content object. When the request for the URL is received, that content object is retrieved and the CMS determines what template should render it. That template is given the content object (and often additional data) and executed to provide output that is returned to the client.

In the prior section I said that templates operate in the context of a specific set of data. For content management specifically, we can say that templates usually execute *in the context of the operative content object*.

In Episerver (using Razor), the operative object is provided as part of the model, under a property called `CurrentPage`:

```
<title>@Model.CurrentPage.Name</title>
```

In Sitecore (also Razor):

```
<title>@Html.Sitecore().Field("Title", Sitecore.Context.Item)</title>
```

In eZ Platform (Symfony and Twig):

```
<title>{{ ez_field_value( content, 'title' ) }}</title>
```

In WordPress (raw PHP):

```
<title><?php wp_title(); ?></title>
```

Note that in WordPress, the title of the post is derived to the point that you don't even have to pass an object to it. When you call that function, the template just assumes you mean the operative content object.

The point here is that the operative content object will be known and provided to the template. In the previous examples, this object was known to the template and referenced as `Model`, `Sitecore.Context.Item`, `content`, and `wp_title()`, respectively.

In a decoupled system that writes files to the filesystem, the URL mapping model is reversed. Instead of a URL being received and mapped to an object, that URL is specified on the object and simply used to generate the file in the appropriate location. Put another way, the file exists before the request. When a request is received, it's handled by the underlying web server without invoking the CMS at all.

Templating Language Functionality

All systems invariably have a language for generating textual output. When it comes time for the merging of content and templating, there is always some type of shorthand for making this happen. It consists of templating code with markers indicating where the managed content should go and how it should behave.

Very few CMSs implement their own custom templating languages. Most modern CMSs use an existing templating language in common use, coupled with some custom extensions and data structures specific to that CMS.

In ASP.NET this is Web Forms or Razor for MVC projects. In PHP, Twig is currently very popular, and Smarty has been well used in the past (to say nothing of just using PHP itself). For Java, FreeMarker and Velocity are popular.

There are three major "levels" of functionality in templating languages. We'll look at these next.

Simple token replacement

By definition, a system will always have the ability to replace "tokens" (or "variables") in the templating code with managed content. A token is simply a placeholder that is replaced with information specific to the operative content object being templated.

Consider the following completely hypothetical code:

```
The name of this article is "{article.title}"
and it was written by {article.author}.
```

In this case, the tokens are clearly the text surrounded by the { and } delimiters (the control characters that identify template code).[3] The system knows to examine this code, find that particular combination of characters, and replace them with the Title and Author attributes of the article that's being rendered, as in:

```
The name of this article is "The Migration Patterns of
the Dodo Bird" and it was written by Bob Jones.
```

In addition to simple token replacement, the templating code might have basic output filtering available to influence the content that replaces the tokens. The pipe character (|) is a common tool for this (taken from the old Unix practice of "piping" command-line output from one program to another).

For example:

```
This article was written on {article.date|"MMM DD, YYYY"}.
```

In this case, the date of the article is output in a specific format. Depending on the platform, "MMM DD, YYYY" might result in "September 3, 2015." The format of this date is dictated by what is placed in the template by the template editor.

---

3 Again, this is fictitious. Different languages will define code embedding differently, but in all cases there will basically be some character combination that specifies code content as opposed to marketing content.

Other common filtering needs include:

- Causing the output to be in currency format with two decimal places:

```
The product costs {product.price|"$#.##"}.
```

- Causing the output to read "5 days ago," rather than a specific date.

```
Posted {article.publish_date|relative} ago.
```

- This might cause the word "result" or "results" to appear, depending on how many search results were available.

```
There are {search.result_count|pluralize:"result"}.
```

Token replacement is core to any templating language. Templating would effectively be impossible without it.

Limited control structures

Where token replacement runs short is when templates need to perform more advanced logic, such as repeating actions for multiple items or deciding whether or not to output something based on criteria. These concepts are foundational to programming in general, and are collectively known as "control structures" or "flow control."

Note that the existence of control structures in a templating language is never *in place of* token replacement—languages with control structures and logical processing as described in this section will also always have the token replacement capabilities described in the previous section. Control structures are an extension of token replacement.

The two core control structures are:

- Looping
- Branching

Consider this (again, hypothetical) templating code:

```
Other articles about this topic include {article.related_articles}.
```

This is problematic, because what does `article.related_articles` output? Clearly, it needs to output a reference to more than one article, but it can do this in many ways—for instance, as a bulleted list or a comma-delimited string—and where is the templating code that dictates that?

What we'd really like to do here is something like this:

```
Other articles about this topic include:
{foreach related_article in article.related_articles}
```

```
* "{related_article.title}" by {related_article.author}
{endforeach}
```

What we've created here is a "for each" loop, which is a programming control structure. Assuming that `related_articles` is a reference attribute to multiple other articles, this code will loop through them, and inside the loop the token `related_article` will be fully populated as an Article content object, from which we can output information. We're saying: "*For each* article in the `related_articles` collection, do this…"

We can usually refer to `related_article` from inside the loop only. Outside the loop —before the `foreach` or after the `endforeach` token—the `related_article` token has no value. This is called "in scope." The token `related_article` is only in scope inside the loop, and it has a different value during each pass through or iteration over the loop. Outside the loop, it has no value (it's "out of scope"), and referring to it might even result in an error.

A `for each` loop is a very common programming construct, and one of multiple ways to loop over a collection of items. The actual implementation will vary from system to system.

In addition to looping, we'll often need to make decisions to output information based on criteria inside a content object. For instance, what if an article had no related articles? In this case, the `related_articles` property would be empty, and there would be nothing to loop over, leaving just this in the output:

```
Other articles about this topic include:
```

This would look odd, and leave visitors wondering if they'd missed something. We need to remove everything referring to related articles if there are none.

In this case, we could attempt something like this:

```
{if article.related_articles.count > 0}
  Other articles about this topic include:
  {foreach related_article in article.related_articles}
    * "{related_article.title}" by {related_article.author}
  {endforeach}
{/endif}
```

Here, we're using an "if…then" control structure. We're saying, "If the number of items in the `related_articles` attribute of our article is greater than zero, then loop over and display the related articles. If this is not true, do nothing between `if` and `endif`." If our article has no related articles nothing will output, which is what we want.

Almost all templating languages have some capacity for at least primitive control structures. Without them, you're limited to basic token replacement, which will quickly fall short of even basic templating tasks.

Native programming language

Templating code can often get complicated. When branching and looping are introduced, templates effectively become little procedural computer programs. The line between the template code and the *actual* code of a CMS can begin to get blurry.

This causes some to ask, why do templating languages exist at all? If native computer languages are available, why not simply use them? It might seem silly or even unfair to constrain a developer into a more primitive language. The underlying language of your CMS—PHP, C#, or Ruby, for example—can no doubt do a great many things, so why can't you just do your templating in that language?

In some cases you can, and this often removes the need for a separate templating language altogether. For example, our original token replacement example could be written in PHP like this:

```
The name of this article is "<?php print $article->title; ?>"
and it was written by <?php print $article->author; ?>
```

Assuming "article" is a populated PHP object representing the operative content object, this would output the same thing as the prior token replacement example. Actually, many systems will allow this. In fact, WordPress—the most ubiquitous CMS in current use—uses PHP as its templating language.[4] Here's some actual WordPress templating from my own blog:

```
<a href="<?php the_permalink(); ?>">
  <?php the_title(); ?>
</a>
<p class="date"><?php echo get_the_date(); ?></p>
<?php the_excerpt(); ?>
```

The code between <?php and ?> is executed by the PHP interpreter.

So, why isn't templating done in a full programming language rather than having access to a templating language?

Remember back in Chapter 4, we identified a subset of developers responsible for the frontend of the website—mainly the HTML/CSS and the templating. This template developer might not be the same person as the backend or server-side developer responsible for completely integrating the CMS. The roles and responsibilities are different. While the server-side developer is concerned with the grand architecture of

---

4 PHP might be unique in that it was originally built with the primary intention of generating web pages. One of my technical reviewers noted: "I would argue that PHP is a templating syntax that grew into a programming language." There's truth to this. The roots of PHP as a web templating language are hinted at in a core function called nl2br, which converts line break characters into the
 HTML tag. This function has no purpose outside generating HTML and has been in the language since version 4, released in 2000.

the entire system, the template developer is only concerned with how things are rendered.

As such, it's generally desirable for a template developer to only work with a subset of programming functionality, rather than having access to the full scope and power of the underlying programming language in use by the CMS. Giving a template developer unrestricted access to the full programming language introduces three problems:

- Complication
- Security
- Stability

First, programming languages can be fundamentally complex. There are often many nonintuitive things that a programmer needs to understand, such as variable scoping, the difference between reference and value types, and recursion. These concepts are far beyond what's necessary to render a simple page of content.

In 2006, Tim Berners-Lee (the founder of the World Wide Web itself) and Noah Mendelsohn edited a paper called "The Rule of Least Power" (*http://www.w3.org/2001/tag/doc/leastPower-2006-02-23.html*). Their abstract states:

> When designing computer systems, one is often faced with a choice between using a more or less powerful language…. The "Rule of Least Power" suggests choosing the least powerful language suitable for a given purpose.

More power almost always involves more complication, and most programming languages are designed to solve problems more complex than templating.

A dedicated templating language can be domain-specific, meaning it is aware of its intended usage and can contain constructs and concepts designed solely to make it easier to achieve that goal—to generate textual (usually HTML) output, in most cases. The full programming language, by contrast, is designed to do anything and everything a programmer may be tasked with doing.

Second, and closely related, is the issue of security. If a full programming language is available to a template developer, that template could then be allowed to do basically anything the programming language allows. Just because the code is executing in the context of a template doesn't make it any less dangerous.

Something like this would cause an error during rendering:

```
Here's what happens when you divide something by zero: <?php print 1/0; ?>.
```

This is fairly benign compared to more potentially destructive practices like raw database access. If a template developer was given such access, he could circumvent the security features of the CMS by going directly to the database for content, perhaps out of genuine frustration over CMS limitations.

Finally, templating languages are designed to be stable by being fault tolerant. If an error occurs, it's often ignored and the template simply carries on with execution. Templates do not (or at least, *should* not) manipulate data, so the risk of data corruption is low. Additionally, template logic issues can be isolated so that they simply affect one portion of a page, and continued execution can still generate usable content. Issues that arise during templating are rarely something that will or should damage the stability of the website as a whole.

The Danger of Prebuilt Interface Widgets

Many CMS vendors relentlessly promote prebuilt interface elements that they claim will automatically generate HTML for common interface needs, like photo galleries, image carousels, comment forms, etc.

Be very careful here. These will certainly generate HTML, but you usually have to simply take what you get. The odds that they generate the *correct* HTML for your project, style library, planned responsive breakpoints, and coding standards are lower than you might think.

These elements often don't save time because other code (CSS and JavaScript, usually) has to be adapted to work with them. And sometimes they become a net time loss, as you find yourself wrestling to get the HTML structures you need, until finally just throwing them out and templating from scratch.

The Surround

When considering a rendered HTML page, there's a need to separate between the managed content of the page and "the surround." The surround is everything that (wait for it) *surrounds* the content object on the page.

The concept of the surround has been with us since long before content management. Server Side Includes have long allowed web developers to provide common markup for headers and footers, and some client-side editing systems provided explicit support for this concept, such as Microsoft Front Page's "Shared Borders" feature.

Consider the news article in Figure 9-2. Several items on this page are the direct result of the operative content object being rendered on the page:

- The title
- The byline
- The body

Then, there's everything else above, below, and to the sides of the news article. The "everything else" is the surround.

Figure 9-2. A news article from the New York Times: everything outlined—the headline, byline, and body of the article—is content from the actual (operative) content object, and everything else is the surround

In most systems, these items are handled by two different templates. The surround is the outer shell of the HTML document, which is common to all content, while the content object has its own template. The content object is rendered by its template, and placed inside the surround template.

Here's an example of a surround from the Razor templating language of ASP.NET MVC:

```
<html>
  <body>
    <h1>Website Title</h1>
@RenderBody()
```

```
    </body>
  </html>
```

The `@RenderBody()` is a method call that will render the subtemplate for the content in that location. Here's an example of that template:

```
<h2>@Article.Title</h2>
<p>
by @Article.Author
</p>
@Article.Body
```

Like in our previous examples, the `@Article.Body` and `@Article.Title` are tokens that are replaced with managed content. The entire result is then embedded in the larger surround and delivered to the end user.

The final result looks like this:

```
<html>
  <body>
    <h1>Website Title</h1>
<h2>The Migration Patterns of the Dodo Bird</h2>
<p>
  by Bob Jones
</p>
<p>Lorem ipsum dolar...</p>
<p>More paragraphs of content here...</p>
  </body>
</html>
```

The surround is valuable because there is often infrastructural HTML that is common to every single page on a website. Every page may require a reference to the same stylesheet in the HEAD tag, or open with the same containing DIV. Keeping this code in one place is simply a good design practice.

Where templates depart from one another is often in the rendering of different content types. Your Employee Bio content type has fundamentally different information than your News Release content type. Each of these types will likely have its own template, though the output of these templates will be placed within the same surround for final delivery.

It's possible that different content types might have entirely different surrounds, but this is more rare than you'd think. Occasionally, a "landing page" content type might have a very bare surround, or certain content designed for machine consumption (an RSS feed, for example) will have no surround at all. However, the vast majority of types in the average content management installation will be rendered in the same surround.

Context in the surround

In the examples just presented, the surround is completely ignorant of the content being ultimately rendered inside of it. Our sample surround will render the exact same way each time regardless of the content type.

But let's add a HEAD and a TITLE tag to the current surround:

```
<html>
  <head>
    <title>...</title>
  <body>
    <h1>Website Title</h1>
{object_template}
  </body>
</html>
```

The question now becomes, what do we put in our TITLE tag and how do we get it there? The article template itself (the "inner" template) clearly knows how to do this with the {article.title} token, but what about the surround? What does it "know" about the content rendering inside of it?

Remember, all the templates we've discussed so far *have known about the operative content object*. They've all executed in the context of a specific content object to which they could refer. Does the surround have this same luxury? Or is it completely ignorant of what happens inside the inner template being placed within it?

This is a matter of *context*, or the ability for the surround to take action based on an understanding of the content that is ultimately being rendered. In our example, we could do this:

```
<title>{article.title}</title>
```

But remember, our surround is universal to all content types. Would an Employee Bio content type have a "title" attribute? (Well, it might, but it would likely refer to the job title, which is not what we want.)

Additionally, would the templating language even understand the token {article}? We're not necessarily rendering an article anymore. The surround has to be generic enough to handle any content type we throw at it.

Here's the brute force approach to solving this problem:

```
<title>
{if object.type == "Article") {
    {article.title}
}
{if object.type == "EmployeeBio") {
    {employee.first_name} {employee.last_name}
}
</title>
```

This would work—and I'm sure it's been done—but it's not very scalable. We'd have to add to this mess of code for every possible content type.

There might be a better way to solve this problem. Back in Chapter 6 when we discussed content modeling, we talked about inheritance, where content types can inherit from more general types and gain all their properties in the process.

Using that, we could create a Web Page content type with a text attribute of Title Tag. Then, our News Article and Employee Bio types could inherit from the Web Page type and get the Title Tag attribute in the process. Then we might do something like this:

```
<title>{object.title_tag}</title>
```

Note that we're using an {object} token in the templating code of the surround. This is purely hypothetical, but common. The surround usually has access to a piece of content in a form *that has information common to all content*. It might not be able to dig into the specifics of the content object, but it can deal in generalities.

Of Abstractions and Polymorphism

The preceding example is what's known in programming as an "abstraction" (more specifically, it's called "polymorphism"). Yes, a News Article is a specific thing, but at the same time, it's a more abstract thing: a Web Page that has a Title Tag. At the same time, it might be an even more abstract type: a Content Object, that has attributes like a Published Date and an Author.

Dealing with content—and especially templating content—often means thinking about it at different levels of abstraction and specificity.

In reality, most web CMSs have specific ways of handling the TITLE tag, but this is just one example of how the surround often needs to deal with functionality that is specific to the content that is being rendered.

Consider the common requirement of "Related Content." CMS integrators see this all the time in wireframes—the idea that content related to the content being viewed can be magically conjured out of thin air.[5] Regardless of the technical challenges involved, this interface element usually appears in a sidebar, or somewhere in the surround.

---

5 If that sounds a little cynical, it is. There is no Grand Unified Theory of Related Content, though wireframe designers usually assume it just magically happens somehow, so they routinely throw it into every sidebar.

To render this, the surround has to know enough about the specific content being viewed—the content in the "inner" template. Will it have this information in enough detail to act on it?

Navigation is another very common contextual requirement. Often, the surround needs to know where the content lives in the larger content geography. For the left navigation menu of the site, perhaps your plan is to render links to all of the "sibling" pages to the one being viewed, or simply to format the link to the current page differently. To do this, the surround has to know what content is currently being rendered. A crumbtrail is another example—a crumbtrail only makes sense when the position of the current content is known in relation to other content.

Is your surround going to have access to this information? Will it be able to get references to the current object so it can query the repository for the sibling pages?

Lack of context in the surround can occasionally be supremely frustrating. While a template for a specific content object is relatively simple, other things can be made unnecessarily complex by a lack of abstraction and lack of awareness when rendering the surround.

Template Selection

Content objects need a template to render. How is that template selected? How are objects and templates matched up for rendering?

In most cases, templates are selected based on content type. This is natural because a content type is the most obvious determinant of what a template needs to do. The templating code required to render an Employee Bio will almost always be very different from the code required to render a News Release.

In some cases, however, the template selected to render a content object can differ based on factors other than type.

Editors may have a selection of templates, usually in order to alter layout. For instance, an editor might select a "two-column" template in order to display a sidebar.

In these instances, confusion might result from the fact that a different template may require different content to render, and the existence of that content might be a better way to do automatic selection.

In the case of our two-column template, content has to exist for that sidebar column. Does the content object have an attribute for Sidebar Content? And if it does, could the regular template simply show or hide the sidebar based on whether that property was populated? It would be confusing for an editor to populate a Sidebar Content attribute but still not see a sidebar simply because she had failed to select a template that supports it.

In other cases, we might want to supply a different template for a specific content object to enable some extended functionality. If, for instance, we had a custom-programmed mortgage calculator, we could create a Mortgage Calculator content type, with its own template based on the type. Depending on the effort required, however, this might be a waste for a content type that will only be used one time—there will be exactly one content object created from that type.

It might be easier to simply create a Page object and call it "Mortgage Calculator," then use a different template for *that specific object* that contains the code to render our calculator. This could be by editorial selection, but that runs the risk of an editor selecting this template for other pages as well. It would likely be better to force this template for that content object at the code or configuration level. (See "Proxy Content Objects" on page 192.)

Some systems do this by filenaming standards, with a defined "fallback" list for how a content object will render. The system will look for a template from most to least specific. For example, say we have an Employee Bio content object that has a unique ID of #632. Our system might look in the templates directory for files named:

- *content-id-632.tpl*[6]
- *content-employee-bio.tpl*
- *content.tpl*

The system will look for a template specific to the ID first (`content-id-632.tpl`). If it doesn't find this, it will look for a template specific to the content type (`content-employee-bio.tpl`). If it doesn't find that, it will use a generic template (`content.tpl`) for *all* content (which, in most cases, would be highly undesirable—one would hope that there would be a template for each content type, at the very least; how would we possibly render completely different content types from the same template?).

While falling back based on file naming is common, other systems have much more elaborate ways of determining template selection, including evaluation of specific properties or specific locations in the geography, and even advanced rules engines involving esoteric combinations of environment and content variables.

---

6 Again, this is hypothetical, but ".tpl" is a very common extension for template files. The files are simple text files, and could just as easily use an ".html" or ".txt" extension, but the ".tpl" extension identifies their purpose by name, which can be helpful.

Finally, many systems will also provide developer tools to override template selection at the code level. A developer might be able to write code that takes any variables into consideration when assigning a template to a content object for rendering.

Proxy Content Objects

The mortgage calculator we discussed in this section is a good example of a "proxy object." In our example, the mortgage calculator was entirely code-driven—all of the functionality was in the template and some backend code written by a developer. In fact, the code might have been written as a standalone executable page, and simply linked to on the filesystem as *calculator.aspx* or *calculator.php*.

Doing this, however, would make that page an "orphan." The CMS probably won't know anything about it, which limits or eliminates any extended functionality the CMS can offer. Ideally, we could find a way to "wrap" this custom functionality in a construct that the CMS knows about and can provide functionality to.

The content object in our example did just this. It was a "wrapper" or "proxy" around this template. We created a content object, then assigned a specific template to *just that object*. This template contained all the functionality required for our calculator.

By creating a proxy object in the CMS to wrap this code, we effectively told our CMS this content exists, and consequently enabled significant editorial functionality around it. For example:

- We can provide a paragraph of help text or an introduction, which can be managed by an editor (perhaps as the Main Body attribute of the page).
- The calculator can be presented in the same surround as the rest of the site.
- The calculator can use our permissions model, perhaps only allowing access to logged-in visitors.
- We can configure the calculator based on its relationship to other content (if it appears in the Commercial Mortgage section, brand it like that; otherwise, brand it as a Residential Mortgage calculator).
- We can configure navigation items (crumbtrails, especially) based on the content's location in the geography.
- If an editor is writing another page and wants to link to the calculator, he can select the calculator as another page in the CMS, rather than having to copy and paste the URL. Then, if the URL of the calculator changes, we won't have to go tracking all those links down.
- We can get a clean URL, as provided by the CMS.

Template Abstraction and Inclusion

In addition to the relationship between the template and its surround, a template will quite often contain "subtemplates" or "included templates," which are separate templates injected into specific places in the "containing" template.

This is the continuation of a very common technique of web programming languages. Server Side Includes have been used for years to insert chunks of HTML and programming code in languages like PHP, Classic ASP, and ColdFusion. And this itself is a continuation of the programming principle of DRY ("Don't Repeat Yourself"), which encourages programmers to elevate common code to central "libraries" that are referenced in multiple places.

The goal of this model is to avoid repetition and ease the maintenance of templates as changes need to be made. If common template code is concentrated in one location, it can be changed once with potentially wide-ranging effects.

For example, in several places in a website, we might want to generate an HTML structure like this:

```
<ul>
  <li><a href="/article1">Article #1</a></li>
  <li><a href="/article2">Article #2</a></li>
  <li><a href="/article3">Article #3</a></li>
</ul>
```

This a simple bulleted list of three articles and their titles. We might use this in our Related Content sidebar, our Latest News menu, and our Other Articles in This Series promotional box. In each case, it would display different articles, but the general presentational structure of displaying a list of articles and titles would apply in all cases.

The code to generate this output might look like this:

```
<ul>
  {foreach article in article_list}
    <li><a href="{article.url}">{article.title}"</a></li>
  {endforeach}
</ul>
```

We could, of course, simply include that template code in all three places in our templates. But what if we wanted to change it? Rather than including it three times, it would be more efficient to have the code in one place, and simply refer to it.

Perhaps instead, we could insert the following code:

```
{include:article_list.tpl}
```

This code would find the *article_list.tpl* file, in which our code lives, and insert the contents in that location. Used in multiple places, this code would have the effect of centralizing the template structure and allowing us to maintain it in one place.

Remember that the actual articles will be different in each of our three use cases, so we need a way to specify what the `article_list` variable means inside the subtemplate. This is usually accomplished by specifying the value when calling the template:

```
{include:article_list.tpl article_list=article.related_articles}
```

In this case, we're calling the subtemplate and telling it that—for this instance only—the `article_list` is comprised of the `related_articles` attribute of the article we're rendering.

Template inclusion is quite common (both in CMSs and web development in general), and is extremely helpful to reduce the complexity of templates by abstracting common output structures into their own templates and managing them there.

Inside-Out Templating

If we consider the operative content object's template as the "main" template, the surround is often described as wrapping this main template. Conceptually, it looks like this:

```
surround.tpl
  content-object.tpl
```

However, there's a subtle difference, and I want to make sure you understand that templating is generally driven *from the inside out*, not the outside in. The surround doesn't pick the inner template; rather, the inner template selects the surround.

Remember that the *content-object.tpl* template is the main template—it is the template that's directly invoked. It's calling the shots, essentially, and can sometimes control what surround is applied. In this way, it "includes itself" in the surround template, which turns the concept inside out.

For example, a Razor template in ASP.NET MVC includes this code at the top:

```
@{
  layout = "/path/to/layout/template.cshtml";
}
```

This says, in effect, "Execute me, then *insert me inside of this particular surround*." The main template specifies the surround that it wants, and remains in control of the rendering flow.

The operative content object is a lot like someone getting ready for a party. First, they get all cleaned up, dressed nicely, and looking great. Then, at the last second, they look through the hall closet for a matching coat that complements their outfit, throw it on, and head out the door. They picked out a coat based on their outfit, they didn't pick their outfit based on their coat. The surround template is the coat that the operative template throws on at the last second.

Template Development and Management

We've spent lots of time talking about templates, but what are they exactly, and how do they differ from content itself?

Templates are almost always file-based. Whereas content exists in the CMS as something editors work with through the interface, templates exist on the filesystem as files that developers work on using their standard development tools. (See "Code Versus Content" on page 28.)

Some systems also allow for template editing through the interface, though this is rare and would usually only be done in an emergency when access to the underlying code was not available. A `textarea` in an HTML page offers very little in the way of the coding support even the most rudimentary code editing tool offers—line numbering, syntax highlighting, autocomplete, etc.[7]

The existence of file-based templates highlights another difference between templates and content—templates are a code asset, not a content asset. A template change will usually be treated as a code-level change and subject to the developer's workflow process, not the editors' workflow process. The two workflow processes are quite different.

Templates are normally stored in a source code management system such as Git or Team Foundation Server. Sometimes they're stored alongside the CMS code itself, and sometimes separately. Changes to templates are often tested and deployed through well-known build tools like Jenkins or Cruise Control (we'll talk more about development tools in Chapter 12).

The relationship between code and content is often misunderstood, and the two are often conflated. Editors might expect content to be handled like code, and code to be handled like content. Understanding the difference between the two and the boundaries between them is critical to an overall understanding of the CMS itself.

Responsive Design and Output Agnosticism

More and more, prospective CMS customers are asking to what extent a CMS enables or inhibits responsive design. The answer to either question should be "not at all." Responsive design is largely a byproduct of HTML and CSS markup, and a CMS

---

7 Very few other systems force template development *solely* through the interface. This is rare, but you see it occasionally, and it often throws developers into disarray. Files are the universal container of web development—they're the thing that developers base their work on and use as an encapsulation and transport mechanism for code. Almost all programming processes and methodologies assume that code exists in files, not database records, and without file artifacts to manage, many programming methodologies and workflows will completely break down.

should neither enable nor inhibit any particular output paradigm. A CMS should ideally strive to be "output-agnostic."

Some CMSs do provide device detection and use this information for template selection (technically, this is *adaptive* design, not responsive), but even in systems that don't, this functionality can be provided by the web server or some other element in the technology stack.

The earlier warning about prebuilt interface widgets looms large here. A canned HTML structure provided by a CMS "feature" will stick out like a sore thumb when it's the only nonresponsive element on a page or doesn't respond in the way everything else does. And given that the HTML for your responsive design will be highly specific to the CSS framework you choose, how will these prebuilt widgets decide what HTML to output?

In a larger sense, this question speaks to the division of responsibilities. Is it the responsibility of a CMS to manage the detection of devices and the generation of responsive HTML? Most developers would say no—this should be handled by other components in the technology stack. So long as the CMS does not hinder the generation of any HTML the template developer desires, then the responsiveness of the output is not the CMS's concern.

 When a CMS gets too cozy with the HTML it generates, in the form of prebuilt widgets or by promoting specific frontend design and coding paradigms, it's said to "infiltrate the browser." It slowly starts to expand its sphere of influence beyond managing content and begins to try to manage what happens when a page is loaded into the browser. *Resist this infiltration.* In most cases, a CMS has no business being there, and it's rarely helpful in the long term.

Publishing Content

Once we understand the relationship between our content and our presentation, and we've developed templates to render content in the format we want, then we need to get this content into a state where someone can consume it. How we do this depends highly on the relationship between our management environment and our delivery environment.

Coupled Versus Decoupled Content Management

One of the more significant architectural principles behind a CMS is the coupling model between its management and delivery environments. By "management," I mean the system in which content is created, edited, and managed. By "delivery," I mean the system from which content is consumed by a visitor.

In many cases, these are the same system. Editors manage content and visitors consume it from the same server, using the same execution environment. For example, an editor working on content in Sitecore and a visitor reading that content are both talking to the same Sitecore installation, just from different sides.

These systems are said to be "coupled." Management and delivery are inextricably linked in the same environment.

Contrast this to a system where the authoring and management environment is on one server, and the delivery environment is on a completely different server, perhaps in a different data center, and even in a different geographic location entirely. Content is created and managed in one place, and is then transmitted to another place where it's consumed by visitors.

The delivery environment might be only vaguely aware the management environment even exists. If content is placed onto it via FTP or file copy, the web server in the delivery environment will dutifully serve the content up without knowing or caring where it came from.

These systems are said to be "decoupled." Management and delivery are separated into two environments.

When it comes to actually publishing content, the two options are handled quite differently:

- With a coupled system, the act of publishing content simply means changing a setting on the content to make it publicly available. From the first moment it's created, content is already in the delivery environment; it's just hidden from public view. Referring back to the versioning discussion in the last chapter, to make it available for public view, we simply mark one of the versions as "published." It's almost anticlimactic.
- With a decoupled system, we have to actually move the data from one environment to another. All content intended for publishing is gathered up from the management environment, then transmitted to another server entirely.[8]

These two models often make the concept of a "staging environment" confusing. In a coupled system, the staging environment is virtual—if you have permission to see draft content and are perhaps in a "preview mode," then you're effectively viewing the staging environment on the same server as the production environment. With a decoupled system, a staging environment might be a literally different environment to which content is transmitted for preview.

---

8 Usually. Some installations might simply publish content to a different location on the same server.

Which is the default architecture?

Back in the early days of content management, decoupling was the default architecture. Content management systems were largely static file generators that simply helped website managers turn data into formatted HTML files that were then copied to the root of the website.

But as web programming languages and websites became more sophisticated, the decoupling model began to show cracks. Having simple, static HTML files worked well when content didn't change much and wasn't required to do anything, but the market was starting to demand that content become active.

Website managers wanted users to interact with content in contextual ways—they wanted to hide some content from users who weren't logged in, or they wanted to change the way content was organized based on the user, or they wanted to enable real-time search of content. Static HTML files didn't adapt well to these needs.

Gradually, the CMS and the content it managed began to become more coupled. Why write out an HTML file when a PHP script could simply query and retrieve content from a database in real time? In the years since, the coupled CMS has become the default model, and decoupled systems are becoming harder to find (though this might be changing; we'll talk about this a bit in Chapter 15).

In situations where decoupling is still used, the CMS normally either publishes scripted web pages (PHP files, for example) that execute on request, or doesn't publish files at all. Some systems publish pure data records into a database,[9] and the website is built to render them live (oddly, now you sort of have two CMSs—a decoupled one populating a database as its destination, and a coupled one using that database as its source).

The argument for decoupling

While not appropriate for many situations, decoupling does have undeniable advantages:

- It allows your repository system and publishing system to be on different architectures. You could have a Java-based CMS pushing content onto a Windows server running .NET. Your delivery environment is not limited by your management environment.

---

9 I've even worked on a highly specialized build that simply populated an entire SQLite database with content and pushed that into the delivery environment. So, the CMS swapped out the *entire data source* of a running website whenever content was published. While clearly not appropriate for many situations, it was the right choice for those particular requirements and demonstrates that decoupled data can be published in many different formats beyond static files.

- It will usually result in a more secure delivery environment. The potential hack points on a stripped-down web server are tiny compared to a full CMS.

- You can publish content to multiple delivery environments. A large media enterprise might have hundreds of servers in dozens of countries on multiple continents. In these situations, deploying content is much more complex than just manipulating the version stack. Caching servers need to be updated, media needs to be pushed into a CDN, reverse proxies need to be reset, failover servers need to be updated, etc.

- Since you don't need to install a CMS on all the delivery servers, you might not need to license them. Depending on the size of your delivery environment, this could save you enormous amounts of money.

- It can be easier to scale a decoupled delivery tier. Adding a simple web server to your load balancer is vastly easier than bringing up a new CMS installation and somehow synchronizing it with the others. Your management environment might actually be quite modest, but it could publish content into a mammoth delivery architecture.

- Reliability is usually higher. Not having a CMS in the delivery environment means fewer moving parts. There are fewer chances for error when serving static HTML files.

- You can publish content from multiple repositories and systems. Your CMS may only be one system of many that generate content, so your delivery tier might need to publish content without knowing (or caring) where it came from. It's easier to blend content from multiple points of origin in a decoupled environment.

- In some cases, the content in a CMS is secondary to the website's primary purpose. An online banking system, for instance, might be a massive, custom-built banking platform that incidentally also displays some content. You can't simply drop a coupled CMS on top of this—the CMS can't "own" the delivery environment. Instead, the CMS has to be subservient to it, exist somewhere else, and push content into it.

- Some editors demand a true "staging environment" from which to develop content. They want a sandbox in which to publish content for preview before public delivery.

Decoupled Publishing Targets

In decoupled environments, the CMS transmits content to "publishing targets," which are environments intended for content delivery. Most systems can support more than one publishing environment and publish content to them simultaneously.

The actual method of transmission is often one of the following:

- FTP or SFTP
- File copy (obviously, the two systems would need to be on the same network or VPN)
- WebDAV
- rsync
- SCP
- Web service

Some transmission methods are universal (almost every server will support FTP), while others need something on the other end to receive the content. There is no universal web service, for example, that would receive content from any CMS. Therefore, a CMS might provide a web service to run in the delivery environment that will be used to get content from one environment to another.

Once this happens, the neutrality of the decoupled model is broken. If the delivery environment needs something running inside it, then that environment becomes an extension of the CMS, to some extent. The CMS no longer publishes to a neutral environment, but instead publishes to a known endpoint that is prepared to receive the content from it.

Some systems are even more specific—they run proprietary software to receive content in the delivery environment. The CMS effectively comes in two pieces, resulting in a system where management software pushes content into delivery software that is required on every delivery server.[10]

Delivery environment synchronization

Here's a seemingly simple question: how does a decoupled system delete published content from the delivery environment? Say your decoupled CMS pushes an HTML file (a database record, whatever) to a delivery server. Later, the content "behind" that file gets deleted from the repository. Does the decoupled system then delete the output file from the delivery server?

Some do, but others might only update the delivery environment when you *publish*, which means that when you delete, there's an orphaned file sitting out there. Over time, these accumulate, and you wind up with a mix of active files that represent con-

---

10 Clearly, another benefit for commercial CMS companies in this model is that all the delivery servers need to be accounted for and subsequently licensed. The cost of licensing the delivery environment might constitute the largest portion of the vendor's total price tag.

tent and orphaned files that have no corresponding content. How can you tell the two apart?

Can you just wipe out the delivery environment and republish the entire repository from scratch? Only if *everything* for your site is in the CMS. Some solutions are just partially managed—supporting files live in the delivery environment (or are deployed there from source control) and content files are published from the CMS, and these files are all intermingled in the same locations on the delivery server. How can you tell which files were published from the CMS and which files exist only in the delivery environment?

This raises a larger question: how does a decoupled CMS ensure it stays perfectly in sync with its published environment? Does it "own" the delivery environment and exert ironclad control over it? Or is it designed to "contribute" to the delivery environment and not disrupt files that are already out there? The answer to this question varies by system.

A Summary of Output Management and Publication Features

The following checklists provide you with some guidance on points to keep in mind when evaluating your output and publication needs.

Architecture

- Is the system a coupled or decoupled system?
- Does the system manage content without reference to delivery on the Web, or does it have web-centric features built in?

Templating

- Is templating done in a domain-specific language, or is it done in the underlying programming language of the CMS itself?
- Does the language allow for token replacement? Does it permit filtering and formatting of replaced values?
- What control structures are available for template logic?
- How does the templating system allow you to manage and include the surround? How can the surround obtain the correct context of the content object being rendered?
- How does the templating system allow you to abstract and include other templates?

- How are templates selected for content? How are you able to affect this selection?
- How are templates developed and managed by template developers?

Decoupled Publishing

- How is content transmitted to publishing targets?
- How are publishing targets configured and managed? Are they required to run CMS-specific software?
- Can the CMS capture publishing events? Can processes be run before or after content is pushed into the delivery environment?
- What data artifacts are actually published? Just files, or can the system publish records to a database or other non-filesystem storage method?
- How does the CMS ensure the delivery environment stays in sync with the repository?
- Is the CMS expected to manage non-content files as well, or should supporting files live in the delivery environment and only content files be published from the CMS?
- What needs to be installed on the delivery servers in order for them to receive content from the management environment?
- How are delivery servers licensed?

CHAPTER 10

Other Features

In prior chapters, we've discussed edge cases, which are usage patterns at the outside edge of what a typical user might do. Edge cases are the bane of software developers because they have to be accounted for, even though they occur infrequently. And sometimes the level of work that goes into handling an edge case will equal or exceed the level of work that goes into developing something that *every* user does, all the time.

One of the problems with writing complicated, feature-rich software is that any individual user of the software might only use 25% of its total features. *But everyone uses a different 25%.* Which means that beyond the basic, core functionality, everything becomes an edge case to some extent.

Once a platform's user base hits a significant size, every edge case can be a huge problem. If 30,000 people are using your software, and a feature is used by only 1% of them, that's still 300 people who expect it work with the same level of polish as everything else.

These users don't know that this is an edge case. They don't know that very few other people are using the feature. Just ask any vendor who has tried to remove a feature it didn't think anyone was using, only to be greeted with howls of protest by a small subset of users who were depending on it.

In the previous four chapters, we've discussed the core features of web content management:

- Content modeling
- Content aggregation
- Editorial workflow

- Output management

It can be safely assumed that every implementation will use these four features to some degree or another. If a system falls down on one or more of these, it's tough to get much done.

However, in this chapter, we're going to talk about features on the edges. These are things that might be used in some implementations, and not in others. Some systems won't implement some of these features, because they haven't had a user base demanding them.

Features that address use cases on the edges often have a "backwater" feel to them. They're somewhere off the mainstream, and might offer functionality that even experienced integrators (or members of the product's development team itself!) have forgotten exists, or never knew about in the first place.

Backwater features are those that don't get nearly the attention of the core features and are sometimes created just so a vendor can check few boxes on an RFP and say it offers them. Consequently, their value tends to fall into narrow usage patterns.

Note that not everything discussed in this chapter is a "backwater feature," but all the features we'll look at here represent functionality that might not be present in all systems.

 A sadly common scenario is when a prospective customer asks to see feature X, and the sales team scrambles to remember if it's handled by the product and, if so, where the functionality exists and how it works. They find someone on the development team who vaguely remembers something that was poorly implemented many years ago and hasn't been touched or updated in years, and then pray that it holds together long enough for them to demo to the prospect and act like it's something they show off every day.

Multiple Language Handling

Content localization is a deep, rich topic. Technical documentation writers have been developing methods to manage multiple translations of their content for decades. Websites have just made the problem more immediate and more granular.[1]

---

1 Multilingual content management was originally much more advanced in systems coming from Europe, because it had to be built in from the start. Europeans are more multilingual than the rest of the world due to the sheer number of different languages spoken in close proximity. As such, the CMS coming from Europe a decade ago tended to be multilingual from their roots, while systems from the rest of the world often had to retrofit this feature later in their lifecycles.

Having your website content in more than one language is often not a binary question, but rather one of degrees. In some cases, you might simply have two versions of your website, with all content translated into both languages. In others, however, you might have some content in your primary language,[2] and some content translated into a secondary language. Not translating all your content into another language might be due to the expense involved, or due to lack of regulatory requirements in situations where an organization is only required to have specific content in multiple languages.

Multiple languages add an additional dimension to your CMS. In terms of your content model, each attribute may or may not require additional versions of itself. The Title attribute of your News Release content type clearly has to exist in multiple versions, one for each language, but other attributes won't be translated. The checkbox for Show Right Sidebar, for instance, is universal. To account for optional translation when modeling content, you might be required to indicate whether a particular attribute is "translatable" or not.

The end result is not a simple duplication of a content type, but rather a more complex selective duplication of individual content attributes. Content objects are populated from the required combination of universal attributes, translated attributes in the correct language, and "fallback" translations for attributes without the correct language.

Nomenclature

When discussing multilanguage content, some terms can be tricky. Here are a few definitions to keep in mind:

- *Localization* is the translation of content into another language.
- *Internationalization* is the development of software in such a way that it supports localization.

For example, a CMS that is "internationalized" has been created in such a way that multiple languages can be supported, in either the content under management or the CMS interface itself.

That last point is worth noting: there's a difference between a CMS that manages content in multiple languages and one that *presents itself* in multiple languages. If your Chinese translator doesn't speak English (let's assume she's translating content from, say, Swedish), having a CMS interface that can only be presented in English can be a problem.

---

2 I'll assume English for the purposes of this chapter, though I apologize for the ethnocentrism.

Language Detection and Selection

The language in which your visitor wants to consume content can be communicated via three common methods:

- The domain name from which the content is accessed
- A URL segment of the local path to the content
- The visitor's browser preferences, communicated via HTTP header

In the first case, the content is delivered under a completely separate domain or subdomain—for example:

```
www.mywebsite.se
se.mywebsite.com
```

In these cases, "se" is the ISO-639[3] abbreviation for Swedish. While the two domains look similar, there's actually a marked difference.

The first example requires that your organization own the country-specific domain name. This might be difficult if a country puts restrictions on who can purchase those domains (you may have to be incorporated or based in the country in question, for example). The second example uses a subdomain, which is available at no cost to the organization that owns the "mywebsite.com" domain.

An additional consideration is that "mywebsite.se" is considered to "belong" to a country, and there are rumors of more search engine optimization (SEO) consideration when using search engines in those countries. In this instance, content served under the "mywebsite.se" domain might perform better when using Google Sweden (*http://google.se*).

The ability to map languages by domain name may or may not be supported by a CMS. In some cases, the alternative domain would be considered another website, while others will allow the mapping of multiple domains to a single site for the purpose of mapping languages to specific domains.

If you don't want to change domain names, many systems will allow for the first URL segment to indicate language. For example:

```
www.mywebsite.com/se/my-news-release
```

---

3 "ISO" refers to the International Organization for Standardization. This is a worldwide organization that collects, manages, and publishes standards across a wide variety of industries and disciplines. The existence of an ISO standard indicates that this is a commonly accepted standard for the relevant subject matter and is used by many organizations. In this case, the language abbreviations contained in ISO-639 are common not only to content management, but across the business world in general. A CMS could implement its own language codes, but that would be fairly pointless.

In this case, the "se" at the beginning of the local path is detected and Swedish-language content is served. In systems where URLs are automatically generated based on site structure, this URL segment is usually added automatically, is transparent to the editor, and will not map to any particular content object. (For now we'll ignore the fact that the remainder of the URL should actually read "mitt-pressmeddelande"; we'll talk more about that in the next section.)

Finally, many systems support automatic detection of the language preference from the inbound request. Hidden in web requests are pieces of information called "headers" that your browser sends to indicate preferences. One such header looks like this:

```
Accept-Language: se, en;q=0.9, fr;q=0.8
```

In this case, the user's browser is saying, "Send me content in Swedish, if you have it. If not, I'll take English. If not that, then use French as a last resort."[4]

This language preference is built into your browser, and can be modified in the browser settings (you may have to look deeply because it's rarely changed, but I promise you it's in there somewhere)—see Figure 10-1 for an example. For most users, this is set (and then never changed) by your operating system based on the version you purchased. If you bought your copy of Windows in Sweden, then the operating system language likely defaulted to Swedish, and Internet Explorer will be automatically set to transmit an `Accept-Language` header preferring Swedish.

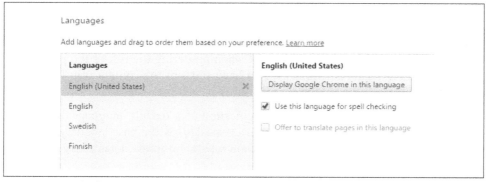

Figure 10-1. The language settings dialog in Chrome—these settings resulted in a header of "Accept-Language: en-US,en;q=0.8,sv;q=0.6,fi;q=0.4"

---

4 While it would make sense to simply list languages in order of preference, the "q=" indicates the "quality factor," which is the order of preference for languages. Why the complication? It's related to a larger concept of "content negotiation" built into the HTTP specification. Other content variations, like quality or type, might be based more granularly on the quality factor. In practice, however, content negotiation is rarely used at this level.

Language Rules

What if a user selects a language for which you do not have content? Your site might only offer its content in English and Swedish. What do you do with a browser requesting Finnish?

First, you need to understand that the information in the Accept-Language header, domain name, or URL segment is simply a request. The user is *asking* for content in that language. Clearly, you can't serve a language you don't have. Nothing is required to break in these cases; you just need to make choices regarding how you want to handle things.

You have a few options:

- *Return a "404 Not Found,"* which tells the visitor that you don't have the content.[5]

- *Serve content in the default language*, perhaps with a notice that the content doesn't exist in the language the user requested. In this case, we would serve English and perhaps explain to the user that Swedish wasn't available by putting a notice at the top of the page.

- *Fall back according to a set of rules.* You could, for example, configure the system to treat Swedish and Finnish the same, so users requesting Finnish content would receive content in Swedish. Clearly, these are different languages, but many Finns also speak Swedish, which would at least get you into the right ballpark.[6]

Assuming the content does exist in the language the user requested, how do you handle requests for specific-language content when rendering the rest of the page, especially the content in the surround? If you have 100% of the content translated, then this isn't a problem, but what if the site is only partially translated?

In most cases, a CMS will require the specification of a "default" language (English, in our example), in which all of the content exists. This is the base language, and any other language is assumed to be a translation of content in the default language. This

---

5 Technically, the correct status code should be "406 Not Acceptable," which means that content can only be produced with "characteristics not acceptable according to the accept headers sent in the request." However, this is rarely used and might be confusing, so most sites will return a 404 Not Found.

6 This is common with "language families" or "proto-languages," which are groups of similar regional languages. For example, Norwegian, Swedish, Danish, Faroese, and Icelandic are all vaguely related to a historic language called Old Norse. Most European languages are also considered to be Germanic, and share many common features (large portions of the alphabet, punctuation, and formatting, such as left-to-right reading direction).

---

might mean, for some systems, that content cannot exist in another language if it doesn't exist in the default language first.[7]

In a partially translated site, there might be content translations for *some* of the content in other languages. If someone requests one of these languages (Swedish, as an example), and you can manage to produce the desired content in that language, you still have the problem of rendering other content on the page—the navigation menu, for example—when parts of it may require content that has *not* been translated.

You have two options here:

- Simply remove any untranslated content.
- Display the content according to fallback rules.

With the first option, the site might shrink, sometimes considerably. If only 30% of the site is translated into Swedish, then the navigation will be considerably smaller. In the second example, all content will be available, but some links will be in Swedish and others in English (our default).

Language Variants

There may also be specific dialects of a language per country. In these cases, in accordance with ISO-639, the language codes are hyphenated. For instance, "fr-ca" is for "French as spoken in Canada," and "en-nz" is for "English as spoken in New Zealand."

Some countries mandate differentiation. For example, Norway has two official written and spoken language variants:

Bokmål
"no-nb," the official variant

Nynorsk
"no-nn," literally "new Norwegian"

All governmental branches are required by law to publish/transmit 25% of their content in Nynorsk. In these cases, fallback rules are common. For the 75% of content that doesn't have to be in Nynorsk, a request for content in "no-nn" would likely be configured to fall back to "no-nb".

---

7 Though not strictly related to your CMS, a little-used variant of the LINK tag can be used to point to equivalent content in other languages: `<link rel="alternate" hreflang="se" href="http://se.myweb site.com/" />`. Some search engine indexers will use this to identify the same content in multiple languages.

Beyond Text

While text is the content most commonly affected by localization, it's not the only content:

- *Images and other media* might have multiple translations, based on language or culture. It's easy to inadvertently offend visitors from some countries by showing images outside their cultural norms. For example, for many years, it was common to avoid showing images of families with more than one child when delivering Chinese content. Similarly, in predominantly Muslim countries, the Red Cross is known as the Red Crescent, with a different logo to match the name.[8]

- *URLs* might be specific per language, as we noted earlier. This results in the additional complication that content can no longer be translated into a different language simply by changing the language indicator (whether this be the domain name, a URL segment, or a request header), since the actual path to the content in another language is different. If someone changes the "se" language indicator to "en," they might get a 404 Not Found because "/en/min-nyheter-releasen" is not a valid path, even though that content does exist in English under another path ("/en/my-news-release").

- *Template text* will need to be changed. The word "Search" on an HTML button is often not content-managed but is baked into the template. It will need to be rendered as "Sök" when accompanying Swedish content. Depending on the platform and templating language, these text snippets are often stored in resource files managed alongside templates and then retrieved and included at render time.

- *Template formatting* is often culture-specific. For example, "$1,000.00" in English is "$1.000,00" in Italian and "$1 000,00" in Swedish. Clearly, the "$" is problematic too, but changing it to the symbol for the euro or krona fundamentally changes the value. This formatting information is often available as a template setting, though this setting will need to be detected and set by the template developer.[9]

- *Template structure* sometimes has to change based on the structural characteristics of the language. French, for example, takes up 30% more space than English on average. German is notoriously long as well.[10] Additionally, some languages are read right-to-left (Hebrew and Arabic, for example), and others vertically

---

8 This is more accurately referred to as "culture translation" rather than "language translation."

9 These settings are often referred to as the "locale settings" of a user.

10 Which, incidentally, might be one reason why Germans use Twitter at a rate markedly less than other countries. It is much harder to shoehorn the German language into 140 characters than other languages.

(multiple East Asian languages). These languages can require major template changes, and sometimes even a specific template set all their own.

Editorial Workflow and Interface Support

Content translation and language management is fundamentally an editorial concern, so the editorial interface and tools can provide functions to assist:

- In many cases, the editorial interface of a CMS can be configured to provide side-by-side presentation of content that needs to be translated. This allows a translator to view the content in one language while simultaneously rewriting the content in another, on the same screen.

- Editing languages can be limited by permissions to ensure that a monolingual English speaker doesn't try to "wing it" and make a change to the Swedish version of a page.

- Translations might be lockable and grouped with the default language so new content can't be published until translations in all other required languages have been added or updated.

- Many systems come with preconfigured workflows and user groups for adding additional translations. User groups can be language-specific, and beginning a workflow for a specific group can automatically add a new translation and route a task to a qualified translator.

- Rich text editors have varying support for multiple languages, especially non-Germanic languages such as Arabic and Japanese. Symbol insertion might be required to add language-specific characters for users not possessing the correct keyboard mappings. An "O" is not an "Ø," and if you don't have this on your keyboard, you're going to need to find a way to insert it.

- Links from one content object to another might need to be language-specific. In some cases, you might want to link to a specific piece of content *in a specific language*. By default, links will likely target the same language as the one used on the page on which they appear (Swedish to Swedish, for example), but if the linked-to content is not available in that language, another language will need to be selected.

External Translation Service Support

Many organizations provide commercial translation support, and your CMS might be able to communicate with the translation service directly through automation.

XLIFF (XML Localisation Interchange File Format; commonly pronounced "ex-lif") is an OASIS-standard XML specification for the transmission of content for translation. Content can be converted to XLIFF and delivered to a translation firm, and the same file will be returned with the translated content included. Many systems will allow direct import of this content, adding the provided language translation (or updating an existing version).

Taking this a step further, many translation vendors offer plug-ins for common CMS platforms that allow you to initiate an external translation workflow that automatically transmits content to the translation service. The content is translated and returned to the CMS, and the content object is updated and either published automatically or presented to an editor for review. Some of these plug-ins are provided at no cost as an enticement to use the translation service that offers them.

Perspective: The Complexity of Internationalization

by Seth Gottlieb

When I hear someone complain about the complexity of managing a single-language website, I feel like a father of ten chuckling at the overwhelmed hysterics of a first-time parent. I remember the stress, but at a scale of one language, it seems so trivial that I can't understand how I got worked up about it. It is especially adorable when I see "supports localization" thrown in with other requirements like "WYSIWYG editor."

The truth is, internationalization is not a feature; it is an aspect that multiplies the complexity of every other feature and facet of the platform. To illustrate this point, let's review some content management challenges and how they are amplified when publishing into multiple languages:

Consensus building
> One of the hardest parts of web projects is discovering latent points of disagreement and building consensus among stakeholders. With a multilingual website, you are bringing in very different perspectives and needs. You might even be asking other groups to give up autonomy and control.

Design
> Remember how much effort was spent obsessing over design? The buttons had to be big enough to fit the words on them, the titles shouldn't wrap, etc. Multilingual websites have to accommodate text expansion (for example, German translations of English use up to 40% more characters). Plus, that nifty font that you selected probably doesn't support all of the characters you need.

Development
> You would be surprised how much content is managed in the templates themselves. For example, the word "search" on the search button was probably hardcoded into the template file. Even worse, a developer could have cut a corner by

putting that word in an image to get the layout just right. To be localizable, all of these strings should be managed in separate files that can be sent to a translator. Moving those strings out of the templates is incredibly labor intensive and error prone. Cutting new images with translated text and keeping them up-to-date is nearly impossible.

Review

Remember how embarrassed you were when that typo got through review? Well, how many typos do you think are in that text that you can't even read? Did you consider the frustration of not being about to publish the source language content until it was translated and those translations were reviewed?

Keeping content fresh

I can't tell you how many companies vow to update the home page every week— "just to keep the content fresh." You expected the CMS to practically update itself, and you probably didn't factor in the cost of translating all of that content. Just getting the content over to the translators and back is nearly a full-time job on a regularly updated website.

The bitter irony is that most organizations are motivated to implement (or reimplement) a CMS because they think managing a website is too hard. They throw internationalization into the mix as a "while we're at it" requirement (or to help justify the budget), and they wind up with more work than they started with.

So, if you are entertaining the idea of multilingual publishing, make serving those markets the core of your business case and prepare to invest the money and effort it takes to get it right.

Seth Gottlieb is the Vice President of Product Development at Lionbridge Technologies, the world's largest localization firm.

Personalization, Analytics, and Marketing Automation

In the current competitive business climate, many organizations are not buying a content *management* system so much as they're buying a content *marketing* system. To explain why requires a little history.

Some time in the last decade, CMS vendors suddenly caught up to customers. For years, customers had been clamoring for more and more editorial and management features, and the vendors were constantly playing catch-up. However, there suddenly came a point where vendors reached rough parity with what editors were asking for, and were finally providing most of the functionality that editors and content managers wanted.

Continually trying to differentiate themselves from the competition, the commercial vendors looked for another audience with unmet needs, and they found the marketers. From there, the race was on to bundle more and more marketing functionality into their CMSs.

The content marketing industry had been around for years—companies like Adobe, HubSpot, eTrigue, and Exact Target had long been providing content targeting and personalization services—but CMS vendors poured into that market. The link between content management and marketing was obvious, so the commercial vendors tried to strengthen their offerings with these tools.

The result has been marketing toolkits of varying functionality and applicability, built on top of and often bundled with a CMS (or available as an add-on or module at additional fee[11]).

Anonymous Personalization

A goal of any marketing-focused website is to adapt to each visitor individually. In theory, a single website could change in response to information about the visitor, and provide content and functionality *that* particular visitor needs at *that* particular moment, in an effort to more effectively prompt visitors to take action.

This functionality is collectively known as "personalization." Two very distinct types exist:

- *Known personalization*, where the identity of the visitor is definitively known over time. Clearly, this only works when visitors proactively identify themselves, usually by logging in. Thus, each user has a permanent identity with the website, and actions and preferences can be tracked and stored for that user specifically. The users might have a "control panel" or other interface where they can modify their own settings.

- *Anonymous personalization*, where the visitor is not known to the website. In these cases, the website has to deduce information about the identity or demographic group of the visitor from clues provided through behavior or other information like geolocation, referring website, or even time of day.

Known personalization has been available for years. In these cases, users clearly know that the website has their identity, and often expect to be able to modify how the website interacts with them. The *New York Times* website, for example, has an entire interface devoted to allowing subscribing users to select their preferred news sections, and this information pervades their interaction with the service (even beyond the website, extending to the *New York Times* mobile applications).

---

11 Several years ago, a system with a list price of $4,999 released a marketing and personalization add-on module at a list price of $14,999—three times the cost of the CMS itself.

But anonymous personalization has been the big trend of the last half-decade.[12] It's still mostly limited to commercial vendors, who as a group tend to be more marketing-focused.

The first step of anonymous personalization requires marketers to create demographic groups into which they can segment visitors. Creating these groups requires the identification and configuration of multiple criteria to evaluate the visitor against. The criteria fall into three general types:

Session

Factors specific to the visitor's current session (e.g., location, incoming search terms, the technical parameters of the web request, etc.)

Global

Factors related to external criteria and universal to all visitors and sessions (e.g., time of day, available content, etc.)

Behavior

Factors related to the accumulated content that a specific visitor has consumed and the actions a visitor has taken on the website (usually in the current session, but optionally including previous sessions as well), with the assumption that users' selection of this content contributes to their audience identification[13]

For example, for a travel agency website, we could decide to apply extra marketing to our Caribbean travel packages by targeting visitors who might be feeling the effects of winter. To do this, we'll identify a demographic group we'll call Icebox Inhabitants. Our criteria for this group are:

- The visitor's location must be north of the 40th latitude, or the current temperature in their location must be less than 50 degrees Fahrenheit.[14]

- The current date must be between October 15 and March 15.

- The visitor must have viewed at least one vacation package to a location we have classified as "Warm Weather."

---

12 The generic term "personalization" once referred solely to *known* personalization when that was the only type available. However, when anonymous personalization tools began to hit the market, the accepted meaning of the term changed, and now it's more commonly used to refer to anonymous personalization. The implication is that known personalization is such an obvious and accepted feature that it no longer requires a differentiating name.

13 Note that user tracking is limited by browser technology and privacy safeguards. A user with strict privacy settings, using a different browser than usual, or even clearing the browser cache will likely disrupt any attempt at this type of personalization.

14 This is surprisingly easy information to get using a combination of geolocation and freely available weather web services.

Anyone falling into this group is "tagged" for their browsing session as an Icebox Inhabitant.

The second step of personalization is to use the information we've gained about the user to modify the site and its content in such a way as to elicit a desired reaction from the user. Some options provided by CMSs that have these capabilities include:

- Changing content elements, such as adding a promotional element in the sidebar, based on group membership
- Showing, hiding, or changing specific paragraphs of text or images inside rich text areas
- Template-level or API-level changes to alter rendering logic or other functionality
- Redirection, allowing the substitution of different content for specific URLs
- Modification of site navigation, by showing or hiding options from different demographic groups

Building on our previous example, we could include a custom promotional element in the sidebar for Icebox Inhabitants highlighting the temperature in Bora Bora and our fantastic vacation packages there. Additionally, we could load a supplemental stylesheet to incrementally change the color palette of the website to warmer colors.

Implemented at a practical level, this allows a marketer to highlight relevant content for users who they think will react to it. At its most absurd extreme, this would allow the management of smaller, individual content elements that are then combined dynamically at request time to render a one-off, bespoke website for each and every user.[15]

Clearly, with great power comes great responsibility. It's quite easy to introduce usability problems by changing a website's structure or content in real time. If a user has viewed personalized content and sends the URL to a friend, that friend might not see the same thing when he visits. The original user might not even see the same thing the next time she visits the site, or even *the second time she navigates to the same page in the same session.*

This also raises the question of how to handle search engine indexing. When the Googlebot (or even the site's own indexer) visits the site, what content does it index? Do you leave it to the default, nonpersonalized content, or do you create a personalization group specifically for search engine indexers and display *all* the content, in an

---

15 If personalization interests you, I highly recommend *The Filter Bubble* by Eli Pariser (Penguin), which delves deeply into the sometimes sinister ways websites and companies use personalization, and the resulting changes to our culture and opinions.

attempt to have as much indexed as possible? But then what happens when a page is returned by a Google search based on content that isn't present unless the user's behavior has put him into a specific personalization group?

Personalization is an exciting feature, certainly but it does call into question one of the core principles of the World Wide Web: *content is singularly identified by a URL.* On a heavily personalized site, a URL is really just the "suggestion" of content. The actual content delivered in response to a URL can be highly variable.

Perspective: Personalization: The Idea Versus The Reality

by Jarrod Gingras

Everyone loves the idea of true personalization. Getting the right content to the right user at the right time is the goal of every marketer. In demos, CMS vendors love to impress selection teams with their product's ability to provide this sophisticated level of content delivery. However, the reality is that while many enterprises buy CMSs that are technically able to provide this functionality, very few enterprises have the internal capacity to properly execute this type of personalization strategy.

The development of a personalization or segmentation strategy goes beyond designing the database and code to feed dynamic, personalized content to users. In many cases, you will need to make sure a CMS has an interface for audience management to enter custom user information, manage groups and profiles, or override automatic processes. You will probably want user- and group-based reporting that typical web log analysis tools will not be able to provide. The effort to implement and customize these administrative and reporting tools should not be underestimated.

Depending on how fine-grained your profiling is, bigger groups might be easier to manage, but the depth of personalization may suffer, since targeting specific content at the individual user level can be very unpredictable. While a CMS can help you by lending a set of features to drive your personalization efforts, a bigger effort lies in the design of your strategy, and picking an efficient and feasible approach.

Any effective personalization strategy requires a significant up-front and ongoing investment. The necessary resource demands make this type of personalization cost prohibitive for most enterprises. Unfortunately, many ambitious enterprises realize that they are in over their heads only when it is too late.

Savvy CMS buyers will not get swept away by vendors' slick personalization demos. Rather, they will be realistic about their internal abilities and resources. Usually this means starting small with broader segmentation and lots of testing and refining until they get to the right level of personalization for them and their consumers.

Jarrod Gingras is Managing Director and Analyst of Real Story Group, a research and advisory firm specializing in helping enterprises make better digital marketing and digital workplace technology decisions.

Analytics Integration

Website analytics systems are not new, but there was a push some years ago to begin including this functionality inside the CMS. The result was analytics packages that were not providing much in the way of new functionality, but were simply offering it inside the CMS interface.

The key question is: what new functionality does integrating with a CMS enable? The answer, seemingly, is not much. Analytics is mainly based on two things:

- The inbound request itself
- Events hooked to activity happening when the page is loaded

The inbound request is usually captured before the CMS has even come into play, and client-side events are tracked using code developed during templating. Given this, the value of analytics integration is questionable.

The trend in the years since then has been to integrate analytics packages from other vendors, the most common being Google Analytics. Many systems now offer the ability to connect to a designated Google Analytics account for the site the CMS manages and show that information inside the interface, mapped to the content itself.

Editors might be able to view a piece of content in the CMS, then move to a different tab or sidebar widget inside the same interface to view analytics information on that content specifically.

With the personalization functionality described in the last section, some analytics reporting might have value in terms of reporting how many visitors fulfilled the criteria for a specific demographic group. This would give editors some idea of how common or rare a particular combination of visitors is.

Marketing Automation and CRM Integration

Beyond the immediate marketing role of the website, there's a larger field of functionality called "marketing automation" that seeks to unify the marketing efforts of an organization through multiple channels. This is what's being used when you get a series of emails from a company, click on a link in one (with a suspiciously long and unique URL), and that action seemingly exposes you to a new round of marketing geared specifically to that subject.

Clearly, your actions are being tracked across multiple platforms, with all your actions feeding a centralized profile based on you in the vendor's customer relationship management (CRM) system.

Many CMSs offer integrations with CRM or marketing automation platforms. Integration goes in two different directions:

- The CMS might include tracking data in links, or otherwise report back to the CRM on actions that known users are taking on the website. In this sense, the CMS "spies" on the users and reports their activity back to a central location.

- The CMS might offer CRM demographic groups as personalization groups or criteria, allowing editors to more easily customize content for groups of users already created and represented inside their CRM.

Some CMS vendors have offered creeping functionality in this space, with the CMS incorporating more and more CRM and marketing automation features into the core. Some go so far as to offer email campaign management directly out of the CMS, complete with link and click tracking, and even direct customer management.

However, as marketing automation vendors such as HubSpot, Marketo, Pardot, and others have become more and more sophisticated, the industry is realizing that pre-built integrations with those systems are more likely to win customers. Thus, the marketing automation vendors are building integrations between their systems and CMS vendors in an effort to present a unified platform that provides a more desirable product on both sides.

Perspective: The Shift to Digital Experience

by Bob Egner

Web content management (WCM) systems have long offered benefits for both IT and business users. With a WCM in place, business users can manage and display content on the Web while relying less on assistance from their IT departments, and in turn, IT departments are free to focus more time on other initiatives after the initial implementation. In an age when the Web served as a form of broadcast media (similar to a billboard or radio ad), these systems provided information technology geared toward solving internal problems.

But just like the Internet, times are changing. Companies that broadcast a "one size fits all" message are losing their competitive edge. This is the age of the customer, and companies who, as Forrester Research put it in a recent report (*http://bit.ly/20jo8z7*), are focused on "understanding, interacting with, and serving empowered customers" are the ones noticing a difference in their bottom line. These companies are using the same technology they once used to make their employees' lives more convenient as a means for transferring that convenience to their customers.

This shift is turning information technology into business technology, turning WCM into digital experiences (DX). By shifting their focus from mass marketing to the individual digital experience, companies like Amazon, Target, and Pizza Hut are tailoring their message according to the interaction: Is this a first time visitor? Or has this visitor already purchased something? What was it they purchased? How close is the visitor to a location, and what can we offer them to entice them to visit?

In the age of the customer, consumers demand contextual relevance combined with immediacy. They are open to letting you know more about them, so that you can make their lives easier. It's up to both IT and business leaders to work together to ensure the step forward from WCM to DX and drive business value. It's time to stop focusing on what your technology does and instead focus on how you can use it to uncover ways to differentiate your company in the marketplace.

Bob Egner is VP of Product Management and Marketing for Episerver.

Form Building

Content management is usually about content *output*; however, most systems have some methods for handling content *intake*, via the generation of forms.

When creating forms, an editor has two main areas of concern:

- Generating the form interface
- Handling the form data once it's submitted

In both cases, the range of possible functionality is wide, and edge cases abound. The market does well at supporting the mainstream use cases, but cases on the edges are often ignored or poorly implemented. The result is usually systems that work for simple data collection, but feel constraining for power editors trying to push the envelope.

Form building in CMSs drives significant overlap between editors and developers. The line between a simple data intake form and a data-driven application can become blurry. Editors might think that form building gives them the ability to do complicated things with data intake and processing, when rarely is that actually true.

Form Editing Interfaces

Editors use two main styles of system to create forms:

- A simple form editor, which allows the insertion and configuration of form fields to allow for content intake.
- A type of "reverse content management," where content to be collected is modeled as a content type and the interface presented to the user is, in effect, "reversed," with the user seeing the edit/creation interface, rather than the output. Unknowingly, users are creating managed content objects with their form input. (e.g., we might create a content type for "Contact Us Data," and the visitor would see the creation form for that and would actually be creating a content object from the type by completing the form).

The former is vastly more common than the latter, and quite a bit more useful. Generation of input forms is usually an editorial task, while content modeling is a developer task. Expecting editors to model content to represent intake from visitors might be too much to ask.

Form editors operate in varying levels of structure:

- A minority are based on rich text editors that allow the free-form insertion of form fields like any other HTML-based element. These are very flexible, allowing for the creation of highly designed forms. Form fields are simply placed alongside information, such their labels and help text, like any other rich, designed content.
- Most editors, however, are structured, meaning users are walked through the process of adding form fields with their accompanying labels and help text. The fields are then rendered in sequence, via a template.

In the latter (and far more common) case, editors can "Add a Form Field" and specify information similar to the following:

- Field type (text box, multiline text box, date picker, drop-down list, checkbox, etc.)
- Field name/label
- Help or additional text
- Validation rules
- Error messages
- Default value

These fields are ordered, then generated in a templated format. This usually generates clean forms that comply with style guidelines, but editors can find it constraining from a design perspective. For example, seemingly simple needs like having two fields stacked next to each other horizontally might not be supported (vertical stacking is a common restriction with form rendering).

Forms Can Be Stylistically Complex

We don't often take note of the fact that forms can be visually complex. For each element, there's often (1) a label, (2) an input element, (3) optional entry instructions, and (4) a validation/error message. And this is repeated for every field on a form. Additionally, all these elements have to work well together (which often means grouping fields by conceptual purpose), flow correctly, and ultimately make sense for the end user.

There's no particular argument about how to read a series of text paragraphs. In comparison, every form is some degree of a UX problem to be solved. Are your editors qualified to solve it?

Whenever you're dealing with user-generated content, edge cases and the sanitizing/validation of data become concerns. As we discussed in Chapter 6, the possible requirements for data formats—and ways for users to circumvent and otherwise abuse them—are almost infinite.

Here are some common validation specifications:

- The input is required.
- The input must match a specified format (numeric, a certain number of digits, or a regex pattern).
- The date input (or numeric input) must be within a specified range.
- The input must be from a specified list of options.

(Does this sound like content modeling? It should. You're essentially modeling the intake of data. This is reification at its most basic level.)

Three additional areas of functionality are commonly requested by editors, but poorly supported in the market. They are:

- *Conditional fields*, which display, hide, or change their selection options based on prior input. The classic example is two drop-down menus, where the options of the second change based on the selection made in the first (e.g., selecting a car manufacturer in one drop-down changes the second drop-down to list all the models offered by that manufacturer).

- *Multipart forms*, which allow users to complete one section of a form, then somehow move to a second section that adds to the data collected by the first. Even more complex, the sections might be conditional, so that the values selected in the first section will dictate what options are offered in subsequent sections (or whether subsequent sections are offered at all).
- *Form elements configured by content*, where the options offered in drop-down menus, radio buttons, or checkbox lists are driven by content data. For example, a class signup form might show a list of classes pulled from content objects stored in the CMS.

These options again bring into focus (or blur further) the line between editorial and developer control. At what point does the complexity of a form cross over from something an editor can handle to something a developer must implement? The line is not clear, but it is quite firm—editors usually don't know where the edges are until they stumble on a requirement that cannot be implemented.

Form Data Handling

Once a form collects data and validates it, a decision needs to be made on what to do with it. Common options include:

- The data can be emailed to a specified set of addresses.
- The data can be stored in the CMS for retrieval, viewing, and exporting.
- The data can be sent to a specified URL, usually as an HTTP POST request or, less commonly, or as a web service payload.

Most systems will allow you to select the first two in parallel.

The third option, while seemingly offering limitless integration possibilities, again causes the form creation and management process to become bifurcated between editors and developers. While an editor can create a form and send the data to a web service that has been developed for it, this limits the value of creating the form editorially in the first place. The web service is likely expecting the data in a specific format, and if an editor changes the form and the resulting data it transmits, there's a good chance that the web service will not function correctly without a developer having to modify it.

The best advice for working with form builders and handlers might be to simply lower your expectations. Your goal should be simple data collection and handling and not much more. Too many editors assume form builders will allow them to create applications or otherwise play a part in complex enterprise data integration *without any developer oversight or assistance*. This is an unreasonable assumption and always leads to unmet expectations.

Simple data collection is quite possible, but an application development platform that completely removes the need for custom development in the future is just not an expectation that can reasonably be met.

Integrating External Form Engines

There are a number of well-adopted form engine services, such as Wufoo (*http://wufoo.com*) and FormSite (*http://formsite.com*), and even Google Docs can be adapted for this purpose. All these services offer ways to embed forms into existing sites.

Perhaps a better way to approach form building is to use an external service and render the forms as some type of embedded content. Editors can create their forms in another service, then embed a reference to the form ID in the managed content, which will render the necessary JavaScript to display the form.

URL Management

In the early days of CMSs, content URLs were commonly "ugly" and betrayed the internal working of the system. For example:

```
/articles/two_column_layout.asp?article_id=354
```

This was in opposition to "friendly" or "pretty" URLs that looked like they were manually crafted from file and folder names, and which imparted some semantic[16] value to the content. For instance:

```
/articles/2015/05/politics/currency-crisis-in-china
```

Today, it's quite rare to find a CMS that doesn't implement some method of semantic URLs. In the case of systems with a content tree (discussed in Chapter 7), these URLs are usually formed by assigning a segment to each content object, then aggregating the segments to form the complete URL (and perhaps adding a language indicator to the beginning).

So, if your tree looked liked this:

- Articles (segment: "articles")
- 2015 ("2015")
- May ("05")
- Politics ("politics")

---

16 "Semantics" is the study of meaning. To describe something as "semantic" is to say that it provides some larger meaning beyond its original or obvious purpose. The actual purpose of a URL is simply to identify content. A *semantic* URL provides some indication of what the content *is*, in addition to identifying it.

- The Currency Crisis in China ("currency-crisis-in-china")

it would result in the URL displayed second.

Other systems without a content tree invariably have some logic for forming URLs, whether by content type, menu position, or folder location. It's rare to find a CMS that doesn't account for semantic URLs in some form.

In most systems, the URL segment for a particular content object is automatically formed based on the name or title of the object, but is also editable both manually and from code. An editor might manually change the URL segment for some reason, and a developer might write code to change it based on other factors (to insert the date to ensure uniqueness, for example).

Forming the URL based on a content object's position in the geography is convenient, efficient, and most of the time results in a correct URL (or at least one that isn't objectionable). However, the "tyranny of the tree" applies here as well—the URL is formed by the tree, but an object might be in some position in the tree for reasons other than the URL, which makes it problematical to form the URL from its position.

For example, our news article example might have been organized in that particular manner (under a year object, then a month object, then a subject object) for convenience in locating content administratively, or for other reasons related to permissions or template selection. However, this organization forces a URL structure as a byproduct, and what if you want something different? For example:

```
/articles/currency-crisis-in-china-0515
```

In this case, for whatever reason, you want the title of the article to form most of the URL, with the year and month appended to the end. Effectively, the year and month need to be "silent" in the URL, and you need to adjust the article's specific URL segment to add the date. Some systems will allow for this, and some won't.

Historical URLs, Vanity URLs, and Custom Redirects

URLs are part of the permanent record of the Internet. They are indexed by search engines, sent in emails, posted to social media, and bookmarked by users. So, changing a URL might introduce broken links. Additionally, when the URL is formed by the tree, changing the URL segment of an object "high" on the tree will necessarily change all the URLs for the content below it, which might amount to *thousands* of pages. Carelessness can be catastrophic in these situations.

Some systems will account for this by storing historical URLs for objects, so if an object's URL changes, the system will remember the old URL and can automatically redirect a request for it. Other systems won't do this, and this functionality has to be added manually.

Editors might also want to provide a completely alternate URL for a content object—for example, a shorter URL to use for other media (print or signage), or a URL with marketing significance for content deep in the site that might have a less advantageous URL naturally.

For example:

```
www.mywebsite.com/free-checking
www.mywebsite.com/signup
```

In these cases, an alternate URL can sometimes be provided that either produces the content directly, or redirects the user to the content. If the former, the content might still be available under the natural URL as well, which raises the question of which URL the site itself uses when referencing the content in navigation.[17]

In addition to reasons of vanity, editors might want alternate URLs for their content to account for vocabulary changes. For example, when the name of your product has changed, and the old name is in 100 different URLs, this presents a marketing problem. Other situations might be to continue to provide access to content after a site migration. In these cases, a series of alternate URLs for a content object might be required in order to provide for continuity.

Some systems will allow for storage of alternate URLs with content, while others might provide an interface to maintain data that maps old URLs to new URLs. Some systems might redirect automatically in the event of a 404, while other systems will have to wire up these redirects manually, usually by including lookup and redirection code in the execution of the 404 page itself. (This means the code only executes and redirects in the event of an old URL access that would otherwise return a 404.)

Multisite Management

If you want to deploy a second website using a CMS that supports multiple sites, you can choose between two solutions:

- Stand up a completely separate instance of the software (on the same server, or even on another server). The new instance of the CMS in question will have no knowledge of, or relation to, the existing website.
- Host the second website inside the existing instance of the CMS. This website will have a more intimate knowledge of the first website, and might be able to share content and assets with it.

---

17 There might also be negative SEO implications to having the same content available under more than one URL.

Hosting more than one website in the same CMS instance can, in theory, reduce your management and development costs by sharing data between the two websites. Items that are often shared include:

- *Content objects*, such as images or other editorial elements. Your two websites might share the same privacy policy, for example, or display the same news releases.
- *Users*, either editorial or visitors. The same editors might be working on content in both sites, and users might expect the same credentials to work across sites.
- *Code*, including backend integration code and templating code. The sites might share functionality, and the ability to develop it for one site and reuse it on another can be a significant advantage.

However, it's hard to generalize about whether or not this is advantageous, because two sites in the same CMS instance might have a wide range of relationships. In some situations, sharing is an advantage, while in others it's a liability.

On one extreme, the second site might just be a reskinning of the first. It might have the exact same content and architecture, just branded in a slightly different way.[18] In this case, sharing editors, content, and code is extremely advantageous.

On the other end of the scale, the second site might be for an entirely different organization (perhaps you're a third party providing SaaS-like CMS hosting). In this case, sharing the same CMS instance is likely to be more trouble than it's worth since *preventing* the sharing of editors, content, and code will be far more important than sharing any of it, and will require policing and increased code complexity.

Somewhere in the middle is the most common scenario: the second site is for the same organization, so sharing editors is beneficial, and the second site requires *some* of the content of the main site, which can also be helpful. But the second site will also bring a lot of unique content, functionality, and formatting, to the point that sharing code and templating is not feasible. This is becoming more common as marketing departments support larger campaigns with individual microsites that are intentionally quite different from the main site in terms of style and format.

Additionally, the second site might need content modeling changes, so sharing content types will be difficult. For instance, if your microsite has a right sidebar on its pages (and the main site does not), how do you handle that? Do you add a Right Sidebar attribute to the Text Page content type for the entire installation, and just ensure

---

18 So-called "affinity sites" are common. My company once performed an implementation for an organization that sold branded financial products. They had 86 individual websites in the same CMS installation, all of which shared 90% of the same content, with just styling changes and minor content changes to differentiate them.

that editors of the main site know that it doesn't apply to them? Or do you create a new content type for the microsite, and suffer through the added complexity of maintaining both Main Site Text Page and Microsite Text Page content types? What happens when the *next* microsite needs to launch with another slightly different content model?

The resulting confusion can make multisite management difficult. The core question comes back to what level of sharing between the two sites is advantageous, and how the CMS makes this easier or more difficult. Organizations have been known to force through a multisite CMS installation on dogmatic principle ("We *should* be able to do this!") when simply setting up another site instance would have been less work and resulted in a better experience for both editors and users.

Reporting Tools and Dashboards

Two things that content editors and managers are consistently looking for are control and peace of mind. Many CMSs are implemented because the organization is unsure of how much content it has, and what condition that content is in. There's a distinct lack of clarity in most organizations about their content, and the metaphor of "getting our arms around our content" comes up often.

For these reasons, simple reporting goes a long way. Editors and content managers *love* to see reports that give them an overhead view of their content. For example, many organizations would like to simply see a list of all the image files in their CMSs not being used by any content that can be safely deleted.

Reporting tends to be glossed over by vendors for two reasons:

- Like all editorial tools, it affects a smaller audience of people (you have fewer editors than visitors), so it can fade in importance compared to more public-facing functionality.
- Developing reporting tools can be frustrating because there are an infinite number of reports that an editor or manager could request. It's virtually impossible to predict what someone might want, so it becomes a huge bundle of edge cases.

Many systems offer reporting dashboards or tools to provide insight into content residing in the system. These systems will usually come with a set of preconfigured reports for common reporting needs. Some examples are:

- Content in draft
- Content scheduled for publication
- Expired content
- Content with broken hyperlinks

- Pending workflow tasks assigned to you
- Workflow states that have been pending for longer than a specified time period

While this is certainly valuable information, no system can anticipate the level of reporting required by any individual user. All it takes is one editor to say, "Well, I really just want to see *articles in the politics section* that are in draft, not everything else" to render a canned report useless.

A lot of reporting is simply ad hoc.[19] The ultimate level of functionality in this space would be for an editor to simply ask a plain-language question of the content repository, Siri-style: "Repository, show me all of the articles in the politics section that have a status of *Draft*." Clearly, technology hasn't caught up to this need just yet, so queries like this would have to be converted to some search format to allow for this level of reporting.

Some systems might have an interface to develop reports. However, the type and range of possible queries are so varied, that a completely generalized interface would be far too complex—take another look at the screencap of the Drupal Views interface from Chapter 7 (Figure 7-10), and increase the complexity an order of magnitude or more.

Additionally, some editors simply don't understand all the intricacies of their content or query logic enough to be trusted to build a report they can depend on. If they don't understand that content Pending Approval can also technically be considered to be in Draft, then they might construct and depend on a report that's fundamentally invalid.

In these cases, a competent API (as discussed in the previous section) coupled with a solid reporting framework is the best solution. Developers who have good searching tools and a framework to quickly build and deploy reports can hopefully respond quickly to editors' needs for developing reports when required.

Content Search

We've discussed variants of search in prior sections—in Chapter 7 we discussed searching for content as a method of aggregation, and we just discussed searching in terms of a system's API or reporting. However, search in these contexts was "parametric" search, or searching by parameter.

This is an exact, or "hard," search. If you want a list of all content published in 2015, reverse-ordered by date, then that's a very clear search operation that's not subject to interpretation. The year—2015 in this case—is a clear, unambiguous parameter, and a

---

19 *Ad hoc* is Latin for "for this purpose," and generally means "something done for a specific or particular reason without prior planning."

content object either matches it or doesn't. The ordering is also unambiguous—dates can easily be reverse-ordered without having to resort to any interpretation.

Content search is the opposite. This is the searching that users do for content—the ubiquitous search box in the upper-right corner of the page. This is a "soft" search, which is inexact by design. The goal is to interpret what the user wants, rather than do exactly what the user says. The results provided should be an aggregation of content related to the query—even if not exactly matching the query—and ordered in such a way that the closest match is at the top.

The Science of Information Retrieval

Information retrieval (IR) is a long-standing field of study. Entire college courses and even advanced degrees are offered in IR, and tens of thousands of pages of theory exist on the subject. The discipline of turning a language-based query into a mathematical formula and using that to evaluate bodies of text is an area of science that has been studied for decades.

Keep in mind that Google, one of the most valuable companies in the world, was fundamentally based on an IR theory that Larry Page and Sergey Brin developed while students at Stanford.[20] In this sense, IR has been solely responsible for billions and billions of dollars in corporate value.

I mention this just to put the discipline in context. IR exists far apart from content management, and has been studied and implemented for far longer than content management. Since search is a subfeature of a CMS, it might be tempting to think that IR is a subdiscipline of content management, when the exact reverse is far more true. Thus, it's not realistic to assume that every CMS platform will also provide Google-level search capabilities on top of all the other features it has to implement.

Search can be very vague and idiosyncratic to implement. Editors and content managers often have specific things they want to see available, and this is exacerbated by "the Google Effect," which postulates that anything Google does simply increases our expectation of having that feature in other contexts. Google offers spellchecking, so this must be a simple feature of search, right? Google does related content, so why can't we?

---

20 "The PageRank Citation Ranking: Bringing Order to the Web," (*http://ilpubs.stanford.edu: 8090/422/1/1999-66.pdf*) January 29, 1998. Interesting side note: the original patent for this was actually owned by Stanford itself. See "Method for Node Ranking in a Linked Database," (*http://patft.uspto.gov/ netacgi/nph-Parser?patentnumber=6285999*) September 4, 2001.

Requested features of content searching can include any of the following:

Full-text indexing
Return results for nonadjacent terms (for example, content that includes the phrase "fishing in the lake" will match when someone searches for "lake fishing").

Spellchecking and fuzzy query matching
Understand search terms that *almost* match and account for them.

Stemming
Conjugate verbs and normalize suffixes (for example, a search for "swimming" also returns results for "swim" and "swam").

Geo-searching
Search for locations based on geographic coordinates—either distance from a point, or locations contained within a "bounding box."

Phonetic or Soundex matching
Calculate how a word might sound and search for terms that sound the same.

Repository isolation
Search only a specific section of the content geography.

Synonyms and authority files
Specify that two terms are similar and should be evaluated identically.

Boolean operators
Allow users to add AND, OR, and NOT logic to their queries.

Biasing
Influence search results by increasing the score for content related to a specific search term, and perhaps allow editors or administrators to change bias settings from the interface.

Result segregation
Allow for the visual separation of specific content at the top of the results.

Related content searching
Suggest content related to the content a user is searching for ("show me more like this").

Type-ahead or predictive searching
Attempt to complete a user's search term in the search box while the user types.

Faceting or filtering
Let users refine their searches to specific parameter values (this represents a mixing of parametric and content search paradigms).

Search analytics and reporting
    Track search terms, result counts, and clickthrough on result pages.

Stopwords
    Remove common words from indexed content.

Some of these might seem bizarre or esoteric, but this is simply because most users don't realize that they're implemented in search engines without being announced or obvious. These technologies have been advanced to the level that they've become an inextricable part of our expectation of how search works.

Now consider the hapless CMS vendors who have to implement and duplicate these features in their systems, out of the box. Commercial search systems exist that rival and exceed the complexity of many content management systems. The average CMS vendor will never be able to compete, especially considering that search isn't the core function of their product.

For this reason, search is likely the feature most often implemented outside the CMS itself. Large CMS implementations usually have search services provided by some other platform, not built into the CMS itself. This has exacerbated the position of the CMS vendors—since many customers look elsewhere for search, there is even less incentive for vendors to spend a lot of time working on it.

This is magnified even further by the difficulty of evaluating search effectiveness. When we see a page of search results, how often do we spend time evaluating whether or not it's accurate, or whether or not the results are in the most correct order? By design, this type of search is fuzzy and inexact, so we're likely to simply accept the default results as optimal since we assume the vendor knows more than we do. Vendors will often simply allow (or even encourage) users to continue to think this.

The result is that search is a feature where CMS vendors simply seek to "check the box." They usually implement search superficially, just so they can say their products have it. They hope that their implementations will suffice for 90% of customers (which is often true), and assume those who have more advanced needs will use another product for search.

Finally, understand that the underlying search technology is only one part of the user's search experience. An enormous amount of the value from search is driven by the user interface. How are the results displayed? How does the predictive search work? How well can users refine their queries? These are fundamentally user experience problems that a searching system cannot solve, and that are fairly specific to the implementation. It's always a bit dangerous for a CMS vendor to add client interface functionality because it runs a very real chance of conflicting with the customer's design or UX standards (remember the discussion about "infiltrating the browser" from Chapter 9).

What support can the CMS offer in these situations? The most crucial is a clear API that allows developers to customize search features as the editors and content managers desire and as the users need. Alternatively, the CMS needs to provide hooks and events to which a developer can attach an external system to allow for searching to be powered by a separate product.

Lucene

Most systems implementing advanced full-text search are using an open source technology called Lucene.[21] Lucene is a search indexing and retrieval system released in 1999. It is the de facto industry standard for text search and is in wide use across the Internet as a whole.

Lucene is wrapped by two major open source search servers: Solr and Elasticsearch. These systems provide a vast range of functionality, and it's very common for vendors to either use them behind the scenes, or offer tools to integrate with them directly.

User and Developer Ecosystem

This might seem to be an odd "feature" with which to round out this chapter, but *the support and development community surrounding a CMS platform is perhaps its most important feature.* There is simply little substitute for the support, discourse, and contributions of a thriving community of users and developers who assist others.

Vendors can help or hamper this effort. Most vendors will provide an official community location for their users through forums and code-sharing platforms. If a vendor does not, one might spring up organically, though its existence might not be known outside a smaller group.

Vendors can further support the community by participating in it. Several CMS community forums are patrolled in part by the developers behind the products, which provides a backchannel support mechanism and, perhaps more importantly, gives these developers a front-row seat to observe the struggles of its users and the ways in which the product should be developing to meet their needs.

Developers contributing code to the community is a huge advantage that can be measured in raw budget. You are often not the first organization to try to solve a particular problem, and tested, vetted code for your exact situation might already exist,

---

21 Yes, the name is unique. Doug Cutting, the original developer, took inspiration from his wife's middle name, which was her maternal grandmother's first name. It appears that the last time "Lucene" was even vaguely popular as a girl's name in the United States was in the 1930s.

saving you the expense of (re)building it. (I maintain that there are few problems that a contributed Drupal module doesn't already exist to solve.)

When evaluating a CMS, evaluate the community in parallel. It will likely have an outsized impact on your experience and satisfaction with the platform.

 Interestingly, the question-and-answer site Stack Overflow (*http://stackoverflow.com*) is becoming home to many impromptu software support communities based around its use of tags.

For instance, at the time of this writing, various permutations of the tag "drupal" have been assigned to over 30,000 questions on Stack Overflow. My own experience has shown that developers experienced in a particular system or library will monitor relevant tags and pick out questions to provide support and answers for.

In the future, CMS vendors may find that their official support communities and forums are increasingly being bypassed by ad hoc, spontaneous groups of developers that come together on sites like Stack Overflow.

CHAPTER 11

APIs and Extensibility

The customization of a CMS is accomplished on two levels. There's templating, which is fully expected in almost every implementation and is handled by a combination of HTML and templating code. Then there are deeper customizations to change or add to the operation of the CMS itself. These customizations are normally done in the native language of the CMS (PHP, C#, Java, etc.).

Editors might assume that the extensibility of the CMS applies only to developers, but it actually has a significant impact on the entire team. When developers respond to an editor's request by saying, "We can't do that," it's often because the extensibility of the CMS has failed them in some way, and they simply have no way to accomplish what the editor wants to do.

Some systems have elegantly designed methods of accessing content and limitless ways of manipulating it, while others are clunky and frustrating and almost seem to be working *against* the developers, rather than with them. Some systems are designed from the ground up to be programming platforms that incorporate and cooperate with code developed by the integrator. Other systems are closed off from this to some degree, either intentionally due to architecture limitations (multitenant SaaS, for example), or because of the product design.

Ultimately, the extensibility of a CMS can be traced back to a core question: did the vendor expect anyone to extend it? I've worked with CMS vendors who were surprised to find out what we were trying to do with their systems. Some of them just never expected that a developer might try to work with the system in a particular way, either due to naïveté or due to the targeting of a different use case. Other systems are little more than raw APIs against which it's expected the integrators will implement their own interfaces and functionality.

I'm using the term "API" loosely in this discussion. The API is technically the attachment points available from code. In a larger sense, all of the extensibility points—code, events, web services, etc.—are often referred to collectively as the API of a system. The functionality in this chapter might be more accurately described as the "extensibility model" of a CMS.

The Code API

The application programming interface (API) behind any software product is the set of programming tools that a developer is given to work with content from code.

For example, here's some code from Episerver to retrieve the title of a page of content in C#:

```
var repo = ServiceLocator.Current.GetInstance<IContentRepositoryService>();
var myPage = repo.Get<TextPage>(new ContentReference(123));
var title = myPage.Property["PageTitle"].Value;
```

The concepts represented in this code—the existence of the repository as an injected service, the content object available as strongly typed TextPage object, the identification of content by numeric ID, the properties of content represented by a keyed dictionary—represent the API available for this particular CMS. The underlying language is C#, but the API is the vocabulary and tools provided to C# to work with Episerver.

For comparison, here's the same general code in Concrete5 (PHP):

```
$my_page = Page::getByID(123);
$title = $page->getAttribute('PageTitle');
```

In Magnolia (Java, using JCR):

```
Session session = MgnlContext.getJCRSession("myWorkspace");
Node myPage = session.getNodeByIdentifier(123);
String title = myPage.getProperty("pageTitle").getString();
```

And in Plone (Python):

```
from plone import api
my_page = api.content.get(UID=123)
title = my_page.page_title
```

The specifics are clearly different, but the general goal and result are the same. The API is the set of tools available to developers from code. (It's worth noting that the preceding code samples are from APIs generally considered to be quite competent. Less capable APIs would have less elegant samples.)

Recently, I've been teaching my 14-year-old daughter how to drive.[1] During this process, I've identified an aspect of driving that I really never noticed before: *you need to be predictable.* A goal as a driver is to do what other people expect you to do. A lot of what happens on the road involves other people making assumptions about what you're planning to do. To be unpredictable is to be unsafe.

The same is true of an API. Consistency and predictability are key. An API should have a consistent interface that a developer can predict. This has actually been named the Principle of Least Astonishment.[2] The ability of a developer to predict how an API might work and what functionality it can offer is of huge benefit when extending a system.

The dynamics of general software development is a topic far beyond the scope of this book, but the quality of the API of any piece of software is driven by how the software was built over time. Software is often built haphazardly, and the API evolves as needed—a product manager or sales rep says, in a panic, "We need feature X to sell the product!" and the development team hurriedly writes feature X, changing the API along the way in whatever way it has to.

A more reasonable development team plans and writes the API *first*, so it has the capacity to anticipate the needs of the product and sales teams, and new features fit into the larger logical model and philosophy of how the CMS models and manages its content. This software tends to be written proactively from the API outward, instead of reactively from the "feature of the day" inward. The API drives the features, not the other way around.

Reality Check

Clearly, this is an idealized description of the process. The fact is, no software product of any significant size is uniformly developed and uniformly adheres to the same standard of quality.

Different teams work on different parts of the system, other companies are acquired and their code is integrated, and technology evolves and renders some parts of the software obsolete or suboptimal. As a result, even the most elegantly architected software has some dark, murky corners that the development team is intending to clean out at some point.

---

1 Yes, you can drive at 14 in South Dakota. This revelation is often greeted with abject horror by people in more restrictive parts of the country.

2 Additionally, usability expert Don Norman has referred to the "conceptual model" of something, which is the mental understanding of how a user expects it to work. Norman was speaking about consumer products, but the same thing is true of an API: the system should strive to work the way most developers expect it to work.

Evaluating APIs can be difficult. Occasionally, an API that appears to be competent has an idiosyncrasy buried deep inside it that a development team runs into at 3 a.m. while trying to get a change out the door and it stops them dead in their tracks.

To mitigate this, it's helpful when a CMS adopts a known development framework and leverages its tools, conventions, and philosophies, as that gives developers some measure of familiarity with it from the start.

For example:

- Many .NET systems are based entirely on the ASP.NET MVC framework. These systems are MVC applications first and just happen to have a CMS behind them. Any .NET developer with some understanding of the styles and conventions of MVC will immediately be right at home.
- Many PHP systems are adopting the Symfony MVC framework to handle the basic tasks of routing and data management, making extension of those systems quite easy for existing Symfony developers.

When trying to determine the competence of the underlying API, the only reasonable method is a code-level walkthrough for your developers by a vendor's technical team. You should require answers to at least the following questions:

- How do you retrieve content from code? Once you have content in code, how can you manipulate it and save a new version?
- How granular can code-level retrieval be? How many different ways can you search for content? Can you get a list of content based on X different criteria and have it ordered by one of more of those criteria?
- How can you create new content from code?
- How can you implement new functionality, which may not even be content-related? How can custom code for your organization live alongside the CMS's code?
- What code-level events, hooks, or triggers are available? When content is published, for instance, can your code detect that event and inject new logic into the process?
- What ability exists to run command-line or scheduled jobs from inside the CMS interface?
- How can the administrative interface be customized to allow for the management of custom functionality?
- Is the API only accessible from code local to the CMS installation, or are there web services or other remote APIs available?

APIs are notoriously idiosyncratic. Once again, there is no Grand Unified Theory of Content Management, so there is no Grand Unified API either.[3]

Additionally, the quality of an API often has no relation to the quality of the product from a user or editor standpoint. Some very slick-looking systems have atrociously difficult APIs behind them that continually frustrate developers, while other systems that appear simplistic have incredible power and elegance from code. (Which, ironically, might be why they look simplistic out of the box—they're simply so easy to customize that most customers do so considerably.)

Again, the only way to ensure and validate the competence of a CMS API is for your developers to actually work with it.

Event Models

One of the problems with any packaged software is inserting logic into it, so that custom code will execute amongst the system's core code. One solution would be to dig into the source code, and just paste new code in places where you want it to execute. Clearly, however, this opens up numerous problems of maintainability and stability, not to mention that source code is simply not provided with many commercial systems.

A more manageable way to achieve this result is by using what's known as an *event model*. Event-based programming is not at all specific to CMSs; it's a common programming architecture.

When code executes, it can raise events. An *event* is a declaration that something has happened inside the executing software. External code can "subscribe" to these events, in effect saying, "When thing X happens, execute this block of code." This code is generically known as an *event handler*.

Event handlers do not need to know exactly where the events occur in the CMS code. Developers simply need to know what events are available, and what information those events provide when they are raised. Any code inside the CMS could raise the event, and so long as an event handler is subscribed, it will execute. More than one event handler might be subscribed to an event, and they will normally execute in the order they were subscribed.

Events usually provide information to a handler about what has occurred. This information might simply be a notification, so that code can be written to take action

---

3 Though attempts have been made. Content Management Interoperability Services (CMIS) and the Content Repository API for Java (JCR) are both attempts to unify the API-level handling of content. They have met with varying degrees of success and have limited implementations in the marketplace, mostly in larger, enterprise systems.

when something occurs. Other events might provide information that the event handler can change. In these cases, the event is giving the subscribing code the opportunity to change how the system functions by hooking into code and changing values as necessary. In effect, the code is saying, "I'm about to perform task X. Before I do this, would you like to give me any advice?"

Most systems will provide some event model to which your custom code can subscribe. There is no standard list of events that a CMS should raise, but most events will be based around the changing state of content during its lifecycle. From inception to final deletion, a content object might raise dozens of events.

Some examples (referenced events are invented, but common):

- A website is heavily cached by a content delivery network (CDN) to provide faster content delivery times around the world. Whenever new content is published, the CDN needs to be notified of the URL of the affected content so that its cache can be cleared and it can retrieve the updated content. For example, an event handler could subscribe to the "After Content Published" event and make a call to the CDN's API with the URL of the published content.

- The editor-in-chief is getting frustrated with editors using acronyms instead of full names. An event handler could subscribe to the "Before Content Saved" event and be provided with content that was about to be saved to the repository. The event handler could scan the text for acronyms and replace them (for example, changing the text string "FBI" to "Federal Bureau of Investigation"). The corrected text would be saved to the repository instead.

- Pricing for events is not announced until 30 days prior to the event. Rather than build and enforce this logic in dozens of places in the templates (and trust template developers to always use it), a developer instead subscribes to the "Attribute Displaying" event. When the requested attribute is Price, and the Start Date is more than 30 days away, an attribute value of "Not Available" is returned.

It's common for two events to "bookend" code. A "before" event will be raised before the code, often providing information to handlers that can be changed to affect how the ensuing code will run. The code will execute, then an "after" event will be raised. The same information will usually be provided to the after event, but modifying it will have no effect.[4]

---

4 In some systems, an "ing/ed" convention is used. Before events are "ing" and after events are "ed" (e.g., "Content Publishing" and "Content Published").

If events seem suspiciously like workflow, that's not entirely wrong. The differences are subtle:

- Editors do not directly invoke events, like they might with a workflow. An event occurs indirectly, usually as a result of some action taken on content.
- Events execute at a single moment in time. They normally do not create a persistent process that outlives the event itself.
- Events usually force the calling code to wait for them to complete execution. Calling code executes subscribed event handlers in order, waiting for each to complete, before it is allowed to continue.
- Events have no user interface, as they neither expect nor allow user input.

Some things accomplished with workflow might instead be implemented in event handlers, and vice versa.

 Since event handlers usually run in the same process as the CMS itself and block the calling code from continuing until they're finished, a poorly implemented event handler can bring an entire system down. Either the event handler throws an error that ends execution completely, or it takes so long to execute that the system feels sluggish. Implement with care, especially when subscribing to frequent events like the retrieval of an attribute value.

In some systems, events are called "hooks" (to represent the idea of "hooking into" things that happen in the CMS code); in other systems they're called "triggers" or "actions."

As a way of illustration, here's an example of subscribing to an event in Episerver (in C#) to execute a method called NotifyCDN after content is published (the first of our earlier examples):

```
DataFactory.Instance.ContentPublished += NotifyCDN;
```

(Note that this is standard C# event-based programming syntax, not anything specific to Episerver.) In this instance, the event handler (the method NotifyCDN) would be provided with a reference to the content that was just published, so that it could find its URL and send an invalidation request to the CDN.

Sitecore uses XML configuration files to specify event handlers:

```
<event name="item:published">
  <handler type="EventHandlers, MySiteAssembly" method="NotifyCDN"/>
</event>
```

WordPress allows developers to specify events by adding "actions" (in PHP):

```
add_action ( 'publish_post', 'notify_CDN' );
```

Event-based programming is not at all specific to CMSs, but rather is an important way for developers to extend the functionality of any system. An event model allows a clear, maintainable way for custom code to be injected into an otherwise closed system.

Perspective: The CMS as a Digital Hub

by Allan Thraen

When I first joined the world of content management, I was expecting it to be a rather boring one. I mean, a CMS is basically a database where you put content in, you edit it, and you pull it out and present it. Big deal, right?!

But what I quickly learned was that as our world becomes more and more online, the role of the WCMS grows from being "just content management" to being the naturally evolving platform the entire business sometimes spins around.

Where websites used to be static brochure-ware, they are becoming a platform for marketing, sales, and customer service. To support this, the WCMS needs to be connected to all the relevant systems: CRM, marketing automation, enterprise resource planning, in-house databases and systems, social media, analytics, business intelligence, search engines, ecommerce, and so on.

The extensibility model of the CMS is essential to ensure that there are good connections to all these other systems. Sure, most CMSs will come with a number of connectors available—either out of the box or as add-ons—but you will often find yourself missing the right connectors to exactly the system you want connected.

A good API and code framework will allow developers to extend the CMS and its administrative interface to be connected in all the places you need to the other business-critical systems as part of the implementation phase.

Imagine you work for an airline about to replace its entire online presence with a new CMS. Aside from the regular implementation work, there are myriad systems you'll want to integrate with:

- You probably have a flight search and booking engine already connected with your flight operations system. That needs to be seamlessly integrated with the CMS in a way that editors can use it and place search or flight-suggestion boxes throughout the site where it makes sense. This will almost always require custom extension of a good API.

- You'll probably want editors writing articles on your website promoting certain destinations to be able to list the current cheapest flight prices to those destinations in their articles dynamically. This requires custom integration to your operations and ticket sales systems.

- When visitors are browsing the site you'll probably want to personalize their content so they only see frequent flyer offers if they are frequent flyers, so you'll need an integration that might very well be custom to your CRM or marketing automation system, or wherever you keep track of your loyalty members.

- After a flight has been purchased you might want to integrate with third-party ad providers to suggest hotel offers or similar to your customers.

Depending on your business, you can imagine how specific integration functionality to your existing systems can improve your online business, improve your conversion rate, or empower visitors to do self-service—and a good API is the underlying key to achieving it.

Allan Thraen is a Technical Fellow with Episerver and a veteran of many integration projects.

Plug-in Architectures

Closely related to the API that a system offers is the ability for customizations to be packaged and distributed, either commercially or via open source solutions. Some systems have vast extensions to their core functionality available through bundles of code variously called plug-ins, add-ons, extensions, components, or modules (we'll use "plug-in").

A "plug-in architecture," therefore, is a set of established API concepts, events, and attachment points that lets a developer create some functionality for a CMS, and then bundle it in some form that can then be installed on another installation of that CMS.

Open source CMSs usually have well-developed plug-in architectures, due to the nature of their development. Open source software is driven by a community of developers, and the plug-in architectures are often created to ensure the integration of new functionality in a uniform way when a large, distributed group of people are contributing. Additionally, the increased user communities of open source systems result in many different people trying many different things. The sheer volume of implementations tends to result in more code spinning off into available plug-ins.

Commercial software, in contrast, has an official organization behind it, and the assumption is that this organization will be providing functionality. Additionally, license fees will naturally reduce the user base compared to open source alternatives, so there will be fewer implementations. Those implementations will be performed by organizations that, on average, tend to be less embracing of open source as a philosophy and more protective of their code.

The number and quality of plug-ins available is usually directly related to the adoption of a particular platform. Systems like WordPress and Drupal have *thousands* of available plug-ins to fulfill almost any requirement. Indeed, for many systems, the most valuable skill a developer can possess is a deep knowledge of what functionality is available through the respective plug-in libraries. A large part of any implementation with these systems is the selection, configuration, and adaption of the most appropriate plug-ins to accomplish the stated requirements.

The downside of plug-ins is issues with security, maintainability, and consistency. When a plug-in is injected into an installation, a third party essentially has access to the environment. The integrator is assuming that this plug-in is reliable, well tested, and doesn't create security holes (inadvertently, or by sinister intent).

 Many security exploits don't target the CMS itself, but instead target common plug-ins, which are usually not subject to the same level of security testing.

Additionally, the implementation is now bound to the plug-in. Once an implementation depends on a plug-in, then it becomes beholden to that plug-in in addition to the core CMS code. If an upgrade for the CMS is available, but a critical plug-in doesn't work with the new version, the upgrade has to wait until the plug-in is updated, replaced, or modified directly (which then divorces it from the original source code, likely rendering it nonupdateable in the future).

Finally, the editorial experience on a site supported by many plug-ins might be inconsistent. You essentially now have a CMS developed by many people who didn't necessarily communicate or plan their functionality to work well together. Most communities have standards and conventions that hopefully are followed by plug-in developers, but you might find plug-ins that deviate considerably from the UX standards and even the core architecture of the system.

I've seen plug-ins that were essentially small applications of their own, just dropped onto the larger CMS without any attempt to integrate with the underlying user experience or design. Working with these plug-ins was almost like working in a completely different software package, somehow embedded inside my CMS. Training and adoption might suffer in these situations.

Some CMS vendors have a process of "certifying" plug-ins, whereby they will inspect a plug-in for security, performance, and compliance with best practices and give it a stamp of approval. This is usually done for a fee, which generally limits it to plug-ins that are sold commercially.

Note that certifying a plug-in doesn't necessarily mean *supporting* it. If something goes wrong with an implementation, the vendor will want to know what plug-ins are installed and will likely be quick to point the finger at one or more plug-ins and simply refer the customer to the plug-in developers for support. And since many plug-ins are open source, there is usually no formal support to speak of.

As with anything, there are advantages and disadvantages, and not all plug-ins are created equal. Some are well known, used by thousands of implementations, and considered almost standard tools necessary when using a particular CMS. Others are just one-off code that a developer somewhere decided someone else might find useful. Make sure you know where your desired plug-in falls on that range.

Core CMS Components as Plug-ins

Some systems consider their plug-in model to be a core part of their architecture, and actually implement large parts of their base functionality as plug-ins to ease the ability to change them when necessary.

Drupal, for instance, bundles its user management features into a plug-in (a Drupal module) called "User." Similarly, basic content functions are handled by a plug-in called "Node" (the description of which innocently states: "Allows content to be submitted to the site and displayed on pages"). Because these are developed as plug-ins, interactions between large sections of the codebase happen in an expected and controlled manner, and developers could conceivably throw away large sections of provided functionality and swap in their own.

Episerver has built its entire administration UI as a plug-in, to ease its ability to upgrade when necessary. An upgrade to the admin UI is now simply a process of updating a plug-in, not the entire core platform.

In most systems, a "plug-in" is some extra functionality to enhance the system. In others, the architecture extends to and defines the communications and interaction paths between large sections of the codebase.

Customizing the Editorial Interface

It's often helpful to customize the editorial interface to add implementation-specific functionality. Editors might need additional links, buttons, and reporting information directly in the interface from which they edit content.

These customizations might be global to all editors. For example, seeing Google Analytics data alongside content is often helpful. In other cases, editors might be able to customize the interface just for themselves, by adding gadgets or widgets to provide information they find helpful that others might not.

In many cases, developers will seek to turn off functionality that's not being used to avoid confusion and the need for support. Streamlining the editorial interface as much as possible is helpful, even more so when this can be done on a per-editor basis. As discussed earlier, different editors have different needs, and the ability to display a specific feature for just a few power editors reduces the chance of inadvertent error, and likely makes all editors less nervous about making a mistake.

Customizing Rich Text Editors

Rich text editors might also need configuration and customization. Most systems implement one of two common JavaScript-based, open source rich text editors: TinyMCE or CKEditor. A smaller number of others use commercial editors such as EditLive! by Ephox or RadEditor by Telerik, and an even smaller number implement their own custom rich text editors.

Here are some common customizations:

- Enabling or disabling of buttons on the interface
- Customization of styling information, such as the list of classes or block elements that can be applied
- Configuration of HTML validation or "cleaning" processes, which enforce allowable HTML tags and remove invalid markup
- Enabling or disabling of access to the HTML source
- Customization of various pop-up interfaces, such as the image or table insertion interface
- Adding custom plug-ins, including buttons that execute arbitrary client-side code (a JavaScript function, for example)
- Styling the contents of the rich text editor to match the final site output

Both TinyMCE and CKEditor have well-documented plug-in and extensibility architectures. A CMS using one of these editors should provide some way to load the required files and inject the JavaScript code necessary to load the plug-in on startup.

Repository Abstraction

It's assumed that most of the content in a CMS installation will be stored in the CMS repository itself. However, this doesn't have to be the case.

Some systems will allow for the abstraction of parts of the repository. The code to actually gather the data for content objects is swappable and can be delegated to other code and other sources. Custom code can allow some data to come from other storage sources, and be presented and manipulated just like content that actually lives in the repository. This might happen for only specific content objects or locations in the geography.

For example:

- An organization maintains its news releases in Microsoft SharePoint. The support team also wants these releases displayed on the website. The CMS repository might be abstracted so that a section of the geography (the children of the News page, for example) will actually retrieve content in real time from SharePoint, presenting this information as if the news releases actually resided in the CMS itself. Visitors (and perhaps even editors) might never be aware that this content isn't actually stored in the repository.

- Technical writers store product code samples as Markdown files in Git. The CMS repository might be abstracted to connect to Git in real time and list the files contained within it as child content objects of a Code Samples page.

Users of the Unix operating system might recognize this as the concept of "mounting a filesystem." In Unix, a completely separate filesystem (System B, we'll say) can be mapped to what appears to be a simple directory in System A. Users navigating through System A might enter a certain directory, and—unbeknownst to them—actually be browsing the filesystem on an entirely different machine.

Repository abstraction is essentially the same thing: a section of the repository might "mount" some other system to provide data. Data exchange between the CMS and the source system takes place silently in the background. Some systems can even write data back to the external source, so an editor might change an object in the CMS and not realize he's actually changing data in a completely separate system, somewhere else entirely.

Clearly, this is an advanced feature, and there's a judgment call to be made as to when this is more appropriate than simply importing the content to the repository and updating it when it changes. Depending on an external data source for real-time access raises issues of performance, network latency, security, and stability. However, in cases where external data might be accessed outside the CMS—by making a direct database query using SQL, for instance—abstracting the repository to present that data as content can increase consistency and simplify templating.

Pluggable Authentication

One of the drawbacks of bringing new software into an organization is having a new set of credentials to manage, and for users to remember. One of the easiest ways for users to feel that a system is an integrated part of their organization is to allow them to use the same credentials they use for other systems. Adding yet another set of credentials creates password fatigue, which usually results in sticky notes containing passwords attached to the sides of monitors.

Many CMSs will allow their systems to either be integrated with common methods of authentication, or be swapped entirely for a custom system. Integration with Microsoft's Active Directory is common, as is more generic LDAP integration. Some systems have OAuth, OpenID, or Facebook Connect integration, allowing users to log in by authenticating against their Google or Facebook accounts.

In the event an organization is using a less well-known or even custom authentication system, code can sometimes be developed and provided to the CMS to handle authentication tasks. In these cases, it's clearly incumbent on the implementing developers to provide well-tested code, as the CMS will be only as secure as this code allows. The CMS will communicate only with this custom code, and will assume it's authenticating users in a secure and rigorous manner.

Note that pluggable authentication and shared credentials does not necessarily mean *single sign-on*. To achieve single sign-on, your editors sign into one system and are seamlessly authenticated across multiple other systems—your CMS included, hopefully. Even if you hook your CMS up to your Active Directory provider, the editors will still need to enter their credentials, but they'll be the same credentials that they use everywhere else, which is helpful in itself.

Web Services

Many systems will provide a web service interface to allow remote interaction with the CMS over HTTP. Systems vary by (1) the specific web service protocol used, and (2) the depth of the interaction allowed.

SOAP (Simple Object Access Protocol) was the standard web service protocol for years, but that position has been usurped by REST (REpresentational State Transfer).[5] Likewise, XML has long been the dominant serialization format, but is being displaced by JSON. Most systems will offer some combination of the two variables (XML via SOAP or JSON via REST, or occasionally vice versa).

Some web services are read-only, but other systems strive to provide complete exposure to their APIs over a web services. Some systems go a step further and run their *own* user interfaces from their web service. Abstraction levels in many programming languages and frameworks have advanced to the point where a web service can be accessed via a common API, and even swapped out underneath that.

---

5 Many developers wouldn't call REST a "protocol," but would rather consider it a convention or philosophy.

If a system's web service API falls short, custom web services can be implemented fairly easily. In many cases, there's little difference between a normally templated content object and a REST service request. Templating languages that generate HTML can usually generate XML or JSON just as easily, and creating custom web service endpoints for specific situations is quite common. Some implementations might even deliver XML or JSON versions of any content simply by appending a designated argument to the query string (e.g., `?format=json`).

RSS is also well suited as a simple API for the delivery of content, and benefits from some level of standardization. RSS feeds can be extended with custom, namespaced tags to deliver more than the traditional blog-based feed of content, and RSS is just as adept at delivering aggregations or single content items.

Scheduled or On-Demand Jobs

In many situations, CMS editors and administrators just need to execute arbitrary code, either on demand or scheduled and unattended. This code usually doesn't need user input and has no visual interface component. It is typically intended to perform batch manipulation of content. Many systems will offer some framework for implementing this code, generally referred to as a "job."

For example:

- Many systems will have a job that checks hyperlinks on a scheduled basis. The job will retrieve all content, examine it for external URLs, then send a request to each of those URLs to ensure they're still valid. URLs that are no longer reachable might be flagged for review, added to a report, or emailed to an administrator.

- An editor-in-chief might want to impose strict editorial guidelines to ensure compliance with governance policies. A scheduled job might run every night, find all content changed since the last execution, and process it to ensure governance policies have been followed: images have ALT tags, usages of the company's name are followed by a trademark symbol, periods are only followed by a single space, etc.

- The information security department might require that certain site content be written out to a flat file once per month and entered into an enterprise content management system for auditing by a regulatory agency.

- A product name might change, and all website references must change as well. A job can be developed to review tens of thousands of content objects and change references from the old name. This job can be installed, executed, then removed once the results have been confirmed.

- During content migration (see Chapter 13), the entire migration script might be implemented as an on-demand job. The developer might execute the job, review the results, modify the script, then execute it again.

The API as a Time-Shifted Relationship

A system's API is the "fingerprint" of the vendor's development team. The API is the crumbtrail the vendor leaves for developers using its product to navigate around sticky problems and unique customizations during an implementation.

In a strange way, developers build a kind of time-shifted relationship with the original vendor team through the API. A clean, consistent, well-documented API gives a good impression of the vendor's team. The implementing developers learn to trust them, and gain confidence that requested customizations can actually be achieved. When a user asks if something can be done, the answer becomes, "I'm pretty sure there's a way."

A poor API is the exact opposite. Inconsistent and awkward APIs breed distrust among developers. In some cases, it seems like the API—and, by proxy, the vendor itself—is actually working against them. It's like having a team member who doesn't pull her weight and drags the rest of the team down. Whenever a customization is asked for, the answer becomes, "I'll check, but I doubt it."

In this way, the competence of a system's API is a critical feature that has an outsized influence on the success or failure of an implementation—especially one requiring heavy customization—*not unlike a human member of the team.*

When evaluating a CMS, allow your developers to "interview" the API to see if they want to make it a member of their team. Demand a code-level walkthrough for your developers and gauge their feelings about what they saw. If this relationship fails, the rest of the project might go with it.

PART III

Implementations

CHAPTER 12

The CMS Implementation

I have two teenage daughters. They're obsessed with their future weddings. They've both planned out the perfect day dozens of times. When they ask why I don't get nearly as excited about it as they do, I always respond the same way: "I'm less concerned with your wedding day than I am with the 50 years that come after it."

In the process of building a content-managed website, organizations often get obsessed with finding the right CMS for their needs. They're dazzled by sales demos and starry-eyed over the things they'll do once it's implemented. Emboldened by finding what they consider a flawless piece of technology, they rush into the implementation, then don't understand why the reality of what they wake up with every day doesn't live up to their dreams.

Identifying and acquiring a CMS is only the first part of building a content-managed website. It's like spending hours and hours at the building materials store, identifying and purchasing everything you need to build a house, and having those things delivered to an empty lot. It doesn't matter how many materials you have, or whether or not they are high quality—*someone still has to build a house with them.*[1]

What plays more into the success or failure of a website: the quality of the CMS, or the quality of the implementation? This is a hotly debated question. Can a fantastic CMS be ruined by a terrible implementation? And can a stellar implementation salvage what is an objectively poor CMS?

The answer to both questions is yes. The greatest CMS in the world can be rendered completely useless by a poor implementation, and a below-average CMS can be made

---

[1] A technical reviewer noted: "Without totally overdoing this metaphor, you could extend it to keeping the house clean. Companies implementing a CMS are often like a family building a new house and then never taking out the garbage. When the house gets too smelly, *they just build a new house.*"

surprisingly functional by a creative integrator who is willing to work around short-comings.

 I've long maintained that being forced to work with a particularly poor CMS for many years had more impact on my professional development than any other experience before or since. Seeing things done the wrong way is the best way to learn how to do things the right way, and having to work around immovable (and often irrational) limitations forces people to think creatively in ways they normally wouldn't.

Clearly, you're ideally looking for both: a solid CMS coupled with a solid implementation. Even a simple understanding and acceptance of the fact that the implementation is just as important as the CMS itself will put you in the right frame of mind.

Principle Construction Versus Everything Else

An old adage of project management says if you want to know how long a project will take, "Add up the time you think it will take to complete all the tasks, then double it." While clearly a joke, it's often not far from the truth.

The amount of time required to implement a content management system is always more than the sum of its parts. Planning out every idiosyncrasy of an implementation before you start is not a straightforward process. During the project there will be bumps in the road that will lengthen the required time considerably: changes, hidden requirements, misunderstandings, staff turnover, bugs, and rework.

We tend to underestimate the time required by concentrating on the activities we consider "principle construction," which are, by nature, development-centric. We look through the functionality required to finish the build, add up the implementation time, and think that's everything that needs to be done.

Along the way, we forget things that fall outside the mainstream path. Things like:

- Environment setup, such as development, test, and integration environments, not to mention source control repositories and build servers
- Testing and QA, including the inevitable "fine-tuning" period in the days or weeks directly prior to launch when bug fixes consume the development team
- Content migration (a subject so chronically overlooked that I'll devote an entire chapter to it)
- Editorial and administrator training—the initial editorial team, future team members, and ad hoc training on specific tasks
- Production environment infrastructure planning

- Deployment planning and execution, including initial launch and postlaunch changes
- Documentation, either of the implementation itself or of the project process
- Project management, including progress reporting
- Internal marketing to affected staff and stakeholders
- User transition management, including moving user accounts, ensuring users are notified of changes, and password resets
- Load and security testing
- Transition of SSL certificates
- DNS changes and propagation
- URL redirection

These are all activities outside of principle construction, and they often get left out of estimates as a result. In some projects, the actual development becomes a minority of the work when compared to all the non-development work surrounding it.

That adage of doubling the initial effort estimate perhaps isn't unreasonable after all.

Types of Implementations

At the most general level, CMS implementations can be grouped into three types, based on their relationship with the current website:

CMS only, or "forklift"[2]
> In this case, the goal is for nothing on the website to change—the design, the content, and the information architecture will carry over identically, but the CMS powering the website will be swapped for another (or, less commonly, a statically managed website will have a CMS introduced). In this type of implementation, the current website is the model for the new website.

CMS plus reskin or reorganization
> This is an extension to the forklift implementation where the organization decides to do some light housekeeping, as they're going to the trouble of implementing the CMS. New designs are often applied since templating has to be redone anyway, and a content migration often means that content can be cleaned up or reorganized without considerable extra work. Some things will change, but the changes are limited to styling and editorial, which means the current website is still somewhat relevant as a model.

---

2 Called a forklift because the website is "lifted up" and a new CMS is swapped in "underneath" it.

Complete rebuild

In these cases, the entire website is reenvisioned. The new CMS might be only one part of a larger digital turnover. The website will get a new design, new content, new information architecture, and new functionality—little or nothing of the old site will remain. The CMS implementation often comes after a large content strategy and UX planning phase. Clearly, the existing website is irrelevant as a model for the new website.

While the first type, the forklift implementation, might seem the most simple, it can be deceptively complex because you're now faced with wrapping an existing base of historic functionality around a new CMS. The new system will invariably do things differently than the old CMS, and the website will likely have adapted over time to fit how the old CMS worked. Implementation teams have often found themselves trying to backport existing functionality into a new system to replicate how a website evolved around an old system.

The edge case adage discussed earlier holds true here as well. Given a sufficient amount of time, editors will have found every nook and cranny of a CMS. As mentioned in Chapter 10, any given editor might only use 25% of the total functionality, but every editor might be using a *different* 25%, meaning the editorial team collectively expects *all* of the old functionality to work in the new system, sometimes in the same manner, even if that's an inefficient way of accomplishing some goal.

On the other end of the extreme, a complete rebuild at least gives you flexibility to weigh new functionality against the new CMS that will power it. Weighing new design and functionality requirements against technical feasibility is an expected dynamic to a rebuild project, which gives an implementation team the opportunity to influence plans toward functionality the new CMS will support.

Perspective: The Hidden Challenges of Forklift Projects

by Jeff Eaton

On large projects, decision makers often push for "forklift" migrations to reduce the cost in both dollars and time. That's not an unreasonable goal, especially given the scale and complexity of many organizations' sites. However, as Deane mentions, there are several common pitfalls to watch for if you go down this path.

First, there's the risk of a creeping redesign. Forklift migrations promise time and cost savings because they reuse the navigation, organization, and appearance of the site's existing design. In the real world, though, stakeholders often get cold feet. With all the time and money spent on a migration, they reason, shouldn't they get *something* that's obvious to the average visitor? "Minor updates" to the site's look and feel are suggested, but soon all of the decisions embodied in the old design are being revisited and questioned. Hold the line at purely superficial updates, or invest in a well-planned design process: "sneaking" a redesign in this way is death by a thousand cuts for timelines and budgets.

The second danger is architectural mismatch. Different CMS platforms approach content organization and presentation in different ways. Sometimes, slavishly duplicating the appearance of the old site can force you into odd, uncomfortable workarounds that consume disproportionate time and resources. The logical choice is to tweak the design to fit the new tool's approach, but if that's not done carefully, it can trigger a ripple effect of design complications.

The last and most serious risk is a distorted content model. Ideally, a site's content model serves an organization's business and communication needs, and a design is developed to effectively present that content. When visual design is the focus of early planning (whether it's new wireframes or the current site's look and feel), the modeling process often focuses on duplicating that design's idiosyncrasies and edge cases rather than the big picture. When the time comes for another redesign, those assumptions baked into the content model can make the process much more difficult.

In my experience, true forklift migrations are rare: most successful ones turn into complete redesigns by the time the project is complete. Keeping these risks in mind, however, makes realizing the promised savings much more likely.

Jeff Eaton is a Digital Strategist at Lullabot, Inc.

Preimplementation

Before you implement, you need to take stock of what you have to work with, then use that to develop a plan.

Discovery and Preimplementation Artifacts

The amount of preimplementation documentation depends highly on the level of change planned from the existing website.

For a forklift implementation, there's a possibility of using the current website as a de facto requirements document. When simply swapping the CMS out from under an existing website, a project mandate might simply be to make things function the same as they have in the past. So long as the development team sufficiently understands the inner workings of the current site and someone from the editorial team is available for questions, this might be enough to suffice.

If the website is being reskinned or reorganized, some consideration needs to be paid to how the changes will affect the CMS. If the changes are limited to the design and content alone—and none of these changes require modification to the content model itself—then they might not be relevant to the development effort. For example, the developer doesn't care if the design calls for a serif or sans serif font, or if the content is written in the first- or third-person perspective. The development effort is the same.

Be careful here—design and content changes need to be thoroughly investigated for potential content model changes. Seemingly simple design and content changes might require significant underlying model changes to support, and these changes have an uncanny way of snowballing. Changing thing A suddenly forces changes to thing B and thing C. Changes beget more changes, until, two weeks later, you're changing thing Z and realizing the initial change went much deeper than you thought.

A Single Screw

One of my technical reviewers relayed this anecdote, which is surprisingly similar to many CMS projects:

> It all started when a screw fell out of our old dishwasher. We could have replaced the screw, but decided that the dishwasher was old and was probably going to fail soon anyway. So we bought a new one. The new dishwasher called more attention to our ugly kitchen. So we renovated that—and the dining room that was attached. When that project was finished the view from our new dining room into our old living room was pathetic. So we gut renovated the third floor, moved the kids there. Made one of the kid's rooms a TV room and turned our living room into a nice sitting room...all because of one screw.

What's the single screw of your project?

For a complete rebuild, significant site documentation is required for an effective implementation. At a minimum, the development team will need the following:

- A set of wireframes that displays the layout of each major content type, including all relevant content elements (see Figure 12-1).
- A set of functional requirements (or equivalent annotations to the wireframes) that explains how nonvisual functionality should work, especially navigation and contextual functionality in the surround
- A sitemap showing an overhead view of how all the content fits together and is organized

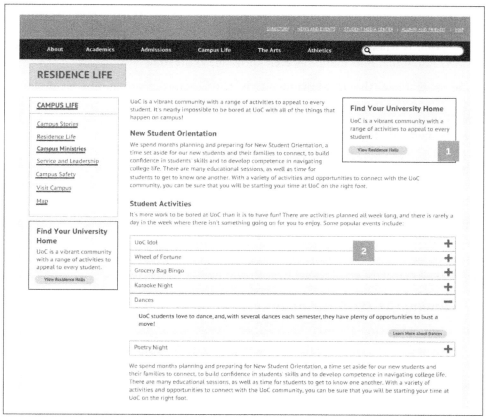

Figure 12-1. A sample wireframe with numbered callouts, which would normally be annotated with nonvisual information about how the elements function—wireframes are helpful to separate content and functionality from the finished design, which can be distracting when developing a technical plan

Depending on the scope of the integrator's responsibilities, they might also need:

- A fully rendered design with all supporting art files
- Frontend HTML/CSS of the implemented design

Over the last half-decade, frontend development has become its own discipline. Implementations used to be achievable with a single set of development skills, but with the advent of responsive design and increased use of client-side technologies, the frontend development is now often assigned its own team. Additionally, many projects will have the frontend development completed before the CMS implementation begins.

The discovery phase of a CMS project is normally handled by a team of content strategists or UX/IA specialists who work with the organization to determine needs. A key point is whether this team needs to work with the knowledge of the intended CMS or not, if that information is even knowable at the time.

Some say that sites should be planned to be CMS-agnostic and that the focus should be on giving the organization the best possible website. However, a more practical school of thought says that if the intended CMS is known, then plans and designs need to be vetted for what can actually be implemented, which means filtering out idealistic and grandiose plans that can't be brought to fruition. Planning a comprehensive personalization strategy, for example, is an expensive waste of time if your CMS doesn't support personalization and you can't integrate the necessary functionality from an external service.

If the intended CMS is known, it's generally wise to have the implementation team review plans and designs for feasibility as they become available. Early discussions about hypothetical functionality can help ground the design team in a firm understanding of which ideas can actually work.

Developing the Technical Plan

There's an old saying among trial lawyers: "Never ask a question you don't already know the answer to." Something similar can be said of implementations: "Don't ever start implementing a wireframe that you don't already have a plan for."

At some point, the implementation team needs to review the preimplementation artifacts and come up with technical plans for everything in them. While it's tempting to try to plan a site from the top down, it's best to start from the bottom up. This means paging through the set of wireframes and asking a lot of questions about each.

These questions need to be answered in some form prior to development. In some cases, the developer will write a formal technical implementation plan (TIP). In other cases, the wireframes are simply reviewed in a "build meeting" to ensure understanding and to make sure there's nothing present that isn't implementable.

For each wireframe, consider the following questions:

- Is there an operative content object present? What type is it? What attributes does it need to support?
- Can a clear line be drawn around the operative content object and the surround? What content will be handled by the object's template, and what content is in the surround?
- Of the content in the surround, what is contextually dependent on the operative content object?

- Of this contextual information, what will be derived from context or geographic position, and what is based on the discrete content present in the object?

- What aggregations are present? Can they be powered through geography alone, or will there need to be secondary structures created to support them?

- What non-content functionality is present? How will this execute alongside the CMS?

- How repeatable do the elements in this wireframe need to be? Are they just for this one page, or do they occur again and again?

- Is this wireframe literal, or simply suggestive of a wide range of possible manifestations? What areas on this wireframe might be swappable by editors?

- How often will this particular content need to be modified? Is this something editors will manage every day, or will this be set on launch and never touched again?

- How much relation is there to future functionality? Should this wireframe be interpreted narrowly as an exact, literal representation of what the site planner wants, or is it indicative or suggestive of other things?

These are all visual questions, driven by what's actually on the wireframe. However, lurking below the surface are several questions about the content represented in the wireframe, which have nothing to do with the wireframe itself:

- What are the URL requirements for this content?

- What are the editorial workflow requirements? Will an editor create this content directly in the CMS interface, or is it coming from somewhere else? What approvals need to be in place for this content?

- Who should have permissions to this content? Who can create it, edit it, or delete it?

- Does the content have to be localized? Into how many languages? What non-text elements (images, for example) will also need to be localized?

- Does this content need to be versioned? Will it need to be archived at some point? In the context of this project and this content, what does that mean?

- What other channels does this content need to be published into? Will this happen on the same schedule? Does it need to happen at any time? Who can initiate this?

- Does this content exist now? If so, where is it, and how can we get access to it for migration? What is the current velocity of this content—how fast does it change or turn over?

To this end, the most valuable question the developer can ask might simply be: "Where does this come from?"

For any element on the wireframe, the site planners, owners, or editors need to explain where it comes from. Is it managed content? Is it from the operative content object? Is it from another content object? Is it from an external data source? Is it contextual logic, like related content or sidebar navigation? If so, on what data is this logic based?

They do not need to have complete technical understanding (this is the developer's job), but they need to have at least some logical idea of where the content sources from. If they don't, the developer can back up and ask more general questions about the nature of the information:

- Is it specific to this page?
- Is it global?
- Is it based on the content type?
- Can everyone see it?
- Is it from someplace outside the CMS?

From the answers, the developer might be able to extrapolate some content model or method of populating the information. This should be repeated for *every single element* on the wireframe: every menu, every sidebar element, every snippet of text.

It's easy to short-circuit this process. It can get tedious, and there's a temptation to think, "Well, I'm sure someone has a plan for that." *Resist this temptation.* The process of answering these questions is vital, both for the developer's understanding and also for the editors and site planners. Many times, the provided answers will be in conflict, and you'll uncover misunderstandings and incorrect assumptions.

 If *no one* can explain where a wireframe element comes from or how it's determined, go ahead and draw a big X through it. If it can't be explained in a simple conversation, then it certainly can't be implemented.

Equally important as the actual answers, the directions these conversations go in will often reveal underlying motivations and goals. The answer to where something comes from will often lead to a discussion about why it's there and what goal the site planner was trying to achieve with it. These discussions help provide context and background, which the developers can use later in the project when they need to make more intricate implementation decisions.

By starting at the bottom and proceeding through the wireframes one by one, larger top-down questions will slowly begin to fill in. Once every interface has been reviewed, the team can back up and look at larger questions such as:

- What is the shape of this content? What content geography is needed to support it?[3]

- What does the aggregate content model look like? Can types be abstracted to base types from which other types might inherit? Can type composition be used to simplify the model?

- What content appears to be global to the installation, and where will that content be stored?

- What larger, nongeographic aggregation structures are needed? Is there a global tagging, categorization, or menuing strategy that ties the content together?

- What is the overall need for page composition? How much of the site is templated, and how much is artisanal?

- What do the aggregate localization requirements look like? How many languages will need to be supported, and how should language preferences and fallbacks be managed?

- What does the user model look like? How many different user groups will need to be created, and what reach will each of them have?

- What external systems need to be integrated with? What APIs are available, and what access is allowed? Can this information be retrieved in real time, or does an import strategy need to be defined?

- What does our overall migration strategy look like?

- If the target CMS is known, how well does the revealed functionality overlay on what's available out of the box? How much customization will be needed to complete the implementation?

- If the target CMS is not known, what CMS might be a good fit?

The answers to both the big and small questions collectively form the technical plan. This plan will drive the implementation process, and, as discussed in Chapter 14, the scoping and budgeting process.

Taking the organization and the team into account

It's important to understand that answers to the questions in the previous section are simply not universal. Many are contextual to the specific combination of *this* organization, *this* particular team, and the long-term plan for *this* website. The same site plan for combination X might be implemented differently for combination Y.

---

3 Of course, if the CMS has already been selected, this might be a moot point, but it could at least inform specifics of how that geography should be formed.

Things the team will need to take into account during a feature-level analysis include:

- How much budget is available for implementation?
- How experienced are the editors? How well can they be trained and be expected to understand technical concepts?
- What portion of the budget will a particular feature consume, and does that need to be balanced against its value? Can it be responsibly implemented at a lower level of functionality or polish to save budget?
- To what extent does the organization want to make structural changes to the site without developer involvement? To what extent will it have users who understand HTML or CSS enough to share some responsibility for output?
- How long will this implementation be used? Is it permanent or temporary?
- What is the future development plan? Is there a phase 2? Does the organization plan to invest in this site over the long term, or is this a one-shot effort? What level of internal developer support does it have?

Here's an example.

Say the site design calls for numerous text callouts, all with different styles. Should there be a visual "palette" of different styles that editors can browse through and select one with a mouse click? Or, on the opposite end of the scale, can these editors be trusted with a simple text box in which to type in the name of a known CSS class that will be applied to the surrounding DIV?

The former is clearly more user-friendly and polished, but it also may cost considerably more to implement and be less flexible. With the second option, new CSS classes might be created on the fly, and editors can simply type them in, while with the first option, the style palette might have to be manually changed to represent a new style.

Some editors want the most user-friendly, controlled experience possible. Others want to get "close to the metal" and have more manual control over these things. These editors might resent being spoon-fed options, and be annoyed that they can't just type in a CSS class that they know exists. Only knowledge of the editor's preferences, skill, training, experience, and governance policies can help you make this decision.[4]

The usage of Markdown and other markup formats is another clear example. Some editors enjoy the precision and speed that Markdown brings with it. Other editors

---

[4] What gets trickier is when the integrator is external and is being paid for its work. While the integrator might pursue the second option in a genuine attempt to increase flexibility, the client might view the first option as clearly better and interpret the integrator's plan as lack of skill, or—worse—a desire to deliver a shoddy product to increase its profit margin.

expect WYSIWYG editing, and might consider Markdown as "low rent" and even question why such an expensive CMS or implementation isn't competent enough to feel like Microsoft Word. In these situations, does the technical plan acquiesce to what the editors expect, or does the case need to be made for the alternative?

This opens up much larger questions to do with user adoption and internal marketing, which are crucial but beyond the scope of this book. Perhaps 10–15% of the effort for any implementation might be social engineering and training to get users on board, both with the system itself and with the decisions that were made during the implementation. Back to our example, do editors simply need to be trained on Markdown, and educated about its benefits and why it's the right solution for this situation? How far down that rabbit hole is the team prepared to go? Will they need to "walk that decision back" to larger concepts like the separation of content and presentation?

The Right Way

We had a raging discussion at my company once on the acceptability of cutting corners and leaving some rough edges to save budget (with the client's understanding, of course).

One of the developers said, "I wouldn't do that because I want to do things the *right* way." Left unsaid there was what "right" meant. Does it mean an architecturally perfect way? Or does it mean a practical but less-polished way that achieves the customer's goals, one of which is staying under budget?

Developers have to make these types of decisions dozens of times during any implementation. (Refer back to "Load-Bearing Walls" on page 176.)

The end goals of a project will also exert an influence on implementation decisions. Consider these two projects:

- A temporary promotional microsite to support a single conference event with content that won't change. This site needs to be launched very quickly, and will stay up for six months at most.

- The main website for the organization. There will be thousands of pages of content, authored by dozens of editors of varying skill levels turning over content multiple times per day. This implementation needs to be functional and relevant for at least the next five years.

These two scenarios will likely result in drastically different implementation decisions. For the temporary microsite, corners might be justifiably cut for the sake of budget, time, and the fact that more complex implementation won't provide much return on investment. However, the main site of the organization has a much longer time span and a larger, distributed editorial base. For this project, a more measured implementation is required. Deeper investments in usability and flexibility will have the breadth and time required to provide value to justify their expense.

Pace Layering

Architect Frank Duffy is known for a concept called "shearing layers" or "pace layering." He considers the design of a building in layers, which move and change at different "paces." There are six layers, all starting with "S":[5]

Site
: The actual ground the building site is on

Structure
: The immovable parts of the building

Skin
: The outer surface of the building

Services
: The underlying electrical, plumbing, and HVAC systems of the building

Space
: The interior design of the building

Stuff
: All the furniture and finishes inside the building

These layers move at different paces. The furniture in a room will be rearranged at a much greater rate than the ground under the building will erode with the passage of time. Likewise, the outer surface of the building is changed much more easily than the foundation or supporting pillars.

The same is true of a website and the content within it. It all changes at different paces. The underlying purpose of the CMS will change at a different pace than the words stored within it. And the logo in the upper corner will change at a different pace than the list of news releases.

Each element has a pace. Those paces need to be taken into account when planning. Items that move at a slower pace might need fewer management tools (or perhaps *less refined* management tools). Clearly, understanding the paces is key to making smart decisions about how to implement.

---

5 Elaborated on by Stewart Brand in *How Buildings Learn: What Happens After They're Built* (Penguin).

The urge to generalize

Developers love to generalize. Specificity gives us a lingering unease, like we're building something too tight around a set of requirements, and what if there's more functionality to be gained by loosening up a bit?

Additionally, developers love to deal in abstractions. Yes, this particular content object is of the type Article, but it could also be considered of the type Web Page, and even more abstractly, it's an instance of some root, generic type like Content Object.

This manifests itself as a desire to interpret wireframes and site plans, and generalize them in such a way as to handle situations that aren't explicitly called for. Developers have mental conversations like this all the time:

> Well, a News Article is really just a Page with a Date and Author. If we add a date field to the Page type, then we can collapse those two types into one. And then, in the future, they can create mixed lists of Pages and News Articles. For that matter, I wonder if we shouldn't just make Help Topic a Page too. We could make just the Subject attribute a category assignment, and now we have one less type and those can be added to lists too. Plus, they could add Subjects to other types of content too. You know, the home page wireframe didn't call for it, but I could see them wanting to add these lists in the sidebars in the future.

Some of this might be interpreted as laziness, but it's mostly a genuine attempt to enlarge the solution to encompass scenarios which the developer is projecting onto the users. If a user wants to do thing X, then the developer naturally thinks ahead that he might want to do thing Y in the future, and the developer can address that need in advance.

There's truly nothing a developer likes more than hearing an editor say, "We're thinking about maybe doing thing Y—" and cutting them off, leaning back in her chair, and saying, "*No problem.* I figured you would want that so I already handled it for you…" [insert exaggerated, magician-like hand flourish here].

Some of this is healthy, but sometimes developers can be a little too clever. We've discussed previously how developers are used to thinking about complex information problems and dealing in abstractions. Occasionally they can be convinced that editors will share in that enjoyment and skill. But usually, editors like concreteness to the same extent that developers like abstraction.

Developers and site planners need to have productive conversations about whether the site plan is suggestive or literal, and those need to be followed by conversations with editors about things they might want to do in the future, and then *those* need to be followed by conversations with project managers about how these things might affect budget and timeline, both for the immediate project and potentially for follow-on projects as well.

In some cases, developers might need to be reminded that they're not building a framework or an abstraction. They are, in fact, building an actual website with a finite set of problems to be solved.

Mike Tyson on Planning

Boxer Mike Tyson is known for many things, but when asked about his opponent's strategy before a match, he made one of his more profound statements: "Everyone has a plan until they get punched in the face."[6]

Mike's point was this: all the planning in the world has a tendency to break down under load. When you're in the middle of a project, a plan is a great starting point and a good guide to keep you on track, but be prepared to adapt when necessary.

Do not stick with a plan *just because it's a plan*. A plan should be a living document. When you get down in the weeds during an implementation, be prepared to change the plan if it becomes obvious that something isn't workable.

The Implementation Process

CMS implementations can be difficult to generalize, but the following description is meant to be as inclusive as possible and to reasonably represent the significant phases through which an implementation will progress.

Environment Setup

In most cases, developers will develop the new website on their local workstations. They will submit their code to a central repository, which is a source code management (SCM) platform such as Git, Subversion, or Team Foundation Server. Multiple developers might be submitting new code, which is then combined and deployed to an integration server for review and testing.

Developers continue a cycle of developing new features, submitting their own code to SCM, and downloading code submitted by others to bring their local workstations up-to-date. Throughout, each developer maintains a fully functioning version of the CMS and developing website on his or her local workstation.

The process of deploying this code to servers is generically known as "building." It is usually accomplished by tools called "build servers." A build server is software running on the integration server that monitors the SCM repository. It detects new code

---

6 Tyson said this, but it wasn't recorded. Accounts differ as to whether he said "in the face," "in the nose," or "in the mouth." Given how hard Iron Mike punched, I doubt this distinction is really necessary.

submissions and launches a process that checks out the code and performs the tasks necessary to get it running on the server—compiling the code, deleting source files, copying the code to the web server directory, injecting license files, etc.[7] Jenkins and Cruise Control are two popular open source build servers.

In addition to the integration server, often a "test" server is used to provide a more stable environment. While the website is built on the integration server, new code (submitted often by developers, sometimes several times per hour) is deployed to the test server less frequently to maintain a semistable environment for testing. The test server usually has a build server of its own, but it's either activated manually or connected to a different branch of the SCM repository where code is merged less frequently. [8]

Installation, Configuration, and Content Reconciliation

Once all necessary environments have been created, the CMS is installed and configured. This is less momentous than it sounds, as many CMSs will install merely through double-clicking an icon, or deploying files to the root of a web server and walking through an installation wizard.[9]

Some CMSs are designed as self-contained web applications that are purposely independent of anything else on the server. In these cases, the CMS isn't installed on the server so much as it's installed within the *web server* process. Others require a more holistic installation where background services and perhaps other files are stored outside the bounds of the web server. In some of these cases, these files and services can be used by more than one implementation of that CMS on the same server.

Once the installation is complete, the resulting website—simple as it is—will need to be checked into SCM, deployed to integration, and then checked out by other developers.

Reconciling the installation and its content between all developers working on the project can be a tricky phase. One of the perennial questions is how to handle the database that powers most CMSs. Does every developer keep their own copy of the

---

7 These tools are also known as "continuous integration" servers. The idea is that new code should continually be integrated into the whole so that problems can be found early, instead of doing infrequent builds of the entire solution that don't reveal problems until late in the process. Submitting code that doesn't work and prevents the solution from being successfully deployed is known as "breaking the build." This is usually a source of ostracism and open derision among a developer's colleagues.

8 Note that the test and integration websites might be on the same server, making them more accurately referred to as test and integration *instances.*

9 Project managers have been known to proudly report to management that they have "Completed the installation of the CMS!" while failing to mention that this impressive-sounding milestone might have been a three-minute process.

database, or do all the developers talk to a central database? And which databases do the integration and test servers work with—their own, or a central version?

If each developer has a copy of the database, they're free to work knowing that their changes won't affect other developers. However, multiple database copies mean that everyone is working from a different copy of the content, and code changes requiring accompanying data changes might require these changes to be replicated on multiple versions of the database. Code might be deployed that breaks other developers' installations because the accompanying data changes haven't been made on their copies of the database.

This can be eased considerably by a CMS that stores and manages configuration as code. In some systems, creating a new content type is accomplished by writing code: in Plone, a new content type is defined as a new Python file; in Episerver, a new content type is a new C# class file. With these systems, deploying code and configuration are the same process. The act of a developer deploying code also deploys the configuration changes necessary for that code to work.

In other systems, new content types might be created by clicking through the administrative interface of the CMS. These type changes are stored in the database to which that copy of the CMS is connected. If a developer creates a new content type on his local workstation, he now has that content type definition local to *his* database. He either needs to re-create the type on the integration server (and then the test server, and then the production server...) or use some external tool to move that data from his database to another.

Finally, how do the developers account for content continuously created by the editorial team? If editors find a bug with new content, or a developer needs to embark on changes that require the latest content, how does the developer bring her local database up-to-date with production?

The process of "reconciling" content changes is the bane of CMS developers. While some systems have developed considerable technology to migrate content changes between environments, other systems simply have a developer community that has gotten used to manually pushing content around. Other CMSs have external vendors that specialize in tools specifically to solve problems of reconciliation.

Developers will usually work off a local database that slowly becomes more and more out of date until they feel it's sufficiently "stale" that they need to refresh it from the production or test data, often via a manual backup and restore.[10]

---

10 And this is to say nothing of all the content files created and managed in production, though thankfully those have to be "brought backward" to development less frequently.

A notable milestone in the implementation process occurs when all developers have a running copy of the codebase on their workstations, this code can be submitted and built successfully in all integration and test environments, and a plan is in place for data reconciliation.

Content Modeling, Aggregation Modeling, and Rough-in

Just like you can't test drive a car without putting gas in it, you can't develop a CMS without having content in it. The content types for the required model need to be created. Types need to be defined and properties need to be added, along with their accompanying validation rules. Custom properties might need to be developed, in the instances where the built-in properties run short.

In addition to the discrete model of each type, relationships between types and objects need to be defined, including properties that reference other objects, and relationships between content types. This means that at least some of the content tree will need to be "roughed in" to represent these relationships before further development can continue.

For example, if you're publishing a magazine, you might have an Issue type, a Section type, and an Article type. An issue will have multiple sections as children, which will have multiple articles as children. You can't work on templating or other functionality until you have a representative set of content roughed in, which means creating "dummy" content as a placeholder to continue developing.

Implicit navigation is similarly dependent on a roughed-in content tree. If the navigation for a site is rendered by iterating through the tree to form primary and secondary content menus, objects will need to be created before development can continue.

Note that it's not uncommon to find problems during rough-in. Plans that seemed to make sense in the abstract may become clearly unworkable when actually creating content. Be prepared that some plans may need to be reworked during this phase. This is a natural part of the implementation process.

Other modeling tasks include:

Defining permissible content aggregations
> To continue the previous example, perhaps we stipulate that an Issue object can only contain children of type Section, which can further only contain children of type Article.

Refining the editorial interface
> Just creating the types and properties isn't enough. The editorial interface needs to be considered from a UX standpoint: Are items labeled clearly? Is there adequate help text? Have unnecessary interface elements been removed? Have

advanced options been hidden from users who won't understand or shouldn't have access to them?

Defining permissions

This requires at least a minimal rough-in of the user model, so that groups can be given varying access to content. Specifically, you need to be careful of allowing delete permission, since many content objects will be the "load-bearing walls" of the content structure, and if they were deleted, then the entire site might stop working.

Beyond actual content, other structures might have to be created at this point to support various aggregations, including:

- Category trees and taxonomies
- Controlled tag sets
- Menus
- Search indexes
- Lists and collections
- Configured searches

Don't Develop in an Administrator Bubble

During development, there's a tendency for a developer to only work as an administrator-level user, which is convenient, but dangerous.

Many times, the editorial team has finally gotten a chance to add some content, and found that half the site doesn't work because the developer did things that require administrator privileges to function. Since the developer was testing code as an administrator, he might never have known this was a problem. The development team needs to log in as editors or users every once in a while, just to make sure they're not depending on access that the average person won't have.

Even worse is when the QA tester works as an administrator. Remember: *a feature doesn't work correctly until it works correctly for the intended user.* Just because an editorial feature works for an administrator, doesn't mean it actually works. To confirm that, someone needs to authenticate as the intended user and test under those privileges.

When content modeling is complete, the basic content structure should be available, and it should be *resilient*, which means protected from careless (or even malicious) usage. Types should be validated correctly, any hierarchies or relationships should be enforced, and the editorial interface should be intuitive and safe for editors.

Early Content Migration

While the entire next chapter is devoted to content migration, it's important to note that it should begin in some form *as soon as a valid content model is available.* Many implementations have run off the rails at the end when "real" content is migrated, revealing multiple problems.

Content migrated at this stage doesn't have to be complete or perfect, but it needs to be pushed into the system regardless. There is just no substitute for having real content in a CMS while it's being developed.

Early content migration can be considered "extended content rough-in." Much like the continuous integration philosophy in development seeks to fully integrate code early and often, a "continuous migration" philosophy seeks to integrate content early and often.

The risk of not doing this is that the development team only works with a theoretical body of content. Sure, they've roughed some in to the extent they need to continue development, but it's not actual content—it was contrived simply so they could keep developing, and it was created by someone with intimate knowledge of how the system works. Consciously or subconsciously, the roughed-in content was designed to avoid delay, not to accurately represent the real world.

Real content has warts. It frequently has bumps and bruises and doesn't quite match up with what you envision. You need to account for missing data, varying formats, problems with length, missing relationships, etc.

The prior warning about developing in an "administrator bubble" holds just as true for content. Don't develop in a "contrived content bubble." Unless the development team occasionally has to stop and deal with content that is representative of what the site will eventually have to manage, they're going to take liberties and ignore edge cases that will cause problems down the road.

Empty House Syndrome

When I got my first apartment, I was so excited to move in. I had the entire layout planned in my head. It was going to be perfect.

On move-in day, I sadly realized that some of the furniture I had bought didn't fit. In particular, the couch was too long for the wall (or perhaps the apartment was too small), and it stuck out into the hallway. The result was that the furnished apartment was less majestic and quite a bit more awkward in reality than the perfect version that had been in my head.

I had been suffering from Empty House Syndrome. A house is perfect with no furniture. When you move things in, you find out that some stuff just doesn't work. There's a nasty glare from the window on the TV, a picture is too small for a vast expanse of wall, and, yes, a couch might stick out into the hallway.

While we can't fix the actual furniture problem, we can do something about content. *Test your content against your website early and often.* Find out what is going to work fine, and what needs to be rearranged or swapped to avoid a move-in day surprise.

Templating

By this point, the environment is set up, the CMS is installed, the content model is created, and roughed-in content is available.

Finally, it is time for templating. This is the moment you've been waiting for, when you actually get to generate some presentations of the content you're implementing this system to manage.

Templating comes in two forms:

- The *surround*, which is the outer shell of each page
- The *object*, which is the specific object you're presenting

Remember, the output of the object template is "injected" into the surround. Your object is templated, then this output is nested inside the shell of the surround.

Surround templating

In most cases, the surround has to work for *all* content. While having multiple surround templates can happen, it's uncommon. In most cases, the template architecture has a single surround that is flexible enough to adapt to all content types. In some cases, surrounds can even nest inside one another, but this is also uncommon.

Templating the surround is unique in that it doesn't execute in a vacuum. The surround is dependent on the object being rendered for information. The information can be of two types:

Discrete
Information drawn from the value of one or more attributes

Relational
Information drawn from the position of the content object in relation to other content

Additionally, the surround will often retrieve other content objects and data structures in addition to the object being rendered, to provide data for other sections of the page.

The primary navigation, for instance, is often explicit, meaning there is a specific content aggregation that drives it. Systems with a content tree might depend on the top-level pages for this, while other systems might have a specific menu structure of some kind that lists these pages.

Again, the "tyranny of the tree" can be a problem here—if the top-level pages are in that position for reasons *other* than being the primary navigation options, then how do you depart from this? It's not uncommon to see explicit menuing for primary navigation, even in systems that otherwise depend on their tree for navigation.

For example, the surround often depends on determining the correct navigation logic. A crumbtrail, clearly, only makes sense in relation to the content object being rendered. Where that object is located in the geography will dictate what appears in the crumbtrail.

Additionally, many sites have a left sidebar menu. How do you know what appears there? Is it dependent on the current content object in some way? For instance, does it render all the items in the same section or group of content as the primary item? Is the menu hierarchical—does it "open"? How do we determine where and how it opens? Based on what criteria?

Despite this emphasis on global and relational information, some items in the surround are more directly contextual to the content being rendered. For example, a common element in the sidebar (the ubiquitous Related Content, for example) is dependent on the actual content item being rendered. It will extract information from that object to render itself. Do all objects have this information, or does the element in the surround have to account for varying information, and even hide itself if the primary object being rendered is not of a compatible type?

A question often becomes: do elements like this get templated in the surround, or do we template them as part of the content object itself and then inject the results into the surround? Content object templates can often be divided into "sections," some of which can be mapped to places in the surround. Thus, if the related content element only appears for one type, then perhaps the more appropriate place for it is with the object templating, rather than the surround templating. If this surround element is required in more than one template, however, this is an inefficient duplication of code, meaning it should be abstracted to an include or moved to the surround template.[11]

Object templating

Inside the surround lives the output created for a particular content object. This is usually far more straightforward than the surround, since the template knows what object it's rendering and can make specific decisions based on safe assumptions about what data is available. The object template doesn't have to work for all content, just a single content type.

Additionally, the operative object template doesn't really have any dependence on the surround template. While the surround depends highly on the object, the inverse is usually not true. The object can often execute neither knowing nor caring what surround it will eventually be wrapped in.

Some content object templates are nothing more than one or two lines, perhaps to simply output the title and the body of a simple text page of content.

A single content object might have multiple templates for the same channel, depending on criteria. Most implementations will have a one-to-one relationship between type and template, but in some cases, the template might vary based on location or content, or on some particular combination of property values inside the content itself. (However, if several content types have multiple templates that vary considerably, some thought might be given to creating different types altogether.)

Templating (both the surround and the objects) can sometimes take the majority of the development time of an implementation. With some teams, a single developer might be responsible for writing the frontend code (the HTML/CSS), while in other situations, a whole team might be responsible for that code specifically, and either provide it to the backend developers or create the templates themselves. If the latter, then the backend developer might "rough in" the templates, then provide access from frontend developers to complete the code.

When templating is complete, the site will be navigable with all objects publishing correctly, and will appear largely complete.

---

11 It's a peculiar truth that some of the most lively arguments in a development project can be philosophical disagreements about *where* code belongs. There might be no argument about the existential validity of a particular block of code or how it works, but two developers can have almost violent disagreements about what place in the codebase is the "correct" location for that code to live.

Non-Content Integration and Development

It's common to find CMS implementations that don't entirely start and stop with the CMS alone. Many implementations involve external systems and data, or custom-programmed elements not dealing with content.

For example, a bank might have a custom-programmed loan application on its website. This is a complicated, standalone application that has absolutely nothing to do with the CMS—it doesn't use CMS content to render, and doesn't create or alter any content by its use. It just needs to "live" in the CMS so it can be viewed alongside all the other content in the CMS.

The ability for non-CMS functionality to exist within a content-managed website varies. Some systems "play nice" with non-CMS code that needs to run inside it, but some systems are "jealous" and make it very difficult to do custom programming within the bounds of the CMS.

A developer can always write custom code outside the system, and simply have the executable application or files accessed without invoking the CMS, but a lot of CMS-related functionality is then lost. Ideally, the custom code can execute within the scope of the CMS and take advantage of the surround templating, URL management, permissions, etc.

Using this method, the output of our loan application could be "wrapped" by the surround, and by using a proxy content object, the page containing the application could be "placed" inside the CMS geography so the surround has context to work from when rendering. (See "Proxy Content Objects" on page 192.)

Problems will arise when migrating from a different system running on an entirely different technology stack. In these cases, the application simply has to be rewritten to comply with the new system's technology stack, which might be a considerable investment—perhaps even greater than the CMS implementation itself.

Some situations might require functionality to be hosted externally and brought into the website via reverse proxy, or—less ideally—an IFRAME. Even less desirable would be to have to transition the user to another website entirely (for example, "loan-app.bigbank.com" for the previous application example). Site transitions often produce jarring visual and UX transitions, along with other technical issues such as cookie domain mismatches and authentication issues.

The practice of content integration

These issues live under the heading of "content integration," which is the process of combining external data with content in a CMS installation. There are dozens of models for accomplishing this, all with advantages and disadvantages, and as with everything, the best fit depends on requirements:

- Where does the external data live?
- How volatile is it? How often does it change?
- Does it need to be moved into the CMS, or can it be accessed where it is?
- If it needs to be moved into the CMS for access, what does the schedule need to be? How "stale" can it be allowed to get before being refreshed?
- Does each record in the external source correspond to a complete content object, or are we simply adding content to an existing object?
- What is the access latency? How fast can it be retrieved?
- How stable is the connection between the CMS and the data source?
- Will it ever need to be modified in the CMS environment and sent back?
- What are the security issues? Can anyone have access to it?
- Do individual records need to be URL addressable, or is the data only meant to be viewed in aggregate?

For example, universities often want to have their course descriptions available on their websites. However, these descriptions are invariably maintained in a separate software system. In these cases, a scheduled job might execute every night, detect course descriptions that have changed in the last 24 hours, and update corresponding content objects in the CMS with that data. The descriptions of the content objects wouldn't be editable directly in the CMS, since that isn't the "home" for this data, and they can be overwritten whenever the external data changes.[12]

The potential needs for content integration are so vast that the discipline largely boils down to a set of practices, tools, and raw experience that are applied individually to each situation.

Production Environment Planning and Setup

Sometime during the development process, the production environment needs to be planned, created, and tested, and the developing website should be deployed. Basic questions need to be answered about physical/logical locations, the organization's relationship to the environment (both technically and administratively), and the technical parameters of the environment.

---

12 Another way to handle this would be via repository abstraction, as discussed in Chapter 11. The course repository might be "mounted" in real time as a section of the repository.

Hosting models

Common hosting models are:

- *On-premise hosting*, in the organization's own data center
- *Third-party hosting under the organization's control*, where the organization creates a hosting account on a platform like Microsoft Azure or Amazon Web Services and manages this environment directly
- *Third-party "managed" hosting under external control*, where the organization cedes control over the hosting to another vendor (often the integrator, as part of a package deal, or the CMS vendor)

Like almost every other type of application, CMSs are trending toward the cloud more than on-premise hosting. Financial institutions and the healthcare sector held out longer than most due to privacy concerns (or the perception of such), but even those organizations are slowly giving up on on-premise installations.

Vendor-provided hosting is becoming more and more common as CMS vendors seek to transition from product companies to service companies. Many are bundling hosting and license fees together in a SaaS-like model. Some vendors are selling on-premise licenses only when directly asked for them—new sales are assumed to be cloud sales.

Hosting environment design

The ease of setting up virtual servers and redundant cloud architectures has completely changed how hosting is initiated and managed. Setting up servers used to be a time- and capital-intensive process.[13] Getting the servers running and the CMS installed was a major milestone. Now it can happen between meetings.

A full discussion of application hosting is beyond the scope of this book, and thankfully it doesn't differ remarkably from hosting other types of applications. When discussing hosting, major points to consider and discuss with your infrastructure team include:

Fault tolerance and redundancy
How redundant is the environment, and how protected is it from architecture failures? Perfect, seamless redundancy is clearly the ideal situation, but it's rarely fully realized and is often expensive.

---

13 I still remember installing and configuring Ektron CMS400.NET from a hastily burned installation CD (the server initially had no network access) for hours while standing in front a physical server in a rack in some freezing data center back in the early 2000s. We've come a long way.

Failover and disaster recovery

If something does go wrong, what's the process to recover? Will you restore from backup in a new environment, or will you maintain a second environment with a version of your content that you can cut away to?

Performance

How much traffic can the website handle? How is it load-tested? How fast can it scale to increased load? Can scaling be scheduled in anticipation of increased load? (For example, can you plan a temporary or "burst" scaling of the environment for 72 hours in anticipation of increased traffic after a major product release?)

Security and access

Who has access to the server? How is new code deployed to the website? Who can approve those deployments?

Regardless of the model and technical features of the environment, the environment needs to be available far enough in advance of launch to be load-tested, have backup and failover procedures established and tested, and have enough test deployments to ensure the process is free from error. What you clearly *don't* want is an environment made available the night before launch.

Once the production environment is available, ensure that code deployments have been pushed all the way through and the development team has verified the site is functional in the environment. Many launch plans have been scrapped at the last minute due to unforeseen problems caused by a production deployment happening for the first time.

Training and Support Planning

Editors and administrators will need to be trained in the operation of the new CMS. Two different types of training exist:

CMS training

This is generic training on the CMS at its defaults, which means training on Concrete5 or Sitecore or BrightSpot or whatever system your website was implemented in. This is usually provided by the vendor.

Implementation training

This is training on *your specific website*, which means understanding how the generic CMS was wrapped around your requirements, and understanding concepts and structures that might exist in your website and no other. This can only be provided by a trainer familiar with the implementation, since the vendor has no knowledge or understanding of how its product was implemented.

Both are valuable, though the latter is more important for most editors. Understanding how the underlying CMS works is not without merit, but editors will primarily need to understand how the features of *their particular site* were implemented. Relevant aspects of the underlying architecture can be worked into that training as necessary, but it's common to have a select few "product champions" in the organization who know the basic system inside and out, and for the rest of the editing team to simply have specific knowledge of the work within their professional jurisdiction.

Beyond the initial training, a plan should be put together for training future editors. In larger, more distributed organizations (e.g., a university), new staff might be hired each month who will need training on how to add and edit content in the CMS.

In addition to formal training hours, an ad hoc training and support process needs to be considered. What happens when an editor has a problem, or needs more in-depth help with a content initiative? Who is available to walk editors through the system on short notice? And how will the CMS fit into the organization's existing IT support infrastructure? Is the IT help desk aware of the new CMS? Do they know how to use it? How do problems get escalated?

Sadly, training is seldom given much attention, and many organizations do as little as possible in the hopes that it will all "just work out." Remember that training is a direct foundation for user adoption. When users understand and are comfortable with the system, they are more likely to embrace it and use it to its fullest capabilities. More than one project has failed due to tepid user response that grew out of a lack of understanding and training.[14]

Final Content Migration, QA, and Launch

We'll be discussing content migrations at length in the next chapter. However, sometime late in the development cycle, final content migration will begin, when content starts entering the system in the form in which it will remain.

This content will need to be QA'd and edited, sometimes considerably. This never fails to take longer than planned, and launch date extensions are common while the editorial team slaves over the content in an attempt to "get it in shape" enough to launch.

The tail end of a CMS integration is never relaxed. Usually, the editors, developers, and project managers are juggling an ever-changing list of QA tickets and content fixes. You need to budget for an "all hands on deck" approach during the last few days or weeks of a CMS launch. The editorial team needs to be on standby for emergency content fixes.

---

14 Michael Sampson has written an entire book of strategies to increase user adoption of new technologies. His *User Adoption Strategies* (*http://michaelsampson.net/books/useradoption*) (The Michael Sampson Company) is one of the few books on the market to specialize in that subject.

Final features might still be under development right up until launch, though it's common for many features to be thrown overboard in the mad scramble to launch. Many get deferred until the ubiquitous "Phase 1.1" project that's invariably planned for immediately after the initial launch (whether it actually happens or not may be hotly debated).

Launch can be a complex affair, depending on whether the new site is taking the place of an existing site in an existing hosting environment or is being deployed to a new environment. The latter is always preferred, since then launch is simply a matter of changing where the domain name (DNS) resolves, rather than having to bring the site down, perform an installation and regression test, then release it. Given the ease of setting up new virtualized environments, it's usually more efficient to deploy the site to a new, parallel environment, launch via DNS change, and then simply archive the old environment.

If you're depending on a DNS change, UGC might have to be shut off temporarily. During DNS propagation—a process ranging from instantaneous to lengthy (up to 24 hours), depending on the user—some users will be interacting with the new site and some with the old site. While the editors should be creating content on the new site exclusively, there's no way to ensure the same for users. In some cases, a user might have a DNS lag, make a comment on the old site, then have the DNS change occur, leaving the user looking at the new site and wondering why that comment is missing.

Plan and rehearse site launches in advance. There's nothing more frustrating than having everything ready to launch and finding out that the one person able to change a DNS record has gone on vacation. Walk through the launch ahead of time, down to a minute-by-minute schedule, if necessary.

Avoiding Development Centrism

If there's one thing this chapter should have demonstrated, it's that the actual development of the website is often a minority of the total work. Yet it's still very common in CMS projects to find a development-centric approach, as if all you need to do is build the site and everything else will work out.

Consider building a new house. The image that comes to mind is a carpenter hammering away on some lumber. However, let's look at the bigger picture. Let's step back and account for everything that goes into the process, from start to finish.

Our hypothetical homeowners have to:

- Decide to build a new house
- Figure out what they didn't like in their existing house, and decide what to change
- Come up with specific plans and designs for the new house

- Get financing for the house
- Get the required city permits
- Interview contractors and get bids and proposals
- Select a contractor
- Find an empty lot to build the house on
- Finance and purchase the lot
- Schedule a time period in which to get the house built

At this point, construction can begin. But the other work is a still a long way from being completed. While the home is being built, our homeowners still need to:

- Explain to their children why they're moving
- Find new schools and reregister their children
- Determine new travel and commute patterns
- Perhaps buy new vehicles to account for new commuting patterns
- Determine what new stores and services they will use from their new house
- Begin packing up the furnishings in their old house
- Pick out finishes and fixtures for the new house
- Perhaps arrange for temporary housing and storage if their first house sells early
- File change of address cards at the post office
- Arrange for new utilities
- Change billing information with all the companies and people who send them mail

Finally, the house is done. But the work isn't. Now our homeowners still have to:

- Actually move all their belongings into the new house
- Buy new belongings to account for changes in décor and room size and type
- Get rid of things that don't work with the new house
- Learn how to work all the new appliances
- Find somewhere to store all of the house documentation and manuals
- Begin maintaining and cleaning the new house, accounting for changes in size, scope, and type of furnishings
- Have a housewarming party for their friends and family

The list could go on and on. And note that we have completely omitted any tasks related to *actually building the new house*. All of these were simply the "meta tasks" *around* building the house.

In saying this, I'm not downplaying the importance and scope of development. But be prepared that there's much more to do than simply implementing a new CMS. From the beginning to the end, a new CMS project is just as much a collection of social, organizational, political, budgetary, and logistical challenges as it is of technical challenges.

The lesson is clear: ignore the vast scope of non-development work at your own peril.

CHAPTER 13

Content Migration

Imagine making the greatest ice cream sundae in the world. First, you start out with the best ingredients—sweet cream, cane sugar, real vanilla—and then you spend hours mixing them together.[1] You add real whipping cream, homemade hot fudge, and the sweetest, most perfectly ripe banana and cherry the world has ever seen.

Then, to complete the masterpiece, you finish it off with a massive squirt of… ketchup.

You were doing great right up until the very end.

This is the story of many content migrations—the task of moving the existing content out of your old CMS and into your new CMS. Just as problems tend to occur when focusing too much on the software rather than the implementation, the exact same thing happens when those two are given too much precedence and the content migration is ignored. Organizations will find the perfect CMS, manage a fantastic implementation, and then completely botch the project at the very end with a disastrous content migration.

Remember, a CMS manages *content*. It's only as good as the content you put into it. And the content your organization currently manages might be the result of years and years of creation, aggregation, and management. There could easily be millions of dollars invested in this content as a business asset. Ignoring this final phase of your project is disrespecting that content and devaluing all the effort that's gone into it.

Migrations are often viewed as "extra" work. However, in some cases, the migration might be the majority of the project. A CMS implementation project might really be a *migration* project with a small development component attached to it.

---

1 Clearly, I know nothing about making ice cream.

More than one project has been cancelled when the organization was confronted with the cost of moving all the existing content. In other cases, this cost drove the decision to simply upgrade and refresh an existing CMS, leaving the content where it was rather than moving it to a new CMS.

And as with content management itself, there is no Grand Unified Theory of Content Migration. Each one is idiosyncratic. Your current website uses a CMS that was modified through hundreds of implementation decisions. Your new website uses *another* CMS, which has likewise been modified by hundreds of *different* implementation decisions.

In this sense, both websites are unique little snowflakes, and there's little way to generalize from migration to migration. The ability to perform a migration is less of a defined methodology, and more of a set of best practices and painful lessons that drive a unique plan for *that* specific migration.

Content migrations are simply an art and science all their own, and are chronically underestimated. Doing them effectively, on time, and within budget might be the hardest part of a project.

Warning: Vagueness Ahead

Talking about content migrations can be extremely vague, since we're discussing a hypothetical existing CMS filled with hypothetical content that is moving to a new hypothetical content model in a new hypothetical CMS. Discussing these things in definitive terms is nigh impossible, so be prepared to consider this subject in theory, with the understanding that the specifics of your situation will always differ.

The Editorial Challenge

While the seemingly central challenge of a migration is to move bytes on disk from one system to another, the first challenge of a migration is actually editorial—what content is migrating, and how will it change?

For some projects (such as forklift implementations, discussed in Chapter 12), the answers are (1) all of the content, and (2) it won't change at all. However, for many others, a migration presents a valuable opportunity to clean house, remove unwanted content, and change existing content to more effectively serve the organization's goals.

A key point: *the easiest content to migrate is content you don't migrate*. Now is the time to clean house.[2] Reviewing your analytics for content that's no longer accessed can remove an enormous amount of migration effort. I've seen intranet projects where 90% of the existing content was simply discarded. For any website that's been in existence for multiple years, there's little doubt that some of the content is simply no longer relevant.

Can these decisions be derived automatically? For instance, is it possible to say, "All news releases over three years old will be discarded"? Or will all these decisions require editorial input?

Many content migrations are preceded by content inventories, where all the existing content is identified and analyzed, and decisions are made regarding its future viability. Inventorying content is an art in itself, and far beyond the scope of this book,[3] but the result of the inventory needs to be recorded somewhere, ideally in a form that can be used to make programmatic decisions about content.

Many inventories are accompanied by an unwieldy spreadsheet that is of little use to the developer trying to move content. A better idea is to record the intended disposition of content *directly with the content itself*, by adding Migrate to New Website or Requires Review checkboxes to the CMS, effectively making the existing CMS the record-keeping location for the content inventory. The developers performing the export of content from the existing CMS can then safely ignore that content in their code.

The first milestone in a content migration will always be a definitive decision and recording of all the content that must be moved to the new system. It's hard to plan any further steps in a migration without knowing at least this.

Automated or Manual?

The most low-tech method of migrating content will always consist of a person copying content from one browser window and pasting it into another. While admittedly tedious, it does have advantages:

- There are no technology incompatibilities.
- A human is available to make real-time editorial decisions about how to adapt content.

---

2 A technical reviewer noted, "Have a yard sale before you move."

3 Paula Land has written a handbook called *Content Inventories and Audits* (*http://xmlpress.net/content-strategy/audits-and-inventories*) on this subject (XML Press). Similarly, David Hobbs (see the sidebar at the end of the chapter) has written a report on the topic called "Rethinking the Content Inventory." (*http://davidhobbsconsulting.com/report/rethinking-content-inventory*)

- File format changes are simpler. Copying content from binary files like Word or PDF isn't much more work than copying from an HTML page. And dynamically composed pages can be more easily deconstructed and reassembled.

The drawback, of course, is that manual migrations are labor intensive and tedious. However, they're not always the wrong answer. For migrations of a small amount of content that will change significantly on the way over, a manual migration might be exactly the right answer.

The argument against manual migration often comes down to volume or cost. Decisions about manual content migrations need to take into account the cost and availability of personnel. Many manual migrations have been performed by interns or college work study students. It might not be glamorous work, but it's often effective.

Crossing a certain threshold of content, however, will make automation the most cost-effective choice. Content migrations that don't require significant editorial decisions during migration can usually be automated far more efficiently.

That said, know that automation has limits, and it's often easier to simply reconstruct selected content in the new CMS manually. Home pages, for example, tend to be very artisanal, with intricate content elements ordered and placed very carefully. Automating the extraction, importation, and placement of elements might be more trouble than it's worth, especially when only a handful of pages need special handling. In these cases, be prepared for a hybrid approach, where certain content is simply rebuilt in place rather than automatically migrated.

The Migration Process

In a perfect world, you'd simply be able to open an administrative console in your new CMS and press a button that says, "Import content from [insert your existing CMS here]." This situation actually exists in some form for highly visible and competitive open source platforms like Drupal and WordPress, but it isn't available for others.

Migrating content between two systems is usually a custom endeavor. There's simply no standardization between systems, and even less standardization between methodologies of architecting content models. Even content coming out of and going into different installations of the *same* CMS might require significant changes, depending on how the content in each installation was modeled and aggregated. It would be rare for the content model in one installation to simply map directly to the content model in another installation.

Successfully migrating content is a loosely structured process, progressing through the following stages:

1. *Extraction*. Content is extracted from the current environment.
2. *Transformation*. Content is altered, to simply clean it up or to change it to work properly in the new environment.
3. *Reassembly*. Content is aggregated to correctly fit the new environment.
4. *Import*. Content is imported to the new environment.
5. *Resolution*. Links between content objects are identified and resolved.
6. *QA*. Imported content is checked for accuracy.

We'll discuss each step in the process in greater depth in the following sections.

Extraction

The content inside your current CMS will need to be accessed and transferred to a neutral format from which it can be transformed and imported. Content needs to be extracted at two levels: (1) individual content objects, which are broken into (2) individual content attributes.

So, you need to extract all of your articles, but also have those articles broken down by attribute.

So long as those two criteria are met, the actual target format doesn't matter. XML is common, as is JSON. Even inserting the content into a simple database might work fine. It simply needs to be in a format that is free from presentation data (such as extra HTML inserted from a rendering template) and is easily manipulated and accessible. I've even seen extracted content simply stored in the new CMS, to be moved and refined later.

In a perfect world, your existing CMS has an export function that can give you all your content in a presentation-free format. Unfortunately, built-in export is often not supported, or it results in a format that isn't workable for future steps in the migration process. Trying to work with a predefined export format over time might reveal that it would have been simpler to write your own export process in the first place.

Without a usable export function, there are two other ways to extract content:

- From the repository, which means using the system's API or even going directly to the database, via SQL (or some other method, for non-SQL repositories)
- From the website itself, which means writing code to request pages and then extracting pieces of the resulting HTML (also known as "screen scraping")

While going directly to the repository might seem the simpler of the two methods, it depends greatly on the capabilities of the system's API. The system might have a poor API, or be in a situation where the API is not available (a hosted system, for example, especially one with a vendor who doesn't know their customer is planning to leave them).

Even if this is possible, there's risk because the repository stores its content optimized for that particular system. It would be uncommon for the CMS to store content in a way designed specifically for export.[4] From repository to screen, content might be transformed. How content sits inside the repository might not be how it's output to the end user. This might be further changed by the templating code, making the actual HTML that is output substantially different from the HTML in the repository.

When screen scraping, you're guaranteed to get the content in the correct output form (given that it is, in fact, being output at that exact moment), but you're limited to the content that is actually output. There might be many unrendered, administrative content properties such as expiration dates, author names, permissions, and metadata that are not output to the end user.[5]

Screen scraping is also limited by the quality of the current HTML. If the current site uses a CMS, then it's probably templated, so you can expect at least a minimum amount of consistency. It's even better when the templates can be modified to make this process easier—it can be very helpful, for instance, to temporarily put some content in clearly defined HTML structures, then simply hide those from the public via CSS during the extraction process. This content will still be available to the screen scraping process, but the page will not appear to have changed to the public.

Sites that are currently static and not templated can be extremely problematic. When the HTML has been hand-coded, there's usually much less consistency, and trying to extract data might be impossible. (Mercifully, sites that have been hand-coded are usually so small that it's easier to just migrate them manually.)

No two extraction scenarios are the same. In any migration, a multitude of factors will need to be analyzed to determine the best method to extract content in a neutral format.

---

4 Some might say that a decoupled system is designed in exactly this way, and that the act of publishing is really a form of export.

5 Not to mention prior versions of content, though I have yet to see a content migration that bothered to bring over any version other than the current, published version. Bringing over the entire version history of every content object would be extremely ambitious. Many systems don't even have the ability to explicitly re-create older versions from the API (by design), so the content would have to be first imported as its oldest known version, then successively overwritten with newer versions, while hoping that all relational content references in use for a particular version would also be available at the time the object was being imported. Suffice it to say that most organizations are satisfied with simply keeping the old CMS available somewhere in case they have to refer to older versions of content.

The Complication of Embedded Content When Migrating

While I extolled the functionality of dynamic page composition and content embedding earlier (see "Content Embedding" on page 97), this vastly increases the complication of migrating between systems. If a content object has another element embedded in it, a hard decision needs to be made on how to handle that during a migration:

- Do we attempt to identify and extract all embedded content and create an equivalent embedded item in the new system? (Does the new system even support this?)

- Do we flag this content as requiring follow-up and have an editor manually reverse engineer and re-create the content embedding?

- Do we abandon the embedding and "flatten" the content—i.e., just scrape the content from the browser as if the embedded content was rendered HTML like everything else?

To date, I have never seen a migration that automatically replicated even a moderate amount of content embedding successfully. The differences in architectural paradigms for that functionality are simply too vast.

Transformation

When content has been extracted, it's rarely in a form appropriate for your new CMS. There's a good chance it came out with extra HTML tags or structure that is not appropriate for your new system and implementation standards.

For example, content that was created many years ago might be full of obsolete HTML tags, such as FONT and even BLINK.[6] More commonly, styling information that was valid in your old implementation will have simply changed. The new implementation might have new CSS classes, new methods of specifying content headers, new methods of aligning images, etc.

HTML content will need to be changed to reflect these new standards. You will usually extract content that contains large blocks of HTML, and you can't treat this HTML as an impenetrable unit. You will often need to "reach into" this HTML and change it in some way.

---

6 Carrying a BLINK tag over to a new implementation might violate international treaties. Check with your attorney.

Common transformations include:

- Removing old HTML tags
- Removing embedded SCRIPT and STYLE tags
- Swapping heading levels (changing all H1 tags to H2 tags, for example)
- Rearranging HTML structures (moving images out of table-based captioning structures, for example)
- Fixing invalid HTML (incorrect nesting, for example)

The end result should be HTML that can be imported into the new CMS and be compatible with new styles, coding standards, and rich text editors.

While rich text requires the lion's share of transformation, other data might need to be modified as well:

- Formally weak attribute references might need to be resolved to their targets and stored as IDs instead.
- Attributes might need to be combined, or split. The old system might have stored first and last name as a single unit, for instance, and the new system requires them to be separated.
- Extraneous data might need to be stripped out of attributes to allow for type conversions. The old system might have stored Price as a text string of "$1,000", while the new system wants a numeric integer of "1000" and will format the number during templating.
- In rare cases, new content objects might need to be created. If the old system stored comments in the Article objects directly and the new system plans to manage them as individual content objects, each comment will need to be parsed out of the parent and created as a new, separate object.

The number of potential transformations is limitless. Once the cleanest possible data has been extracted from the old CMS, the developer of the new implementation needs to evaluate it for potential problems and identify all the ways in which it must change before import.

Reassembly

When discussing content modeling in Chapter 6, we differentiated between discrete modeling and relational modeling. The former was describing the information about content that is limited to the content object itself. The latter is about how that content fits into ("relates") to other content.

After you've extracted hundreds or thousands of content objects from your existing CMS, these objects will need to be assembled and organized to correctly reflect their relationships in the new system. It's not only the content that has to be migrated, but the *relationships* between content as well.

Content trees, in particular, need to be transferred, which means content needs to be extracted in such a way that parent/child relationships remain intact or can be reconstructed. In some cases, this might mean exporting the parent ID with each content object. If you're screen scraping, this might mean outputting the parent ID in a META tag, or even attempting to reverse engineer the hierarchy from the URL paths (assuming they correctly reflect the tree structure).[7]

Changing Geographies

Moving from tree-based system to tree-based system is intuitive, but more problems result when trying to switch geographies. If your old system is based on a content tree and your new CMS is based on a folder structure, how do you handle this? Content has parentage in the old system, but in the new system, the parent is a folder.

There is no universal answer here. Hard decisions need to be made about how to adapt content for foundational geography changes.

In some cases, there is simply no way to reconstruct the structure of content. This might be due to an inherent structural parameter (thousands of blog posts ordered by nothing but date, for example), or because of poor organization and architecture in a legacy site.

Sites that have grown organically over time often reflect poor and idiosyncratic navigation, where menu options were added on an ad hoc basis to create a desired navigation pattern without any thought to an overarching content geography. These sites can be notoriously hard to migrate since it's hard to impose structure on something that was poorly structured at best, and wildly unstructured at worst.

In these cases, content might have to be imported without relational structure and then structured in the new system. Groups of content can be imported to a "holding area" on the new site, then organized using the tools of the new system.

---

7 I remember a particularly difficult project with an existing CMS that had no built-in hierarchy and a new CMS with a very strong content tree. Unfortunately, the URLs had been "SEO optimized" to make all content appear to be on the top level, containing just a single URL segment. With absolutely no other way to figure out content geography, we were reduced to parsing the HTML that formed the crumbtrails and reconstructing the hierarchy from that information.

Content Stubbing

In some situations, content reassembly becomes a critical problem. The new system might require a precise geography, but content from the old system contains no extractable structure that can be reused.

In these cases, it might be a valid option to "stub" content in the new system. Using this method, you manually create empty content objects in the new system, organized into the correct relational structure but each containing nothing but a reference to the corresponding object in the existing system (and perhaps a title, to easily identify them).

Using this method, editors create the "shell" of a new content geography, while inputting nothing but the existing content IDs. When this structure is complete, the references to the existing content items are used to automatically extract content from the existing CMS and populate the corresponding objects in the new CMS.

The larger principle at work here is that content references can be structured in the new system to represent a new relational content geography, *without any actual discrete content*. You're stubbing out the geographic relationships of content as placeholders, which can be populated at a later time. In this way, you're separating the discrete from the relational migration.

Import

Up until this point, we've only been getting content *out* of the old system. Once content has been extracted, transformed, and reassembled into a workable structure, the content actually needs to be brought into the new CMS. This is usually a task involving custom programming.

The only exception would be when your new system has an import function, and it has a known, documented format where you can organize your exported content. This is rare.

In most systems, a developer will write a custom job to get new content into the system. This can either be in the form of a standalone program that uses a web service or similar API to "push" content, or as code that runs inside the new system that "pulls" content.

In many cases, the developer will not just have to import the content, but will have to create other data structures to support secondary geographies, such as tags, categories, or menus.

For example, if your content objects are assigned to categories in the old system, then these categories will need to be created in the new system in advance of a migration (perhaps through a separate "pre-import" script), or created in real time as content is imported. Either way, incoming content will have to be checked for category assignments, which will need to be created at that time.

Also, given the iterative nature of content migrations (discussed more later in this chapter), an import job cannot assume the content hasn't already been imported once before. Any particular execution of an import job might be a rerun to update or refine imported content. This being the case, any import job needs to determine if the content object being imported already exists. If so, the existing object should be updated in place.

There might be a temptation to simply delete the imported object and re-create it, but this becomes complicated when dealing with relational content. Once imported object X has a "resolved" relationship (see the next section) to imported object Y, a deletion and recreation will break that relationship. As such, once created, imported objects should be updated.

Resolution

Content objects have links between them. They might exist in a geography that was re-created during the reassembly phase discussed earlier, but they might also have explicit references—the Author property of an Article object, for example, might link to another content object. Additionally, there might be numerous HTML links inside rich text.

These links will likely break during extraction and import. If an HTML link deep inside the rich text of content object X links to content object Y, you need to ensure that link is still valid once X and Y have moved into their new system. When migrating content, the URL structure of content often changes. These internal links need to be found and corrected to represent the new URL structure.

To do this, you must always store an old identifier with the new content object. The imported content object *must know where it came from*, which means it needs to know the ID or URL[8] of the corresponding content object in the old CMS. It's quite common to create temporary properties on content types in the new CMS to hold these values during development and migration, then delete these fields and their values after a successful launch, when they're no longer needed.

The ability to discover links between content objects depends highly on the API of the existing system. When processing an Article, can you simply export the ID of the Author? Or does your existing CMS store that as the public URL to the author? Or

---

8 Which is, let's face it, just another form of ID.

does the API of the system give you the entire Author content object when that property is referenced?

For referential attributes, attempt to export an identifier if at all possible. If your article links to an author, bring over the ID of that Author object as the value of the attribute. You'd much rather know that the Author is content object #634 than that it's "Bob Jones." In the latter case, you're going to have search for authors named "Bob Jones," and hope there's only one of them.

The process of reconnecting or "resolving" all these references happens at the end of an import job. Content is imported with broken links, then once all the content is in the new system, those links are resolved to point back to the correct objects. This cannot be done *as* content is imported, because there's no guarantee that the target object is already in the system—an Article might be imported before its Author is imported, for example.

In some cases, you might have to adjust your content model to allow weaker references during import. For example, if the Author property of your Article content type is intended to be required, you might have to relax this during import to allow Articles to be imported without an Author, then have the Author resolved later in the process. Once all content is in, the references can be resolved, and required restrictions can be reenabled.

To resolve HTML links, you will usually have to parse the HTML, which means finding a competent parsing library such as AngleSharp for .NET or Beautiful Soup for Python. All HTML needs to be processed, looking for all anchor or media tags, which then must be examined to determine if they link to external websites or internal content objects. For anchors linking to other objects that are imported, those objects need to be found based on the link and have the target of the link changed to reflect the new URL (or alternative method of linking). The URL should be inserted in the correct repository format for the new CMS, which might not be the public URL, but rather a placeholder URL intended for request-time resolution.

Normally, the resolution of content references doesn't happen immediately. It's common for several import jobs to occur before all the content is imported successfully and reference resolution can begin.

This is great for SEO, but it might not actually help your import process. In many systems, embedded URLs are actually stored as ID references to the target content. So, the URL inside the repository might look like this:

```
<a href="CMSLINK:634">
```

At render time, CMSLINK:634 is detected and replaced with the actual URL to content object #634 *at that instant*. It's unlikely that both CMSs support the same ID format and sequence, and you normally can't specify a new ID when creating new content. This means that keeping your URLs the same likely won't help you, because the ID of the target content object ("634" in the example) will almost certainly change on import.[9]

QA

Once content is in the new CMS and the links are resolved, migration QA can begin. Migration QA is designed to verify that content was moved into the new system successfully.

It has two levels:

Functional QA

This can be performed by someone with no domain knowledge, which means no knowledge of what the content actually means. All this tester is reviewing is whether or not the content is generally intact—whether all the content properties are populated, all the links work, any images are broken, etc. This person does not need to understand the content itself.

Domain QA

This needs to be performed by someone with domain knowledge, which means an understanding of the subject matter of the content. This tester is reviewing whether content is in the right place in the navigation, whether it was categorized correctly, if it's responding to search queries correctly, etc. This person needs to be qualified to make editorial decisions about content.

Ideally, there will be a specific checklist of content to review and a highly structured method of recording problems. If a tester finds a problem with content, where is that information logged? In many cases, adding temporary content properties is helpful,

---

9 In some cases, a CMS will use a 32-bit GUID as an ID. With these systems, explicitly specifying the ID on content creation is sometimes possible. If both CMSs have this format, it's theoretically possible to retain the same IDs during a migration. Clearly, however, this would be rare, and even then, the actual text of the link (which is detected and replaced) would be different.

such as a checkbox for Migration QA Complete or a text box to record migration defects directly in the content object itself. Alternatively, the ticket or issue management system used for functional QA can be used for migration defects.

When a defect is found, it needs to be evaluated for scope. Defects can be one of two types:

Import defects
> These are defects that need to be fixed at the import level, which means they're likely widespread. Often, small defects are harbingers of a larger problem. Finding one or two articles that have no Author property populated might reveal that a large portion of Author objects were accidentally skipped during migration and the only solution is to rerun the import and start over. Import defects can be very disruptive, and the entire migration team might need to stop in the middle of what they're doing while the import is corrected and rerun.

Object defects
> These are defects specific to a particular content object. These aren't the result of the import, but are issues that were either present on the old site and carried over, or resulted from something introduced through interaction with the new CMS—a missing style or JavaScript library, for instance. You do not have to reexecute the entire import for these, but they need to be marked for manual correction *after* the import has run for the final time.

Efficiency is key in these situations. Having the new website on one screen and the old website on another screen can ease the process of comparing versions of content. If the old URL is stored with the new content object, the old page could even be displayed under the new page in a temporary IFRAME, so testers can review both simultaneously.

Automated QA can be helpful during migration testing. Having a link checker running once a day and delivering a report of broken links can increase the testers' ability to find problems.

Migration Script Development

The process of automated migration tends to be iterative, with phases running in cycles. It's very much a process of performing some action, reviewing the result, modifying the process, then repeating.

The goal is to develop a *migration script* that exports content, transforms it correctly, imports it, and resolves all the references in one uninterrupted execution that might take minutes or hours. Then this script can be executed immediately prior to launch. All prior work during the migration cycle might be considered a "dry run" for the actual migration to take place closer to launch.

The word "script" here has dual meaning: it usually takes the form of an actual programming script that is executed, and in a more generic sense, it refers to a choreographed series of actions—both machine-powered and human-powered—that are intended to be executed in sequence at a later time.

Migration script development often looks like this:

1. Concurrently with the start of implementation of the new CMS, a developer begins investigating options for exporting content from the existing CMS. Multiple methods might be tested until one is identified that provides the least number of obstacles.

2. Once a workable method of export is found, the developer performs a test export. The results are reviewed, often found to be deficient in some way (a property is missing, the references are not correct, etc.), and the export is repeated. The developer might iterate through this cycle for days or weeks until arriving at an export that is deemed acceptable.

3. The exported content is compared against the requirements for the new CMS (which, in many cases, are still developing), and required transformations are identified. Methods of making these transformations are developed and incorporated into the export job, which can then be rerun with the transformations executed in real time.

4. When the new CMS has reached a state where content can be imported (at the very least, the content model must be implemented), an import job is developed to bring the exported content into the new CMS. Like the export, the import is performed once, reviewed, often found to be lacking, modified, and run again. This process is repeated multiple times until the imported content is found to be satisfactory. Often, the process of importing reveals a defect with the export or transformation, which moves the developer backward in the process.

At a certain point, the migration script has been refined to the point where further work is inefficient. If the launch date is still far in the future, development on the migration script might halt for weeks or months at this stage until the launch date approaches.

The One-to-One Migration

There's a school of thought that says a migration should simply be as direct as possible. Content types in the old system should be mapped to identical types in the new system. Templates should be mapped to identical templates. The content tree should be identical, navigation should be rendered using the same logic, etc.

Even if you *can* do this, it's often not a great idea. Different systems do things different ways, and what worked well in one system might not be the best way to do something in another system. Trying to force-fit the paradigms of one CMS onto another is a perfect recipe for a suboptimal implementation.

For example, perhaps your old system had "global attributes," which were applied to every content type, but your new system doesn't have these. It *does* have content type inheritance, which can accomplish the same thing, but this involves creating a more general abstraction type, then inheriting all types from it. A one-to-one migration would completely miss this technique, and the implementation would suffer for it.

Content Velocity and Migration Timing

The rate of content change on a particular website can be referred to as its "velocity." A news website has a high velocity of content, meaning new content is added multiple times per day. A small website for, say, a dental office might have a slower velocity, with pages that change every few months at most.

Even different areas on the same website can have differing velocities. On a high-traffic media site, content like the privacy policy likely has an extremely low velocity. It may be reviewed once a year, at most, and change once every few years.

The perfect content for migration has a velocity of zero, meaning the content will not change from the beginning of migration to the launch of the new website. Referring to the migration cycle we just discussed, a developer can begin exporting content and know that none of that content will change during the inevitable trial and error process that might take weeks or months.

In the real world, content *will* change. The content that is initially exported early in the cycle might change the very next day. Thus, the ideal situation is to refine the migration script to the point that nothing further is required to migrate content, and then run the completed script *immediately prior to launch*.

This type of "push-button migration" is a bit of a mirage. It can be done, but usually takes an enormous amount of work. Migrations can be idiosyncratic, in that specific content items might need intricate fine-tuning that's not easily scriptable. These will surface as object defects in the QA process. These one-off content corrections are quite common in order to fix problems with individual content items that are not efficient to incorporate into the migration script.

What normally happens is that a developer refines the migration script until further refinement is impossible or inefficient. The developer might get the migration script to the point where the content is extremely close to a launchable state. Even so, there will almost always be some amount of manual correction that needs to take place after the script completes execution.

The goal is to run this script as close to launch as possible, in order to include the most recent content changes from the existing site, then plan and execute the manual interventions immediately between that moment and launch.

At a scheduled point prior to launch, the migration script is executed for the final time. Rehearsal is over, and this is the actual migration. Content brought over during this execution will be officially considered "rehomed" in the new CMS. Unless mass import defects are found during QA, *the migration script will not be executed again.*

This period of time starts what's known as a "content freeze," because the editorial team is told to cease content changes on the existing site. Once the migration script has executed for the final time, the old site should not be changed because those changes will never make it to the new site. Content on the existing site is considered frozen, and cannot be changed until the new site is launched and it is changed there.

 The alternative to a content freeze is editorial duplication, meaning content is changed in both locations. This is clearly inefficient, but often happens when content is frozen and a critical content change needs to be made. While sometimes unavoidable, content editing during a freeze should be minimized as much as possible.

Content freezes are always stressful, as the editorial team has their hands tied while the organization has one foot in the old system and one foot in the new system. The goal is to resolve the object defects and finish the fine-tuning required to launch the new site as soon as possible and to allow the editorial team to begin managing content in the new system.

Sadly, some projects can run into major problems right before launch that push the launch date back. In these cases, staying in a content freeze might not be reasonable, and it makes sense to allow content editing to resume in the existing system with the intention of rerunning the migration script closer to the new launch date. Any manual interventions that were already made to the migrated content might be lost and have to be repeated during the new content freeze prior to the new launch date.

For these reasons, the timing of a migration can be an intricate balance between the velocity of content changes and the intended launch date. The goal is to refine a migration script to the point where manual interventions are minimal, and to schedule and execute those interventions during a content freeze window that is kept as short as is reasonably possible.

A Final Word of Warning

Do not underestimate a content migration. It can easily be the most labor-intensive and riskiest portion of a CMS implementation.

As soon as the CMS project is identified, a content inventory should be started to identify which content is moving and how it needs to be changed. You do not need to even know the new CMS platform to start this. If you know a migration will have to occur, it's time to start planning.

If you're ambitious and have the capacity, a developer might even start on extraction prior to any activity on the new CMS. Remember, the content has to be extracted at some point, and the extraction is fairly universal and not particularly dependent on the new CMS.

Work on the actual migration script should begin concurrently with development, as show-stopping problems with content import, export, and transformation are common. Do not simply lump migration script development in with other development work. Development of the migration script should be an assigned task, just like any other, and the developer should be given adequate time to complete it. In migration-intensive projects, a developer might be assigned to migration work and nothing else.

The migration script can often be some of the most complicated code in the entire project. And while it is temporary code, resist the urge to treat it as such. Good development practices should still be followed, including source control, testing, and continuous integration. This code is just as important to the success of the implementation as anything else the development team does.

Editorial staff need to be acutely aware of the migration schedule. They need to know, long in advance, when a content freeze will be imposed. During this time, it usually becomes an "all hands on deck" environment as the team works to QA and fine-tune migrated content in preparation for launch. Having half your editorial team go on vacation during the final weeks prior to launch is a recipe for a failed migration attempt.

Finally, overbudget for your migration, in terms of both time and funding. Too many projects have fallen over right before launch because of a migration that simply wasn't planned adequately. The industry is saturated with stories of new CMS implementations that stood idle for months, or even years, waiting for content to be migrated.

Perspective: Forecasting a Content Migration

by David Hobbs

Migrations—especially large ones—are complex beasts. They must be tamed. The good news is that organizations have more control over them than may be obvious.

Deane's ketchup analogy is apt since many organizations put off even seriously thinking about migrations until it is time to

migrate, at which time we have to do what's easy (squirt the ketchup bottle that's just sitting there) rather than what's important (perhaps preparing a sauce that would have completely transformed the dish but taken far more lead time). Although there are always migration surprises, we want to reduce those surprises. The key is early planning, which needs to happen even before those early migration tests that Deane rightly points out as important in the previous chapter.

Even light, early migration planning goes a long way. For instance, a healthy dose of "How is that content going to happen?" when looking at beautiful wireframes goes a long way, quickly pointing out areas where a last-minute dump of content from one system to another isn't going to achieve the vision everyone rallied behind via the wireframes. Aside from generally keeping migration in mind, a way to drive very concrete migration discussions (and broader discussions about the project goals) is to estimate the migration effort—perhaps even before sending RFPs to implementers— to make sure you are ready to actually execute upon what you are envisioning (and modify the plans or budget if not).

At its core, we have three migration control knobs:

- Weight (how much is moving)
- Quality (what quality we are attaining)
- Distance (how much of a change from the current content/site we are attempting)

We need to play with those control knobs in planning, and estimation gives us feedback as we turn the knobs. Even wild estimates will squeeze out useful dialog about all the other aspects of content management that Deane talks about in the book (for instance, you may discover that you need significant content modeling changes in addition to content changes).

An effective way to estimate is to attempt to consider buckets of content (for instance, product descriptions), look at samples (from your content inventory), and then consider what steps will need to be taken to handle the content during the migration (to decide which can be skipped, which can be automated, and how much effort the manual ones will take) to achieve a particular quality level. Then you can tweak and reestimate as needed going forward in the project.

But above all: plan for the migration early!

David Hobbs helps organizations make higher-impact web and intranet changes through early planning, and is the author of Website Migration Handbook v2 *and* "Rethinking the Content Inventory" *(David Hobbs Consulting).*

CHAPTER 14

Working with External Integrators

When it comes time to actually start an implementation, who does it? The organization wanting the CMS can certainly do it themselves, but there also exists a vast network of professional integration firms. Some CMS vendors will also integrate their own CMSs for their customers. Which option is the right one?

Many organizations have no development staff, making the decision clear. Even if an organization *does* have internal development staff, they might still seek an integrator for several different reasons:

- Their development staff is too busy with other work, and they simply don't have the capacity to do the work in-house.

- Their development staff is not focused on the Web; in many cases these resources are concentrated on internal, line-of-business applications, not what they view as a marketing exercise.

- Their development staff might do web development, but have no experience with this particular CMS.

- The reality of organizational politics and relationships often makes going outside the company more attractive. Marketing and IT have not normally been good bedfellows, and this often manifests itself as a search for an external integrator in an attempt to avoid IT restrictions or conflicts.

In these situations, contracting the CMS implementation can be a wise choice, through varying engagement models discussed in the following section.

Before considering a project, organizations should look at their internal resources and determine where they fit in. The result of that inventory will likely inform any decisions made about strategy, functionality, and system selection.

To ease confusion, this chapter will use the following definitions:

- The *organization* is the entity purchasing the CMS to use it in the future.
- The *vendor* is the entity selling the CMS software.
- The *integrator* is the entity installing, configuring, and templating the software for the project; in some cases (noted below), the vendor and the integrator might be the same.

This organizational trifecta is quite common in CMS implementations.

From this point forward, this chapter is targeted toward the *organization*. Henceforth, all usages of the pronoun "you" are intended to refer to the implementing organization, specifically.

Engagement Models

There are a number of ways of working with an integrator, based on the distribution of work:

Integrator develops
> In this case, you simply write a check and get a website in return. In some cases, you might even contract with the integrator for hosting and support, which means you might not ever actually take possession of the implementation.

Integrator and organization codevelop
> In this situation, you and the integrator develop the website together, splitting the work through some agreed-on method.

Organization develops, integrator consults
> In situations where you want to do most of the work in-house, you might still engage with an integrator for expert consulting. During scheduled or ad hoc meetings, the integrator can review the current work, discuss upcoming challenges, and provide guidance for how to handle specific situations or challenges.

Organization develops
> Technically, there is no integrator in this situation, though occasionally the software will be sold through another party. Either you will purchase from the vendor, or the software will be resold through an integrator.

The range is single-party on the extremes—solely the integrator on one end, and solely your organization on the other—with varying shades of gray in between.

Of the two options in the middle, the codevelopment model is the most logistically challenging. Collaborating on the same codebase can often be difficult, especially between teams spread across two otherwise unrelated organizations. How do you

---

split development? Along functional lines? Or does your organization want to be embedded in every decision?

Knowledge transfer incurs overhead. Some engagements quickly turn into long-term training relationships. Hopefully, this training is solely about the CMS, though in some cases integrators find themselves training on more fundamental questions of web development or development operations. Unfortunately, the need for this level of training is often not obvious until the project is underway.

Differences in experience between teams will quickly become apparent. An integrator might implement anywhere from 10 to 100 websites per year, whereas the average organization might reimplement their own website only once every three to five years.

These difficulties can be magnified when you consider deeper, subtler differences between a professional integrator and the typical organization:

Motivations
The integrator might be paid by the hour, while salaries at an organization are sunk costs.

Success metrics and time horizons
An organization has to live with the result, whereas the integrator typically disengages after the project is delivered.

Competition for attention
The integrator's clients have no affinity with each other—one client doesn't care about the other clients' projects, and is essentially competing with other clients for attention. By contrast, the employees at an organization are ostensibly working to advance a single mission and "client"—the organization itself.

Project styles
Integrators are often more agile and iterative than larger organizations. Conversely, an organization has the benefit of a more open-ended project—they can keep working to make an implementation better over time, while the integrator has to define a "hard" stopping point.

Interpersonal skills and experience
An integrator works with many clients and organizational styles, while an organization might be more insular and more accustomed to vendors adapting to it.

CMS Vendor Professional Services

Many CMS vendors offer "professional services," which are integration services for the CMSs they produce. For some vendors, this is simply a side business, meant to provide real-world exposure to their own products and to give customers an expert-services option to make a license purchase more attractive.

However, for other vendors, professional services represent a significant portion of their revenue. For a small subset, the CMS might even be sold at break-even or a loss and exist solely to position the vendor to sell integration services. For these vendors, a license sale without a professional services component might be viewed as a failure by the sales team.

The benefit of this arrangement is ostensibly that the vendors know their own systems better than anyone else and have unparalleled access to the product and technical teams. While this is undeniably true, the use of vendor professional services is polarizing for many in the industry—it can be viewed positively for the aforementioned reasons, or negatively due to problems of insularity.

The issue here is that when the only CMS a vendor works with is their own, the vendor might become insulated to other developments in the industry. More than once, I've observed vendor professional services teams that were unaware of developments and techniques in use by the broader CMS community. In these cases, a vendor might fall into the "my way or the highway" trap—they've always done task X this way, and their product is designed to do task X this way, so clearly this is the correct way to do task X.

Additionally, a vendor might be loath to admit their product has a shortcoming, and will therefore be resistant to helpful workarounds or external integrations. Whereas a third-party integrator might be willing to say, "This CMS is bad at task X, so we're going to use hack Y to fix that," a vendor typically won't do this because that might raise the awkward question of why they don't fix the underlying problem.

 A trickier gray area is when the integrator recommends a CMS product to the organization for purchase, which happens quite often as organizations will often begin their search at the integrator level, not the vendor level. In these cases, the integrator is not the vendor, but the integrator has tacitly *endorsed* the vendor, meaning the integrator has some skin in that game and will be expected to answer for vendor shortcomings at some level.

In the end, there are just as many arguments to use vendor professional services as there are not to. Vendors will often push professional services just as hard as they push their products, sometimes to the point of competing with other integrators that work with their products for the services business.

Sales and Scoping

Without question, the hardest problem for an integrator is defining the scope of the project. You and the vendor have to come to some agreement about the work that has to be done. This is harder than you might think.

You know what you want. Your website is already built in your heads. You have a vision of what the final product looks like. The integrator doesn't share this vision. They can't read your mind.

Furthermore, if you haven't integrated this particular CMS before, you are very likely making assumptions about how it works. You assume that feature X works in some particular way, or perhaps you don't know how it works, but you assume that for the amount of money you paid for the system, you should certainly be able to achieve result X through some method.

In Chapter 6, we defined the term reification, which is Latin for "to make real." Projects are a constant process of reification—taking a vague idea or goal and making it real through the application of information structures.

Consider these statements:

- "We're really failing at digital. We need to do better."
- "Our customers are uninformed. We need to keep them updated."
- "We need a database of technical notes that customers can subscribe to."

These statements are a progressive reification. They're a movement down a continuum toward a goal. Knowing that your organization is not doing well digitally is one thing. Defining exactly *where* you think you're failing is better. Defining a potential solution is even better yet. The problem is slowly being reified over time.

Unfortunately, all these statements have something in common: *none of them can be bid by an implementation firm.* The last one is the only one with an actionable plan, but it's still missing key information:

- What does a technical note look like?
- How many will there be?
- Who is authoring them?
- In what system will they be authored?
- How do they need to look?
- How do they need to be delivered?
- How does access need to be controlled?

- What does it mean to "subscribe" to the database?

I could go on—there are at least 50 questions that need to be answered here, and the answers to those questions would likely spark 100 more.

In many cases, these questions are assumptively answered by a common understanding of similar use cases with which both the organization and the integrator have experience. If the organization wants an RSS feed, this is something that's been done many times before, and both the organization and the integrator have a fairly common understanding of it and a common vision of where to start.

Other needs are far more variable: message boards, calendars, profile systems, commenting, etc. These things have also been done before, but the range of functionality from one example to another is so vast that the "common" understanding between organization and integrator might not be nearly as common as one or both of them think—the organization may think feature X is obvious and should be included, but only because it was present in the one example they've seen.

Websites are simply *highly* variable things. There are patterns, certainly, but two descriptions of a problem could result in wildly different websites, just as the phrase "single-family dwelling" could result in wildly different houses being built.

Preimplementation Artifacts

A key factor in trying to get a scope from an implementer is what you are bringing to the relationship. The integrator has to start from somewhere. What are you providing them with to guide their scoping process?

Consider these starting points:

- You have a vague idea of a shortcoming: "We need a new website."
- You have an existing website that has a problem: "We don't like the design," or "Our CMS is too hard to use."
- You have some narrative explaining what you want: "Here are the different sections we want the new website to have."
- You have detailed analysis by a qualified consultant: "Here is a functional specification, annotated wireframes, and a sitemap."

Of those, the last one is the only one that could conceivably be scoped and bid without further elaboration. The documents described—a functional specification, annotated wireframes, and a sitemap—are collectively referred to as "pre-implementation artifacts." This is the plan from which a website can be scoped.

Just as you wouldn't walk into a contractor's office and say, "How much for a house?" you can't really ask an integrator, "How much for a website?" The integrator will want a plan.

The Problem Behind the Problem

Although coming to an integrator well armed with a plan is better than the alternative, be careful of attempting to solve your own problem. Many times, problem statements like the one we saw earlier ("Our customers are uninformed…") are just the symptom of a bigger problem that's hiding behind the first.

Why are customers uninformed? Perhaps your documentation is poorly written. No CMS will fix this. Perhaps the problem is even bigger. Maybe your products are poorly named, and this causes confusion. Even bigger: maybe your product line is bloated with too much overlap.

This is not a book on general business practices, but just know that a CMS often gets blamed for problems that come from sources far removed from what a CMS can control. Before laying blame anywhere, do some research and make sure you're solving the right problem.

As we discussed in Chapter 12, the documents that most integrators need are:

Functional specification
> This is a narrative document explaining how the website should work. It should describe all content types and aggregations, users and groups, workflows and permissions, etc.

Annotated wireframes
> These are line drawings of how each interface should look. There should be at least one wireframe for each content type and aggregation, and there should be wireframes showing those at different responsive breakpoints (tablet, phone, etc.). Callouts should explain how specific functionality should work.

Sitemap or IA diagram
> This is the classic "boxes and arrows" diagram showing *all* the content on the website (or content groups; news articles in aggregate, for example). It should show logical and geographical relationships between content, and it should seek to be as comprehensive as possible.

This is the generally accepted minimum for a comprehensive, firm bid. A smart integrator, when presented with less than this, will seek to get to this point before providing you with a number.

If you don't bring this information with you to the integrator, expect to be referred to another firm to develop the information, or expect the integrator to do it for you *and charge you for it.*

Perhaps even consider treating the development of this set of documentation as a separate project with the integrator. If you're having trouble coming to a well-defined scope, the integrator can help you develop and document that scope as a self-contained project (perhaps even at a flat fee), then *bid the resulting plan.* Do not consider this an "extra" expense, since it has to be done at some point (remember, architects design houses for a reason). Breaking it off into its own project gives you the benefit of both a defined cost for it and more realistic and firm pricing for the larger project, due to better documentation.

With any project of moderate scope or larger, there will likely always be some level of misunderstanding between you and the integrator about scope. Experienced integrators know this and have planned for a certain amount of leeway in this respect. A shared goal is to limit these misunderstandings to the point where none of them have a material effect on the project.

Reality Check: Padding Costs as a Defensive Measure

Do websites get scoped and bid with less information than what I've described here? Yes, all the time. This is the optimal method of scoping a project, but I absolutely concede that this standard is often not reached.

The important point to understand is this: *vagueness will result in padding.*

If an integrator doesn't know exactly how you want feature X to work, they have two choices:

- Push you harder to define your requirements.
- Increase (or "pad") their bid to cover things they think you *might* want to do.

The first choice is the correct one, clearly, but the second choice is what often ends up happening. The integrator might fear losing the work, or they may have a hole in their schedule and need to get the work started, so they just pad their bid and hope for the best. If your actual requirements grow, they're covered; if they don't, the vendor pockets the padding.

An intelligent, rational scoping process is often the first casualty of the realities of running a professional services firm.

Costs

In years past, the rule of thumb was that a CMS implementation will cost three to four times what the CMS itself cost. Thus, a CMS that cost $50,000 to purchase will cost between $150,000 and $200,000 to implement, making the total cost of the project roughly four to five times the cost of the software (or estimated equivalent expense for an open source system).

This is a crude measure and not universally applicable, but it's valuable to at least frame how expensive implementations can be. They are almost always the majority cost in the total budget. Exhausting most of your budget on the CMS license will limit your ability to have it implemented, whether you do it internally or hire a third party.

In practice, content management implementations run the gamut from simple blogs that might work out of the box to incredibly complex content aggregation platforms that require massive development efforts. Consequently, there's no simple way to generalize about budget scope. Some of the factors that go into a budget include:

- The number of content types required
- The number of content aggregations required and their complexity
- The number of unique templates required and their selection rules and criteria
- The complexity of the design, and the number of pages that require advanced page composition
- The level of content migration and transformation required to bring existing content into the new CMS
- The amount of integration required with systems external to the CMS and the level of risk that brings with it
- The amount of editorial workflow and customizations required to support the editorial process
- The amount of project coordination and project documentation required
- The number of "one-off" page designs, not seemingly related to any other design

These factors can be combined in almost unlimited degrees for a wide range of budgets.

Perhaps surprisingly, aside from migration QA effort, total volume of content doesn't play as big a part in the budget or level of effort as you might think.

Consider a website with 100,000 content objects, all having the same content type, structure, and aggregation requirements. The implementing developer is really working with that content at the content *type* level, not the content *object* level. Even though there are 100,000 objects, there's still only one type. It's only a slight exaggeration to say that the developer cares very little if there are 100 objects or 100,000—the level of effort required to create the types, aggregations, and editorial tools is largely the same.

This is the same reason that "one-off" page designs can inflate the cost of an implementation. UX firms have been known to run wild, delivering detailed, individual designs for dozens and dozens of pages, each introducing a content management or templating idiosyncrasy for which the integrator will have to account. Remember that inconsistency is the bane of templating, and each unique page design comes with a price tag.

Even dynamic page composition has limits, because those systems work from a palette of available interface elements. Each of those elements has to be identified along with all of its variations, and then developed, templated, and managed in such a way that the page fits together the way the designer intended.

Finally, when budgeting, things that are unknown are what get an outsized allotment of time and funds. External integration is likely the best example. When your CMS has to work with Other System X, unless the implementation team has worked with both, the schedule and budget will suffer for it. Making two systems work together can be difficult, or sometimes impossible. The effort required for even seemingly simple integrations can sometimes dwarf that expended on the remainder of the project.

Written Agreements

At some point, the agreement between you and the integrator will need to be codified and executed via some written instrument. This document is ostensibly the enforceable agreement for both parties.

Nomenclature is a problem here, because there's no agreed-upon vocabulary for this industry, especially when it comes to project documentation. What one firm calls a "proposal" might be a "statement of work" or a "memorandum of understanding" to another.[1]

In general, documentation falls into the following types. You'll often see all three of these when working with an integrator:

Marketing proposal
> This is an attractive sales package meant to sell you on a firm's capabilities. It might not speak to your project at all, or even your organization, but instead promotes the integrator's capabilities in general terms. You might see this package

---

[1] My company generally titles its proposal documents as "Proposal for Professional Services." A few times, a prospective customer has said, "This looks great, now we just need a Statement of Work." These situations have sometimes been resolved by simply changing the title on the document and resubmitting it.

one time, when your organization is initially being courted by the integrator. This is not an executable document (there is no signature line).

General Services Agreement (GSA)

This is a highly legal document spelling out things like warranties, required insurance coverage, intellectual property rules, etc. GSAs are usually drafted and reviewed by attorneys. There will likely not be a mention of a specific project, as these documents are usually meant to govern the life of the *entire relationship* between the integrator and the organization. These are executable documents, and often the subject of significant negotiation and revision. These documents are also known as "Master Services Agreements" or "Master Vendor Agreements."

Statement of Work (SOW)

This is the project-specific document that explains exactly what the integrator is doing for *this specific project*. If you do more than one project with an integrator, you will likely have one SOW for each project. As the title implies, a Statement of Work is an explanation of the details around a specific unit of work. This is an executable document. The SOW is sometimes referred to as a "proposal" or a "project proposal."

When it comes to the General Services Agreement, a key question is: which side generates it? The integrator no doubt has one of their own, but there's a good chance your organization has one as well. Do you execute both? What if they conflict? Do you need to review both and come to a third, resolved version? For many compliance departments in larger organizations, this isn't acceptable as they want *their* GSA executed, specifically.

Many times, the side with the most lawyers wins. The integrator will submit their GSA for execution, and the client will return it with so many changes that the integrator decides it's easier to review the organization's GSA and just ensure nothing in it is objectionable.

When negotiating a project, there's often an unspoken vibe as to which organization is going to require the more stringent documentation. That organization usually gets *their* document executed, even if it doesn't differ remarkably from the other side's version. So long as both parties agree to the contents, who "owned" the document in the beginning is of little import.

The Statement of Work is important enough to require its own section for discussion.

The Statement of Work

The Statement of Work is the guiding document for any particular project. If there is a disagreement about some aspect of a project, the SOW is usually the arbitrating document. If something isn't in the SOW, then it doesn't legally exist.

At a minimum, the SOW needs to explain:

- *What* is being done
- *When* it is being done
- *How much* will it cost

What, when, and how much. Those are the critical questions in any implementation.

What is being done?

The SOW has to clearly state the scope of the project. In many cases, the preimplementation artifacts discussed previously will be attached to this document and referenced as exhibits.

The scope in the SOW often says something to the effect of, "Integrator will develop a website to fulfill the functionality and requirements described in Exhibit A." In other cases, the functionality will be described in the document itself, though this is more rare since the requirements can be lengthy.

The SOW should also state what form the deliverables should take. Is the integrator delivering the website as a set of files and a database backup for the organization to deploy? Or is the integrator actually deploying the website to a server somewhere? Are they hosting it?[2]

In practice, there is a constant debate on the required depth of this documentation. To what level of detail does the website need to be described?

This is hard to quantify, for the simple reason that *a website can always be described in more detail.* No matter how specific you are, you can always be *more* specific, and what level of description is "good enough"?

The desire to describe every last aspect of a website can turn into a black hole of time lost, and it often drifts past simple scoping and into deeper consulting as technical questions get more detailed and are answered with more and more specificity. There's only so much analysis an integrator will do without being paid, and there's only so much time either side will wait before they need to get started.

Where to draw this line varies for every organization and integrator, and it's often simply a level of comfort and trust. When both sides agree that the level of description is enough and they feel comfortable moving forward, they do. There are no hard and fast rules here.

---

2 Note that hosting agreements are almost always separate from integration agreements. The model of engagement for hosting a website over time as opposed to a one-time integration makes the nature of the agreements entirely different.

Nonimplementation Consulting

Occasionally you might engage with an integrator for reasons other than an implementation. They might be consulting to answer some questions, or evaluating a poorly performing implementation, or perhaps helping you evaluate and plan some new functionality.

For these agreements, it's best to concentrate on deliverables. What is the integrator delivering in exchange for payment? A document? A set number of hours of analysis? A series of phone calls? Some prototyped code?

When a project doesn't involve a concrete implementation, it can be vague and ill-defined. Clearly defining what the integrator is delivering helps all parties understand the goal the project is moving toward.

When is it being done?

The Statement of Work needs to address dates in the following two ways:

Start date
> When is the integrator available to start? Expect a delay for the start—it will be rare for an integrator to have enough staff just sitting around that they can start right away. Some integrators might be booked three to four months in advance.[3]

Project duration
> Regardless of when it starts, how long will the project take? This shouldn't be discussed in hours, because that's generally a function of project cost (projects are almost always priced against some nominal hourly rate). Rather, you want to know actual calendar duration. From the start date, how many weeks will there be until launch?

It's wise to be clear with the integrator whether your project is date-driven or quality- and feature-driven. Do you have a desired launch date, and is this date set in stone? Should the integrator plan their development to hit a specific date no matter what, or should they plan on delivering the best final product possible, even if that means investing more time?

How much will it cost?

Clearly, you need to have some idea of your final cost, but determining this is rarely simple. Projects can be priced in several ways:

---

3 If an integrator can get started on a huge project instantly, it might be a good idea to ask why. Sometimes the integrator just happens to have a convenient hole in their schedule. In other cases, they may be overstaffed or not have enough business to sustain themselves.

Flat fee

You will get website X for $Y, full stop. Expect this on projects where you've defined your requirements clearly. If your requirements are vague and exploratory, the only way you'll get a flat fee is with significant padding (or foolishness on the part of the integrator).

Time and materials

The integrator will perform work for $X per hour or per day. The integrator should give you an estimate of total hours. If they don't, then you're simply agreeing to pay a certain hourly rate, open-ended.

Fee-capped

You will spend $X, and the integrator will get as much functionality done for that amount as possible.

Clearly, the first option is the most rigid and therefore the safest for both sides. With that option, both scope and cost are defined in the SOW. However, because this is so rigid, it leads to two other phenomena that we've discussed previously: a tendency for cost padding, and a need to excessively define the scope of work, often leading to delays.

The other two options are both more flexible. A time-and-materials project has the scope defined, but the cost is open-ended. The integrator will simply keep working by the hour until the job is done. This can be risky for the organization. A fee-capped project has a hard limit on expense, but no expectation of delivered functionality. The integrator could theoretically hit the cap with only 50% of the project finished.

In the end, deals are fundamentally negotiated around the assignment of risk. Both sides—the organization and the integrator—are trying to minimize their risk. Rigid deals are risky for the integrator, so they're often padded to compensate (which implies a type of risk for the organization—the risk of overpayment). On the other hand, flexible deals are risky for the organization in that there's no clear correlation between functionality and expense.

It's entirely possible to pursue a hybrid approach. If 90% of your project is straightforward, consider a fixed fee for that portion of work. The 10% that's exploratory and risky might be handled under different terms—time and materials or fee-capped. This method allows work to start quickly on the mainstream part of the project, instead of the entire project being delayed while details of the more complicated sections are labored over.

Regardless of deal structure, the payment terms and schedule need to be defined:

- When is payment due?
- Are payments tied to milestones?

- If it's a time-and-materials project, how are hours recorded? Can they be audited?
- What are the terms of acceptance in order for the integrator to request payment?
- Is there a deposit required before work can begin?

Beware of large deposit requirements. On smaller, shorter projects and consulting engagements where there is no functioning deliverable, 50% is common. But on longer projects, a requirement to pay half up front may be indicative of an integrator who needs the money to fund current payroll and liabilities. Some professional services firms can be extended to the point where they need deposits in order to stay in business. This is clearly dangerous.

When discussing deal structure and payment terms, remind yourself that at some point, your Accounts Payable department will need to write a check to pay an invoice from the integrator. What information will they need to be able to do that?

You Are Not Buying a Used Car

This is not a book on business negotiation, but when discussing implementation costs, my experience has made one point very clear: *you do not want to be the client an integrator is losing money on.*

This relationship is not brief—it needs to last for a significant period of time, both during the implementation and through post-launch and the inevitable changes that come later. My firm has clients that we've been actively working with for almost a decade. Additionally, remember that your integrator has other clients, and in some respects, you're competing with them for attention.

With all due respect to used car salesmen, taking advantage of one is usually something to be celebrated. It's not the same with your integrator. They have a business to run. When their capacity gets tight, you absolutely do *not* want to be known as "the unprofitable client."

Production

There's a temptation to think that since you're paying the integrator specifically for production, once the project is started, you're hands-off. Resist this thought process. You have several critical things to keep track of during production.

Team Proximity and Dedication

What will your relationship with the project team be? While it's common to work with a remote team, other firms might work on a staff augmentation model, where the developers come to your site and work in-house.

This is getting rarer, and is almost always unnecessary, but some organizations require it. Some organizations have such stringent security requirements that access is controlled down to geographic locations (this is quite common in banking and finance). In other cases, the code might have to interact closely with other parts of the organization's infrastructure that are only available on their network.

Define your proximity to the team. If they are coming on-site, do you have the physical accommodations for them? More than one project has gotten off to an awkward start because no one thought to ask where the project team would sit while they're in the building.

Additionally, to what extent is the production team dedicated to your project specifically? Are you employing them full time, or are you sharing them with other clients? Can you expect that they will always be working on your project?

Unless specifically stated, assume that the production team is working on more than just your project. As such, you usually can't micromanage their work schedule or their process.

Development and Testing Infrastructure

Where will the work in progress be located, and what will your access be to it? Developers commonly work on their local workstations and deploy code at regular intervals to an integration environment. Who controls this environment? Will it be on your infrastructure, or on a server controlled by the integrator?

Where will the source code be stored? It's quite common for an integrator to store source code in their own environment, but at what times are they required to turn it over to you? Additionally, what level of visibility do you have into the source code management system? Can you inspect it at any time?

How do you record issues? During development, you might bring up a concern, only to be told it will be addressed later. How does this issue get tracked? Is there a ticket management system or a wiki where these items can be tracked so they don't fall through the cracks? Unless your concerns are recorded somewhere, the likelihood of a production team remembering each of them and circling back proactively is quite small.

Project Communication and Check-in

You need to establish what level of communication you will have with the integrator's production team, and what level of visibility you will have into the project.

It's very common to have a scheduled project call with the project team to discuss the work in progress. Define the schedule for this call in advance. Weekly is common. If you have an extremely intensive project with a larger, dedicated team, perhaps a subset of the team might have a daily "standup" meeting to discuss progress. However, daily meetings are often unnecessary.

Remember that your project often won't be the only project the developers are working on. Additionally, they might not work on your project every day. If they're waiting on something, or had to fight a fire on another project, there's a good chance that they simply won't have done anything on your project that day. For this reason, daily meetings are usually too much. They'll often be cancelled because no one has anything to report, and when they're cancelled multiple days in a row is usually the time it becomes obvious that they were overkill to start with.

As with any meeting, be careful of inviting people who don't need to be there. In some cases, having the development team in a design meeting is helpful, but only if you need their specific input. Having them on the phone "just in case" wastes their time, and you should expect to be charged for this.

 Meeting costs add up quickly. Having a five-person development team on a one-hour call at a rate of $150/hour makes it a $750 meeting. There are not a lot of situations where this is money well spent.

You need to define your point of communication at the integrator. Will you have a dedicated project manager? If you have a concern, who do you contact, and how will this concern be escalated if you're not satisfied with the result? What will be your level of ad hoc, unscheduled contact with the development team? Can you call a developer out of the blue? Will you have access to developers directly via email or instant message?

It's common for integrators to limit direct access to developers. This isn't to make things difficult, but just to limit interruptions, which can be deadly to productivity. You might think, "Well, it's just a quick question," but when this happens with multiple clients, multiple times per day, it becomes a serious drain on progress.[4]

Work Acceptance and QA

At some point, the integrator will invoice for the project, which is contingent (explicitly or implicitly) on the organization accepting the work product. What does this

---

4 Programmers are usually trying to reach that ideal state of "flow," where they're in the zone and making extraordinary progress. This phenomenon is well known and much heralded in programming, and interruptions are antithetical to it. It might be worth reading the seminal paper on this concept: "Flow: The Psychology of Optimal Experience" (*https://www.researchgate.net/publication/224927532_Flow_The_Psychology_of_Optimal_Experience*) by Mihaly Csikszentmihalyi.

process look like? This can get closely intertwined with the methodology and development style the integration firm uses.

To describe what they do, many development teams throw around the term "agile." This term only makes sense when looking at how software used to be built.

In years past, software development used what was informally known as a "waterfall" methodology. The development process proceeded down a serial line of tasks. Just like water can't go back up and fall down a waterfall a second time, each task built on the first, moving slowly and steadily forward. The result was that the software product tended to not come together until the very end of the process. There might have been nothing to see until the project was almost complete.

The problem here should be obvious: with nothing to see, how do you know if the product is coming together well? A huge problem might be only identified upon testing the final product, and by then it's too late to change anything.

In 2001, a group of software engineers released what they called "The Agile Manifesto," (*http://agilemanifesto.org/principles.html*) which was a declaration that the old methodology wasn't working well. The manifesto has 12 principles, but the first one is key:

> Our highest priority is to satisfy the customer through early and continuous delivery of valuable software.

This is the key to agile software development: deliver early and often. Get something into the hands of the client as soon as possible, no matter how rough or stripped down, then collect feedback and iterate back through the process. Refine the product over time with the client's feedback an integral part of the process.

The term "agile" is overused (and is often thrown around by developers too young to have even been exposed to a "non-agile" process), but it should be accepted as a standard practice. The key is for the integrator to avoid the "crawl into a cave" syndrome of building the website without you seeing it until immediately before launch.

 Back in 1999, my business partner and I built the website for an NFL football team. The team's marketing department approved a design comp, then saw nothing else for *months*. I remember a phone call one week before the site launched in which the client said, "The site is actually getting built, right?" They first laid eyes on it a few days before we changed DNS to coincide with a planned marketing campaign that could not be delayed. I present this as a textbook case of what *not* to do.

In practical terms, you need to know how often you will be given the opportunity to inspect and pass judgment on the work product. There should be scheduled times during the project where parts of the final product are released for your inspection.

These will usually coincide with invoicing. You will often be asked to inspect, approve, and officially accept the work product at these points.

Related to this, at what point do you officially "take possession" of the work product? This is likely related to the final disposition of the code. If it's meant to be deployed to your environment, the integrator might state that this happens upon deployment, but it gets murkier when the code is to be hosted by the integrator themselves, or by a third party. At what moment do you state that the work product is acceptable and fulfills the agreement? This should be clearly defined in advance.

Define the level of QA you require in advance. Will you require the integrator to develop formal test scripts and provide you with results for each iteration, including regressions of prior tests? Or will you just take the integrator's word that everything works fine? Do you want to see the code? Do you want line-level input on coding decisions? Different organizations require different levels of QA and documentation, and don't let this be a surprise when it comes time to accept the work. If you have high expectations of formal QA, the integrator needs to know this so they can build that into their scope.

Content Development

It's very likely that the implementation project will change your website in such a way that content changes will be required. Content will have to be reorganized, or new content will have to be created. And this doesn't take into account all the content that will have to be migrated.

Who will make these changes or create this content? Are you paying the integrator for these changes? Are you paying another firm? Or do you need to make these changes yourself?

The scope of content development is often underestimated by the organization, and is consequently delayed. Many websites have been completed and have sat for months waiting for necessary content changes to happen. "We'll launch as soon as we get the content in shape" is a common refrain.

Define what needs to be done on your side prior to launch, and dedicate staff and resources to this. Make sure the timing is clear. When does your content have to be complete, and what disposition should it be in? Can you input it directly into the developing website, or will you need to stage it in some neutral location such as Google Docs or a service specifically designed for this, such as Gather Content (*http://gathercontent.com*)? More than one integrator has gotten an unexpected ZIP file of hundreds of Word documents right before launch with the note, "Here's all our content. Let us know when it's in the system!"

There's a joke in this industry (and many others, I'm sure) that "this job would be great if not for the clients." While clearly dark humor, understand that the biggest threat to your project might actually be *you*. Make sure you have your own bases covered during the implementation process.

Don't Be THAT Client

Every integrator has dozens of horror stories of clients who dragged their feet on every task assigned to them. No matter how clear the integrator is on what needs to be done and when, some clients never hold up their side of the bargain.

Worse: when the client finally *does* come through with what they were supposed to supply, they expect the integrator to drop everything and get back on their project *immediately*. These clients don't understand that an integrator has to avoid schedule holes, and when it becomes obvious that a client isn't going to deliver, they're removed from the production schedule.

Always remember that your integrator has other clients. If you cause your project to come grinding to a halt, expect the integrator to move on. When and if you finally come through, expect to suffer through a delay while you're slotted back into their production schedule.

Training and Support

As we discussed in Chapter 12, training and support can be tricky because the website is often a combination of a vendor's software and an integrator's implementation.

When planning training, determine who in your organization needs to get trained at what level. How many people need to know basic, foundational principles about the CMS software? On the other extreme, how many people need to know nothing more than what it takes to get the job done?

Most integrators won't do the basic, fundamental training, for the reason that the vendors use training as a revenue stream. Vendors make money from training and would frown on integrators offering formalized training courses on their software as competition.

Most vendors offer training in one or more of several models:

On-site
    A trainer from the vendor travels to your organization, which is appropriate for training larger groups.

Hosted
    Your employees fly to the vendor's location (either their actual location, or a remote location from which they're offering training at a particular time); this is

appropriate to train a smaller number of people than would justify flying a trainer in.

Remote
> The vendor runs a training class online, usually in real time, for a group of participants.

Unlike the basic training, implementation training is something only the integrator can provide. The most effective training is likely a mixture of both, though participants might have to be prepared to unlearn some vendor training principles when undergoing the implementation training ("I know they told you it worked like that, but *this* is how we actually implemented it…").

Much like training, support becomes a jurisdictional issue between vendor and integrator. If problems arise, are they related to the software (vendor) or the implementation (integrator)?

A running website being actively managed also brings in the variables of the hosting environment and the editors themselves. There are dozens of combinations of variables that might be the source of any given problem.

There are four major types of support that an integrator may provide to an organization:

Downtime support
> In these situations, the site is significantly and obviously impaired for some reason that an editor cannot fix. Thankfully, critical software errors in mainstream CMS products are relatively rare. Most products are tested to such an extent that glaring, show-stopping bugs aren't common. When such a problem does happen, it's often infrastructure-related (the hard drive is full, DNS is broken, the database server stopped working, etc.).

Error support
> In these situations, a user has encountered an error that may or may not be public (it might only be visible to editors). The user is doing the task correctly, but something in the software has clearly failed. The editor cannot fix this problem and needs external assistance.

User support
> Sometimes there is no error, but the editor does not know how to accomplish a specific, defined task that she feels she should be able to complete. This is often due to a training deficiency.

Consulting support
> Again, there is no error in these cases, but the editor wants to accomplish a larger, more systemic goal, and doesn't know the best way to do this. This is less

support, and more *advice*. The editor needs to know the most optimal route to bring about some larger goal.

The last two types—user and consulting support—can get tricky because the lines between support, training, and consulting can be blurry. At what point is this less of a support issue and more of a consulting issue, where the integrator is being asked to explain foundational concepts of content management and web development, and assist the organization in planning out new functionality? By the same token, at what point is it obvious that some people just didn't pay attention during training and the integrator is explaining the same thing for the tenth time? These conversations can get awkward.

Much like with the scoping process, there's only so much an integrator will do without being paid. The line between what's considered support and what's considered consulting or additional, unscoped training can be tricky to navigate.

It's becoming quite common in professional services to pursue retainer-style agreements where organizations pay a monthly fee for access to a development and consulting team as necessary. These are generally "use or lose" hours that allow ad hoc access to expert services but do not carry over between periods. Even if such support is not needed long term, it's still quite beneficial to have such access in the months immediately following launch, when most questions and issues are bound to arise.

A Final Word

While it would be ideal if the relationship between organization and integrator was perfectly business-like and free from interpersonal issues, this is never the case. The organization and the integrator (and, to a lesser extent, the vendor) will work together closely, usually for an extended period of time. This relationship can stretch for years after launch in some cases.

In a relationship like this, human factors will come into play over time. Organizational politics can and will have an influence on the project. Development teams at the organization might be resentful of an external vendor coming in, marketing teams might have had bad experiences in the past, or an integrator might not be able to look past their perception of the organization's unsophisticated thinking.

 A friend once remarked that "some of the most childish, immature people I know are sitting in corner offices, hiding behind six-figure salaries."

It's crucial to establish a relationship of trust and communication between both parties. If you don't feel like this exists, *keep looking*. A poor relationship at the beginning of the project often doesn't improve, and barriers between teams can fester over years and have a devastating negative effect on the project over time.

Perspective: Mutual Trust Is the Key to an Integrator Relationship

by Joe Kepley

I've been working in consulting relationships for around fifteen years, and what I've found is that like any relationship, the relationship between an integrator and a client thrives on mutual trust and respect.

In the best client relationships, we've worked with a client long enough to understand their business well. Our team trusts the client to know their business, and they trust us to provide a great CMS experience. When there's a problem, we work through it together, and we have each other's best interests at heart because we all think of ourselves as part of the same team.

The relationships that don't work, like any relationship, are the ones where one side wants to squeeze the most out of the other party and move on to something else. We've had clients that made it clear that we were the means to an end, felt our time or advice should be free, or just wanted to use us as leverage against an internal team.

CMS experts are rare, and if Blend as an organization continually subjects our team to groups that are willing to grind them down or ignore their advice, we're telling them they're not important. If we're willing to keep pushing ourselves into client relationships where we're not a good fit, we're saying the invoice has more value than the success of the project.

As a professional services firm, we've spent years building a team of CMS experts. That team is the most valuable asset our company has. We owe it to both our clients and our employees to maximize the healthy relationships, and minimize the unhealthy ones.

When we have a client that values our work and our input, participates in their solution by taking the time to communicate, and treats us as a trusted partner, we'll bend over backwards to make sure they have a great site and a great experience with us. Every group on both the client and integrator side of the relationship should work together to develop that.

Joe Kepley is the CTO of Blend Interactive, a CMS integration firm.

CHAPTER 15

Where Content Management Is Going

Web content management is constantly in a state of flux. As a discipline, it rides on the back of the Internet itself, and as the Internet landscape changes, content management changes with it.

In writing this book, I've had to navigate the blurry line between what aspects of content management are foundational and unlikely to change (content modeling, for example) and what aspects are still being defined by the marketplace (marketing automation and personalization, to name but two). In five years, parts of this book will still be wholly relevant, other parts will be showing their age, and a half-dozen new chapters will need to be added.

As a preemptive strike, I'd like to look forward a bit and consider where content management might be headed in the future. This is a practical exercise in that I'd like you to be ready for what might be around the corner, but it's also an exercise in perspective, as I want you to understand the axes and inflection points along which this industry might expand, to give you some sense of the elasticity of content management—the industry, the software, and the discipline.

Chapters like this are difficult to write because they're always a combination of legitimate prediction, documenting the obvious, and unavoidably spinning the conversation in the direction the author would *like* something to go. While I think evidence exists for all of the following predictions, only time will tell how accurate they are. In five years, I'm quite prepared for someone to find me at a conference and mock me for how wrong some of them turned out to be.

Additionally, predictions like these inevitably involve looking back at history and making interpretations of what has happened in the industry. My preferences and opinions will show through here. If you have a long history in this industry, you will no doubt disagree with my perspective on some of what has gone before. All that said, let's take a look…

Fewer Open Source CMSs Will Get Traction

The open source CMS market is already crowded. I've long maintained that developers like to architect new CMS platforms more than any other type of software. This is due largely to a quick ramp-up time (a lot can get done in a short period of time, before development inevitably hockey sticks upward), but it's also due to the Lure of the Framework.

Developers simply *love* writing frameworks. We love solving problems that stay theoretical. And that's basically what a CMS does: it solves a problem that doesn't exist yet. Someday, the CMS we build will solve an *actual* problem, certainly. But initially, it's just a framework for a website, and the developer receives all the joy and endorphin rush of "solving" that problem, while the associated problems remain safely hypothetical. It's all of the fun with none of the accountability.

Ten years ago, there was a dizzying array of open source projects launching seemingly every week, each one claiming some new angle on the content problem. Every once in a while, one would get a toehold in the collective attention span of CMS developers and claw its way toward some user base of note. All the others would fall away.

But even getting that initial toehold is becoming harder and harder. So many products are available in the marketplace that developers are seemingly retreating into what's well known as a defensive mechanism. Existing open source systems are exerting something of a gravitational pull, drawing in more and more developers while slowly getting larger and larger, which allows them to draw in even more developers.

Very few new open source platforms have gotten traction in the last five years, especially compared to the five years before that. Systems like Concrete5 (*http://www.concrete5.org*) and ProcessWire (*https://processwire.com*) are still young, but have managed to knit together vibrant and dedicated communities.

In contrast, Microsoft's open source CMS offering, Orchard (*http://www.orchardproject.net*), has been unable to gain much traction or mindshare, even with a gigantic community of ASP.NET MVC developers to draw from and relatively few open source options in that space. And there are dozens of other new entrants that will simply never reach critical mass.

The thing that sustains and grows an open source project is the ability to attract developers, and the excitement of a new system is quickly tempered by the lack of a community and installed base in which the system might grow and be tested.

What *will* give birth to new systems is the adoption of new web frameworks. Every time a new language or programming paradigm gets traction, a handful of open source projects will spin off of early projects written for those platforms.

At the time of writing, the new darling of web developers is Node.js. We will no doubt see a handful of CMS options for that framework in the coming years, and those frameworks will have the benefit of few competitors. They will sink or swim based on the adoption of the underlying platform—if it withers, so will they.

In no way am I predicting that the development of open source CMSs will completely dry up, but there is simply less and less reason to roll the dice on a new system. While some developers enjoy being contrarian and iconoclastic as a rule, most others will simply be seduced by the array of plug-ins and support available for the larger platforms.

Decoupling Will Make a Comeback

Decoupled CMSs built the Web. When I first entered this industry, we didn't even have the term "CMS." We barely had the term "content." As I noted in the preface, we just had a bunch of files sitting around and were forced to manage them by raw necessity.

Some of the first CMSs, in fact, were simply collections of Perl scripts that templated data and made aggregations easier to manage. Movable Type—one of the earliest blogging platforms, launched in 2001—was a Perl-based scripting system that generated static HTML.

But decoupled CMSs suffered from a need for active delivery environments. The need for real-time interactivity (message boards, commenting, rating) never lent itself well to static files. As websites became more variable, immediate access to the repository was required and the concept of a clearly defined "moment of publication" got blurrier and blurrier. Small changes in the delivery environment (a comment, a rating, etc.) were forcing full republishing, which became problematic.

Over time, more and more functionality was pushed into the delivery environment, until it became obvious to new developers that content should be managed there as well. With this, decoupled architectures began to decline.

At the same time, managed websites got smaller and smaller. While CMSs were used on larger sites, many smaller websites were still managed with client-side editors like Microsoft FrontPage and Adobe Dreamweaver. As CMSs began to filter downward, a generation of sites came online that couldn't suffer through the complexities of decoupling and required the latest delivery-side interactivity. This further spurred the adoption of coupled CMS platforms.

But the tide is slowly turning back. What seems to have happened is that the interactivity needed in the delivery environment has become detached from the CMS—it's now serviceable by systems that might not need interaction with the CMS at all. Adding commenting to a website now is as simple as using a pluggable system like Disqus, IntenseDebate, or even Facebook. Client-side technologies have advanced to the point where integration with social networking platforms is simply done with a JavaScript include. Marketing automation vendors can integrate solely on the client side, and even A/B testing is available with virtually no templating changes.

This means that rich, variable user experiences can now ride "on top" of static HTML files. The HTML files containing the content simply play host for a dizzying array of interactivity provided by other services. Most client-side technologies neither know nor care whether their HTML hosts exist in files written to disk 10 years ago or generated on the fly a millisecond ago.

Even further down this road, the relationship between server-generated content and client technologies may be on the verge of flipping entirely. Full-stack JavaScript frameworks like AngularJS, React, and Dojo are giving rise to "single-page apps," where what's delivered to the client is not content at all, but an application that runs in the browser and might retrieve content based on user behavior. In these situations, instead of content delivering the client functionality, we now have the opposite—*the client functionality is delivering the content*. In effect, we're installing a templating and output engine in the browser every time a visitor comes to the website.

All of these changes are eliminating some significant benefits of coupled CMSs. Removing post-publication functionality, and sometimes even templating, leaves an editorial core that can survive just as well as a decoupled system and might be the better for it.

As noted in Chapter 9, decoupled publishing brings unique advantages in terms of scalability, stability, and security. And delivery environments are becoming simpler and simpler to create and maintain. Amazon Web Services allows the hosting of static content from the Amazon S3 storage framework, and with a couple of mouse clicks this can be integrated into CloudFront, its content delivery network. Combine this with a decoupled CMS and you can literally have an almost endlessly scalable environment to stage content for optimized worldwide delivery in five minutes. (For developers who have been working in this space since the mid-'90s, the mind *boggles*.)

We may very well see the CMS withdrawing back into its core, which has traditionally been the modeling, management, and aggregation of content. When and if this happens, decoupling is poised to play an enormous role in the landscape that results.

The Rise of Static Site Generators

A new wave of static site generators coupled with grid hosting is an interesting development.[1] Many command-line tools now exist to template and assemble content stored in flat files, usually in Markdown. The resulting HTML is then pushed into a hosting environment.

Some tools even turn CMS-powered sites into static sites. You might have a Drupal or WordPress site on your local workstation or behind your corporate firewall, and these tools connect to it and "flatten" it into static HTML for hosting elsewhere.

Tools like these are effectively turning coupled CMSs into decoupled ones. All the editorial features are still used to model, manage, aggregate, and template content, but the delivery features are abandoned in favor of all the other benefits that decoupling provides.

Focus on Marketing Tools and Integration Will Increase

Two years ago, I attended a networking event for CMS professionals on the East Coast. One of the speakers was the web marketing manager for a services company, who came in to explain how they handled their content. For an hour, he detailed the remarkable process and techniques they used to monitor, personalize, deliver, and optimize their content. It was obvious that his team was the focus of an enormous amount of attention and budget at this organization.

I was interested to know what CMS they were using that supported this level of marketing optimization. When I asked, he mentioned the name of a marketing automation vendor. I knew this particular vendor wasn't a CMS provider, so I pressed him on what *content management platform* they were using.

He simply didn't know. He explained that he was notified by the editorial team of what the content calendar looked like so his team could prepare, and then given a URL just before that content was published. He had no idea how the content was managed or generated. He and his team didn't need to know.

I've already made the point that many organizations aren't looking for a content *management* system as much as they're looking for a content *marketing* system. The fact

---

1 See *https://www.staticgen.com* for a comprehensive list of these tools.

is, most corporate websites don't turn over that much—their content velocity is extremely low, and content might change monthly, at most.[2]

However, even though the content might not be new, most user interactions with it *are* new. That page explaining the features of the product might have been unchanged on the website for two years, but Bob is looking at it for the first time, and this scenario repeats itself a hundred times a day.

Every combination of visitor + content is a brand new *experience*, which needs to be managed. We might not change the content, but we need to optimize this visitor's interaction with it through an arsenal of marketing and optimization tools such as personalization, A/B testing, and predictive analytics.

How the industry reacts to this need over time remains to be seen. There are two camps:

- Do it internally, by developing large marketing automation and customer experience suites inside the system itself
- Integrate externally with existing marketing automation vendors

The open source community is generally concentrated on the latter option. They're content to leave marketing automation to specialized vendors, and keep their systems centered around management.

The commercial vendors are hedging their bets on both. Many are building marketing suites inside their systems. While some claim this is to provide high levels of integration between management and marketing, one has to assume that they simply see another market and source of revenue to capture. At the same time, most commercial vendors are also offering integrations to popular marketing automation vendors.[3]

What we may see is commercial vendors pushing further and further into this market until it becomes obvious that they're going to be outdone by dedicated marketing automation vendors that don't need to worry about core management features. When this happens, some management vendors will likely acquire marketing platforms, others will spend less on their own systems and more on integrations, and a select few

---

2 During the writing process the website for this book, *http://flyingsquirrelbook.com*, was a single page of content for almost a year and only changed through the addition of chapter titles as they were written. There simply wasn't much content to present, and the entire purpose of the website was to drive the visitor to the ordering page at O'Reilly's website.

3 It's worth noting that some of these "integrations" are ridiculously thin. One commercial vendor offered a plug-in for an A/B optimization tool. After installation, it became apparent that the only thing this plug-in did was add a single JavaScript reference at the top of every page, something that would take a template developer 10 seconds to add manually.

might break off their marketing platforms into separate products and recenter their efforts around core management.

Entry-Level SaaS Will Eat Away the Lower End of the Market

In Chapter 3, I expressed skepticism about pure multitenant SaaS offerings at the higher end of the market where customers require heavy customization. However, the entry-level SaaS market appears to be thriving and will continue to shake up that end of the CMS spectrum.

By "entry-level," I'm referring to SaaS products that can generally be set up with nothing but a credit card and some personal information. Services like Squarespace and Wix have been popular in this space for years—and this is to say nothing of the blogging platforms like WordPress that can be repurposed into basic, limited CMSs without much trouble.

These systems will chew up the lower fringes of the CMS market, as organizations decide this level of management is good enough and concentrate their budget and staffing on marketing optimization using many of the platforms, tools, and methodologies discussed previously.

Yes, the functionality of these systems is undeniably limited, but they will still exceed the need of many organizations, or the organizations' more demanding requirements will be abandoned or delayed in the face of the immediate availability and low cost of the platforms.

With these entry-level options, with nothing more than a credit card, a couple of hours, and some knowledge of the marketplace, an organization can come away with a simple website platform and an extensive marketing suite (which, admittedly, still needs to be visually themed and populated with content, but this is a task that needs to be done no matter how the website is actually acquired).

What will be key to the success of these platforms is the ability to balance the needs of a massive range of users. There will be the aforementioned organizations that "just need a website," but there will inevitably also be a group that requires more and more customization. As these systems evolve, the ability to balance these groups—providing the latter with more and more ability to customize while not making the platform too expensive for the former—will drive or destroy adoption.

Beyond pure user adoption, these platforms are redefining functionality. Previously, we talked about "the Google Effect" which drives our expectation of how search platforms work. Perhaps "the WordPress Effect" is that which drives our expectations of how CMSs should work.

I envision vendor salespeople having to reorganize their sales decks as entry-level platforms develop. When WordPress finally began offering versioning, for example, that was no longer a competitive advantage for systems costing tens of thousands of dollars. This will begin to happen throughout the entry-level SaaS market. Vendors will have to reorient their systems and sales processes around what they offer *beyond* these platforms.

A system that costs $15/month today is quite similar to a system you might have paid $30,000 for a decade ago. This is healthy. Not only do customers with modest budgets get more functionality, but it pushes the industry forward. Lack of a vibrant entry-level market allows the higher-end vendors to stagnate.

Multichannel Distribution Will Increase

For years, vendors paid lip service to multichannel publishing. They claimed their systems would publish content into many distribution channels (wink, wink), but they knew the average user would never build more than a single website with them.

However, the rise of social networking has forced the multichannel issue. Massive amounts of content are being created that will never see the inside of an organization's website. This content will spend its entire lifecycle in third-party, hosted distribution platforms. Facebook, Twitter, and Pinterest are enormous marketing and communication channels, and some organizations could simply forgo a formal website entirely and market solely through those channels.[4] *But this content still needs to be managed.*

What we're seeing is the rise of the "social networking CMS" in the form of management platforms for social media updates. Platforms like Hootsuite, Buffer, and Tweet-Deck abstract content creators away from the actual platforms, allowing authoring and management in centralized applications. The line between these and more traditional CMSs is getting blurrier.

What we'll likely see in the future is more vendors encouraging social media management from their core CMS products. Some have done this through add-ons and subsystems, but others will pursue a more "pure" approach, where a social media update is treated as a content object like any other, subject to workflow, permissions, auditing, etc. When content is published, it doesn't appear on the website; it's simply injected to the various social networking platforms through various APIs.

---

4 There was a huge trend a few years back among smaller organizations toward using Facebook as an official website, and having a domain name simply redirect to the Facebook page. At the time, Facebook was essentially letting organizations build static websites as their Facebook pages. However, this architecture was changed to force more of a timeline-style page with continuing, serial content. With this change, the platform became less attractive and the trend lost steam.

Social networking is just one channel among many. Marketing departments have been quick to embrace microsites, where a multitude of smaller websites are created to support ad campaigns. While these sites can often be managed out of the same CMS, the complication and overhead (not to mention the potential licensing costs) might encourage organizations to create static websites or use smaller SaaS platforms and push selected content to them from their core CMSs.

And while mainstream usage of RSS continues to (sadly) wane, RSS is still a valuable content distribution mechanism. Many platforms and systems consume RSS feeds, and one might envision a CMS that "publishes" content simply by including it in an RSS feed, where it's devoured to be repurposed by dozens of other systems.

Electronic book formats continue to evolve, but repurposing content in a format like PDF, EPUB, or MOBI might be a preferred way for visitors to consume it, especially for long-form, reference content.

Finally, how about offline channels? Video billboards are becoming more and more popular (and distracting). As different as this application may seem, it's still content that needs to be managed. I look forward to the day when my publication target menu includes options for "10th Street at 63rd" and "I-90, west of Sioux Falls."

Distributed Content Intake Will Start to Grow

Services are starting to appear that are targeted directly at the editorial and content creation process. Platforms like GatherContent (*https://gathercontent.com*) and Divvy (*http://divvyhq.com*) are centered around managing editorial calendars, task creation, and collaboration. They have effectively broken off that set of functionality from the CMS, and are concentrating on it specifically.

Some organizations will turn to these services as editorial process tools inside their CMSs run short. Teams will begin working on the sometimes laborious process of content creation, with an API call that actually creates or updates the content in the CMS at the last moment.

Additionally, organizations will begin demanding more and more distributed content intake. I don't think it'll be long before we see a CMS offering content editing and collaboration directly from Google Docs, for instance. Other systems, like Beegit (*http://beegit.com*) and O'Reilly's own Atlas (*http://atlas.oreilly.com*) platform, provide high-end document collaboration based on traditional source control and Markdown-like syntax.

Organizations might likewise begin to distribute their content management, having multiple systems internally but one external CMS that delivers all content. Internal blog authors, for example, might write their posts on a private WordPress installation that then pushes content into a more robust marketing CMS for delivery.

To date, the default assumption of a CMS vendor is that all content will begin life in the CMS itself. This will start to change, as vendors begin to realize and adapt to the fact that other platforms are handling the editorial process with more focus and functionality.

COPE, CAPE, and the CMS as Content Middleware

In 2009, two developers at National Public Radio (NPR) delivered a conference talk about a system they called COPE, which stood for Create Once Publish Everywhere. NPR had built a content platform that allowed for the creation and management of content in a neutral format, and then used this platform to push it to dozens of endpoints: its own website, affiliates' websites, mobile apps, third-party portals, iTunes, etc.

This was multichannel publishing, which was the picture that CMS vendors had painted for years about what we could do with their products. However, the COPE presentation was one of the first examples many people had seen of this idea practically implemented at scale. The industry was fascinated by it.

I interviewed Zach Brand, one of the architects of COPE, several years ago, and he told me that the system eventually morphed into what they informally called CAPE: Create *Anywhere* Publish Everywhere. Instead of a single interface for entering content, they developed the API to accept content from multiple different channels. After content intake (from "anywhere"), the system provided management functions, then pushed the content out (to "everywhere").

In this sense, their platform had become content middleware. It was the "glue" that connected many different content creation methods with many different content delivery methods. Content streamed in from multiple points to an editorial "traffic cop," then streamed out to be delivered to end consumers.

Is this the future of the CMS? Vendors have given us all the tools we need for distributed content delivery, and, as we discussed earlier, social networking has been the impetus for many customers to move forward on that front. What will be the companion development to kick-start distributed content intake and creation?

I have no doubt that the majority of web content will continue to be developed inside a CMS itself, but organizations will increasingly look for the ability to push non-CMS content to their CMSs, solely to be delivered alongside everything else.

Afterword

Content management is simply not a static discipline. We're constantly rearranging the sails on a ship that is floating on rough seas. We never stop changing and stretching the boundaries of something that is built on a platform—the Internet itself—that never stops changing either.

It can sometimes seem hopeless to try to keep up, and I can assure you that trying to write a book about the topic took this problem to another order of magnitude. I shudder to think how quaint and naïve sections of this book might appear a decade from now.

However, no matter how variable the current industry is, it's important to note that web content management is a new spin on a set of very old disciplines.

Always remember the four pillars of content management:

- Content modeling
- Content aggregation
- Editorial workflow
- Output management

We have been practicing these disciplines in some form or another for millennia. Scribes in Ancient Egypt still had to structure content, organize content, control the workflow of creating it, and find a way to distribute it.

This industry can often be self-important. There's a tendency to believe what we're doing is wholly new and original. But while the superficial constructs of the moment might change, the practice of managing content manifested in these four disciplines is transcendent.

All the rest is merely details.

Next Steps

To continue learning about web content management, I invite you to do two things:

- Visit this book's glossary at *http://flyingsquirrelbook.com/glossary*. There, I define and relate hundreds of terms used throughout this book and include links to related resources.[1]

- Please don't hesitate to contact me if you'd like to discuss any of the topics in this book further, or if you have any comments or objections about anything you've read here. I enjoy and welcome raging debates about content management. My email is *deane@blendinteractive.com* and I can be found on Twitter at @gadgeto-pia.

- Since 2003, I've been blogging about web technology at Gadgetopia. My content management-specific writing is aggregated at *http://gadgetopia.com/cm*. Some of these blog posts are over a decade old, and it's occasionally interesting (and mildly embarrassing) to see how my thinking has evolved over that time.

---

1 Ironically, the website for this book does not use a content management system. The glossary is maintained in Markdown and the website is generated by a wonderful static site generator called Wyam (*http://wyam.io*).

Index

and CMS, 5-7
basic characteristics, 1-14
content delivery vs., 5, 25
content in, 3-5
data modeling and, 80
discipline vs. software, 6
early days of, xv
evolving role of, 60
four pillars of, 339
future of, 329-338
multilingual (see multilingual content management)
systems vs. implementations, 17
content management systems (CMSs)
acquiring (see acquisition, CMS)
actual vs. theoretical benefits, 19
and commercial software syndrome, 23
and editorial efficiency, 11
and technical debt, 32
as digital hub, 242
code vs. configuration, 29
code vs. content, 28
content automation/aggregation, 11
content control, 9
content formatting limitations, 13
content reuse, 10
core functions, 9-12
coupled vs. decoupled, 26
defined, 5-7
extensibility of (see extensibility)
feature analysis (see feature analysis)
functions not handled by, 12-14
homebuilding analogy for, 14
implementation (see implementation)
implementations vs. systems, 17
installed vs. SaaS, 27
management vs. delivery, 5, 25
multisite management, 226-228
open-source vs. commercial software, 20-23
page-based, 84
platform-style vs. product-style, 18
points of comparison for choosing a system, 15-33
practicality vs. elegance, 32
systems vs. implementations, 17
target site types, 16
technology stack, 23-25
types of, 7-9
uni- vs. bi-directional publishing, 30

content management team, 53-61
administrators, 58
and project stakeholders, 59
developers, 57
editors, 54-56
site planners, 56
content middleware, 338
content migration, 285-303
and content velocity, 300
and embedded content, 291
automated vs. manual, 287
changing geographies during, 293
dangers of underestimating, 301
early in implementation process, 273
editorial challenge, 286
extraction, 289-291
final, 281
import, 294
migration script development, 298
one-to-one, 299
planning, 302
process, 288-298
QA for, 297
reassembly, 292-294
resolution of migrated content, 295-297
stubbing, 294
timing, 300
transformation, 291
content modeling, 75-108
and content embedding, 97-103
as editorial issue, 106
attribute validation, 91
attributes and datatypes, 88-90
attributes as editorial metadata, 92
built-in attributes, 90
composition, 104
content type, 85-88
content type inheritance, 93-96
content vs. presentation, 83
data modeling and content management, 80
data modeling basics, 76-79
defining a model, 85-104
features checklist, 107
for implementation, 271-273
manageability, 105
page-based CMS, 84
relationships, 103
separating content and presentation, 81-85
types, 85-88

information retrieval (IR), 230
Ingenuix, 15
inheritance, 93-96
inner template, 194
installation, 269
integrators, external
    as starting point for CMS acquisition, 35
    CMS vendor professional services, 307
    content development, 323
    costs, 313
    development and testing infrastructure, 320
    during production, 319-324
    engagement models, 306-308
    nonimplementation consulting, 317
    pre-implementation artifacts, 310-312
    project communication and check-in with,
        320
    QA, 323
    relationship with, 327
    scoping of project, 309-312
    support provided by, 325
    team proximity and dedication, 319
    training models, 324
    trust and, 327
    work acceptance, 321-323
    working with, 305-327
    written agreements with, 314-319
IntenseDebate, 332
interface widgets, prebuilt, 185
internationalization, 205
    (see also multilingual content management)
IR (information retrieval), 230
ISO (International Organization for Standardi-
    zation), 206
IT department, organizations requirements vs.,
    44

J
Jenkins, 269
jobs, scheduled/on-demand, 249

K
known personalization, 214

L
languages
    native programming languages vs. templat-
        ing code, 183-185

spoken (see multilingual content manage-
    ment)
launch, 282
learning management systems (LMSs), 8
licensing
    commercial CMS software, 40
    open source software, 39
lifecycle (see content lifecycle)
lists, 100, 118
LMSs (learning management systems), 8
localization, 205
Lucene, 233

M
managed hosting, 38
management (see content management) (see
    content management systems (CMSs))
manual content migration, 287
manual ordering, derived ordering vs., 125-127
marketing
    analytics integration, 218
    and CRM integration, 218
    anonymous personalization, 214-217
    as beyond scope of CMS, 12
    as editorial role, 55
    automation, 213-220
    future of marketing tools/integration,
        333-335
    proposal document, 314
Media Wiki, 112
meetings, with integrators, 320
Mendelsohn, Noah, 184
menus, as secondary geography, 118
metadata
    attributes as, 92
    defined, 92
Microsoft FrontPage, 11, 331
middleware, 338
migration (see content migration)
migration script, 298
modeling (see content modeling)
multichannel distribution, 336
multilingual content management, 204-213
    content management challenges, 212
    external translation service support, 211
    language detection/selection, 206
    language rules, 208-209
    language variants, 209
    nomenclature, 205

Q

QA
   for content migration, 297
   of migrated content, 281
   with integrators, 323

R

RadEditor, 246
React, 332
reassembly
   and stubbing, 294
   content migration, 292-294
reconciliation (see content reconciliation)
records management (RM), 7
recurring revenue, 43
regions, in templates, 101
regular expressions (regex), 146
reification, 77, 309
relational content, 112
relational content modeling, 103
relational information, 274
renditions, 81
reporting tools, 228
repository, abstraction of, 246
requirements gathering, 44
resolution of migrated content, 295-297
responsive design, 195
REST (REpresentational State Transfer), 248
reuse, content, 10
reverse content management, 221
rich text
   defined, 90
   editing interface for, 146
   editor interface customization, 246
   embedding, 97-100
RM (records management), 7
rough-in, 271-273

S

SaaS CMS systems (see software-as-a-service
   CMS systems)
scale/scaling, 140
scheduling, 155, 171
SCM (source code management) platform, 268
scoping, 309-312
screen scraping, 289
script, migration (see migration script)
searches

as dynamic variable aggregation, 125
content, 229-233
criteria in dynamic aggregations, 123
Lucene, 233
supplemental indexes for, 124
selecting, CMS (see acquisition, CMS)
selection consultant, 35
selection process (see acquisition, CMS)
serial content, 111
server administrators, 58
Server Side Includes, 11, 185, 193
shape of content, 111-113
shearing layers, 266
single-page apps, 332
site planners, 56
sitemap, 311
SOAP (Simple Object Access Protocol), 248
social networking, 336
software-as-a-service (SaaS) CMS systems
   acquisition of, 45-47
   future of, 335
   installed software vs., 27
source code management (SCM) platform, 268
SOW (statement of work), 315-319
Spolsky, Joel, 21, 67
stack (technology stack), 23-25
Stack Overflow (website), 234
stacking (web page composition), 103
stakeholders, content management team and,
   59
statement of work (SOW), 315-319
static aggregation, 123-125
storage administrators, 58
StringTemplate, 177
stubbing, 294
subscriptions, software, 42
Summary field, 91
supplemental indexes, 124
support
   by integrators, 325
   of implementation, 280
   of open source software, 39
surround, the
   and inner template, 194
   and templating, 185-190, 274
   context in, 188

T

tabular content, 112

About the Author

Deane Barker has been working in web content management since the mid-'90s—before the discipline even had a name. He is the veteran of hundreds of implementations ranging from small marketing sites to massive publishing operations. Deane has worked on almost all programming architectures and dozens of different CMS platforms. He has been writing about content management for over a decade, and speaks frequently on the content management conference circuit.

About the Technical Reviewers

Seth Gottlieb transforms ideas into technology platforms and is equal parts developer, architect, and team builder. As VP of Product Development at Lionbridge Technologies, Seth designs and implements technology to support strategic business initiatives. Seth draws from a deep background in software development and integration. For more than 20 years, he has led consulting and in-house project teams and built performance-oriented engineering cultures.

Lynsey Struthers developed her CMS chops wrangling content for higher education—helping to create her employer college's first home-grown content management system in the early 2000s. Since then, she's consulted with organizations large and small on implementing and maintaining an effective web presence. Lynsey is currently a senior user experience consultant with Evantage Consulting in Minneapolis, Minnesota.

Arild Henrichsen has been building websites, portals, and intranets for over a decade, specializing in content management systems. He's a certified developer, architect, tech lead, trainer, speaker, and blogger—and an Episerver MVP.

Colophon

The animal on the cover of *Web Content Management* is a *pygmy flying squirrel*. This smallest species of flying squirrel can be found in the jungles of Borneo and Malaysia.

A flying squirrel is more appropriately called a gliding squirrel. A large flap of skin, called the patagium, extends from the animal's flanks all the way up to its wrists and ankles. It launches itself into the air with arms and legs extended, pulling the patagium taught. Like a furry kite, the pygmy flying squirrel floats outward and downward, sailing three feet for every one-foot drop. It uses its long whiskers to detect branches and lands with its eyes closed.

Pygmy flying squirrels have an omnivorous diet consisting of nuts, seeds, fruits, berries, insects, and bird eggs. It forages under the cover of night to avoid predators.